Word 2013

FOR

DUMMIES®

Word 2013

FOR

DUMMIES®

by Dan Gookin

WILEY

John Wiley & Sons, Inc.

Word 2013 For Dummies®

Published by
John Wiley & Sons, Inc.
111 River Street
Hoboken, NJ 07030-5774

www.wiley.com

Copyright © 2013 by John Wiley & Sons, Inc., Hoboken, New Jersey

Published by John Wiley & Sons, Inc., Hoboken, New Jersey

Published simultaneously in Canada

For general information on our other products and services, please contact our Customer Care Department within the U.S. at 877-762-2974, outside the U.S. at 317-572-3993, or fax 317-572-4002.

For technical support, please visit www.wiley.com/techsupport.

Wiley also publishes its books in a variety of electronic formats and by print-on-demand. Not all content that is available in standard print versions of this book may appear or be packaged in all book formats. If you have purchased a version of this book that did not include media that is referenced by or accompanies a standard print version, you may request this media by visiting http://booksupport.wiley.com. For more information about Wiley products, visit us www.wiley.com.

Library of Congress Control Number: 2012956410

ISBN 978-1-118-49123-2 (pbk); ISBN 978-1-118-49147-8 (ebk); ISBN 978-1-118-49153-9 (ebk); ISBN 978-1-118-49130-0 (ebk)

Manufactured in the United States of America

10 9 8 7 6 5 4 3 2

About the Author

Dan Gookin has been writing about technology for over 250 years. He combines his love of writing with his gizmo fascination to create books that are informative, entertaining, and not boring. Having written over 130 titles with 12 million copies in print translated into over 30 languages, Dan can attest that his method of crafting computer tomes seems to work.

Perhaps his most famous title is the original *DOS For Dummies*, published in 1991. It became the world's fastest-selling computer book, at one time moving more copies per week than the *New York Times* number-one bestseller (though, as a reference, it could not be listed on the *Times'* Best Sellers list). That book spawned the entire line of *For Dummies* books, which remains a publishing phenomenon to this day.

Dan's most popular titles include *PCs For Dummies, Word For Dummies, Laptops For Dummies*, and *Android Phones For Dummies*. He also maintains the vast and helpful website www.wambooli.com.

Dan holds a degree in Communications/Visual Arts from the University of California, San Diego. He lives in the Pacific Northwest, where he enjoys spending time with his sons playing video games indoors while they enjoy the gentle woods of Idaho.

Publisher's Acknowledgments

We're proud of this book; please send us your comments at http://dummies.custhelp.com. For other comments, please contact our Customer Care Department within the U.S. at 877-762-2974, outside the U.S. at 317-572-3993, or fax 317-572-4002.

Some of the people who helped bring this book to market include the following:

Acquisitions and Editorial

Sr. Project Editor: Mark Enochs

Acquisitions Editor: Katie Mohr

Copy Editor: Rebecca Whitney

Editorial Manager: Leah Michael

Editorial Assistant: Annie Sullivan

Sr. Editorial Assistant: Cherie Case

Cover Photo: © malerapaso / iStockphoto.com

Composition Services

Project Coordinator: Patrick Redmond

Layout and Graphics: Carrie A. Cesavice, Joyce Haughey

Proofreaders: Lindsay Amones, Bonnie Mikkelson

Indexer: BIM Indexing & Proofreading Services

Publishing and Editorial for Technology Dummies

Richard Swadley, Vice President and Executive Group Publisher

Andy Cummings, Vice President and Publisher

Mary Bednarek, Executive Acquisitions Director

Mary C. Corder, Editorial Director

Publishing for Consumer Dummies

Kathy Nebenhaus, Vice President and Executive Publisher

Composition Services

Debbie Stailey, Director of Composition Services

Contents at a Glance

Table of Contents

Introduction

. . . .

The only thing standing between you and your writing is your word processor. Yeah, I know: It's supposed to be helpful. Well, it tries. Computers can do only so much. But you, as a smart person, are capable of so much more. I'm guessing that's why you opened this book.

Welcome to *Word 2013 For Dummies,* which removes the pain from using Microsoft's latest, greatest, most confusing word processing software ever! This book is your friendly, informative, and entertaining guide to the routine of processing words that is Word 2013.

Be warned: I'm not out to make you love Word. I don't want you to enjoy the program. Use it, yes. Tolerate it, of course. The only promise I'm offering is to ease the pain that most people feel from using Microsoft Word. Along the way, I kick Word in the butt, and I hope you enjoy reading about it.

About This Book

I don't intend for you to read this book from cover to cover. It's not a novel, and if it were, it would be a political space opera with an antihero and a princess fighting elected officials who are in cahoots with a galactic urban renewal development corporation. The ending would be extremely satisfying, but it would be a long novel because I need something on my bookshelf to balance out *Atlas Shrugged.*

This book is a reference. Each chapter covers a specific topic or task you can accomplish by using Word 2013. Within a chapter, you find self-contained sections, each of which describes how to perform a specific task or get something done. Sample sections you encounter in this book include

- Moving a block
- Check your spelling
- Save your stuff!
- How to format a paragraph
- Working with tables in Word
- Inserting clip art
- Mail merge, ho!

I give you no keys to memorize, no secret codes, no tricks, no presentations to sleep through, and no wall charts. Instead, each section explains a topic as though it's the first thing you read in this book. Nothing is assumed, and everything is cross-referenced. Technical terms and topics, when they come up, are neatly shoved to the side, where you can easily avoid reading them. The idea here isn't for you to master anything. This book's philosophy is to help you look it up, figure it out, and get back to work.

How to Use This Book

You hold in your hands an active book. The topics between this book's yellow-and-black covers are all geared toward getting things done in Word 2013. Because nothing is assumed, all you need to do is find the topic that interests you and read.

Word uses the mouse and keyboard to get things done. If your computer has a multi-touch monitor or you're using a tablet, you can touch the screen to get things done, though Word works best with a keyboard and mouse.

I use the word *click* to describe the action of clicking the mouse's main (left) button. Likewise, on a touchscreen, you can touch the screen rather than click with the mouse.

This is a keyboard shortcut:

   Ctrl+P

Simply press and hold the Ctrl (control) key and type the letter *P*, just as you would press Shift+P to create a capital *P*.

When you're using the onscreen keyboard on a multi-touch monitor, keyboard shortcuts require two steps: First tap the Ctrl key, and then tap the P key, for example.

Sometimes, you must press more than two keys at the same time:

   Ctrl+Shift+T

In this line, you press Ctrl and Shift together and then press the T key. Release all three keys. (These key combinations are not possible when using the onscreen keyboard.)

 I use the word *Win* to refer to the Windows key on the keyboard. The key sports the Windows logo, shown in the margin. So, *Win+D* refers to pressing the Windows key in combination with the D key.

Commands in Word 2013 exist as *command buttons* on the Ribbon interface. I may refer to the tab, the command group, and then the button itself to help you locate that command button — for example, the Page Color button in the Page Background group on the Design tab. Or I might write, "the Page Color button, found in the Design tab's Page Background group."

Menu commands are listed like this:

Table➪Insert Table

Choosing this command tells you to choose from the Table menu the command named Insert Table. The Table menu appears as a button on the Ribbon.

 The main menu in Word 2013 is the File tab menu. It replaces the File menu from older versions of Word, and the Office Button menu, found in Microsoft Office 2007. Clicking the File tab displays the File screen, which fills the entire Word window. To return to Word, click the Back button, found in the upper-left corner of the File screen and shown in the margin. Or you can press the Esc key.

When I describe a message or something else you see onscreen, it looks like this:

```
Why should I bother to love Evelyn when robots will
eventually destroy the human race?
```

If you need further help in operating your computer, I can recommend my book *PCs For Dummies.* It contains lots of useful information to supplement what you find in this book.

Foolish Assumptions

Though this book was written with the beginner in mind, I still make a few assumptions. Foremost, I assume that you're a human being, though you might also be an alien from another planet. If so, welcome to Earth. When you conquer our planet, please do Idaho last. Thanks.

Another foolish assumption I make is that you use Windows as the computer's operating system, either Windows 8 or Windows 7, which are the only two versions of Windows capable of handling the Word 2013 beast. Differences between the two versions of Windows are covered where applicable in the text. Keep in mind that this book isn't about Windows.

This book can also apply to running Word 2013 on a tablet computing device running Windows RC. Though I do mention some tablet-related tricks in the text, the book doesn't cover basic tablet operations and procedures.

Your word processor is Microsoft Word 2013. It is *not* Microsoft Works. It is not an earlier version of Word. It is not WordPerfect. It is not a version of Word that runs on a Macintosh.

Throughout this book, I use the term *Word* to refer to the Microsoft Word program. The program may also be called Word 2013 or even Microsoft Office Word 2013. It's all Word as far as this book is concerned. Word 2013 is a part of the Microsoft Office 2013 suite of programs. This book doesn't cover any other part of Microsoft Office, though I mention Excel and Outlook wherever they encroach upon Word's turf.

How This Book Is Organized

This book contains six major parts, each of which is divided into two or more chapters. The chapters themselves have been sliced into smaller, modular sections. You can pick up the book and read any section without necessarily knowing what has already been covered in the rest of the book. Start anywhere.

Here's a breakdown of the parts and what you can find in them:

Part I: Getting Started with Word 2013

This part provides a quick introduction to Word and word processing. You can find information on how to start and quit Word and a simple overview of the typical word processing day.

Part II: Your Basic Word

The chapters in this part of the book cover the seven basic tasks of any word processor: Move around a document, edit text, search and replace, work with blocks of text, proof documents, save and open, and, finally, publish. (Publishing has replaced printing as the final result of your word processing efforts, though printing is still covered as part of the whole publishing milieu.)

Part III: Fun with Formatting

This part deals with formatting, from the smallest iota of text to formatting commands that span an entire document and more. Formatting is the art of making your document look less ugly.

Part IV: Spruce Up a Dull Document

This part is formatting dessert, or tasks you can do beyond regular formatting to help make your document look like more than a typical, boring document. Part IV covers lines, borders, tables, columns, lists, graphical goodness, and all sorts of stuff that makes Word more than a typical word processor.

Part V: The Rest of Word

This part covers a few dangling details that I consider myself fortunate to write about, such as outlining, collaboration, mail merge, label making, and other interesting things that Word does.

Part VI: The Part of Tens

The traditional last part of any *For Dummies* book contains chapters with lists of ten items. You find lots of helpful information there, some weird things you may not know about, plus even more useful tips, tricks, and good suggestions.

What's Not Here

Word is one heck of a program. Covering the entire thing would fill a book several thousand pages long. (I kid you not.) My approach in this book is to cover as much basic word processing as possible. For that reason, some advanced features got pushed off the table of contents.

I give you some information about macros, though it's not meaty. Covering macros without a technical description is difficult. If the publisher ever lets me increase this book's size to more than 400 pages, I'd be happy to add a macro chapter; the publisher's address is in this book's front matter, in case you want to lobby on my behalf.

Some of Word's more esoteric features are touched upon lightly here. For example, I could spend about 70 pages detailing what can be done with graphics in Word, but I limit myself to only a dozen pages.

Finally, this book doesn't cover using Word to make a blog post or create a web page or how to use Word as your e-mail program. Word does these things, but I consider this a word processing book rather than a Word-does-whatever book.

Icons Used in This Book

 This icon flags useful, helpful tips or shortcuts.

 This icon marks a friendly reminder to do something.

 This icon marks a friendly reminder *not* to do something.

 This icon alerts you to overly nerdy information and technical discussions of the topic at hand. The information is optional reading, but it may enhance your reputation at cocktail parties if you repeat it.

Where to Go from Here

Start reading! Observe the table of contents and find something that interests you. Or look up your puzzle in the index.

If you've been using a version of Word earlier than version 2007, you're probably somewhat surprised at the look of Word 2013. Therefore, I recommend that you start reading at Chapter 1.

Read! Write! Let your brilliance shine!

My e-mail address is dgookin@wambooli.com. Yes, that's my real address. I reply to all e-mail I receive, and you'll get a quick reply if you keep your question short and specific to this book or to Word itself. Although I enjoy saying "Hi," I cannot answer technical support questions or help you troubleshoot your computer. Thanks for understanding.

You can also visit my web page for more information or as a diversion:

www.wambooli.com

Occasionally, there are updates to technology books. If this book has technical updates they will be posted at:

www.dummies.com/go/word2013fdupdates

Enjoy this book. And enjoy Word. Or at least tolerate it.

Part I

Getting Started with Word 2013

In this part . . .

- ✔ Learn how to start Word 2013 and decipher the Word screen.

- ✔ Familiarize yourself with how to quit and minimize Word 2013.

- ✔ Get to know the PC keyboard and the touchscreen.

- ✔ Learn how to read the status bar and discover secret symbols representing special characters in your text.

- ✔ Visit www.dummies.com for great Dummies content online.

Chapter 1

Hello, Word!

*Y*ou can't do squat with a computer until you start the thing. Likewise, you can't even write the word *squat* until you start a word processing program. Because you bought *this* book and not *Pencils For Dummies,* the program you need to start is Microsoft Word. This chapter tells you how to get Word started and begin your word processing day. Let me also mention that reading this chapter is a far more enriching experience than reading *Pencils For Dummies,* which is barely a pamphlet, albeit one that's charmingly illustrated.

Get into Word

The Windows operating system is rife with various and sundry ways of getting things done. One victim of that variety is the way to start a program. Rather than bore you by listing all those ways, I figure that you simply want to know the best way to start Word. This section offers three solid choices.

- ✔ Before you can use Word, your computer must be on and toasty. Log in to Windows. Start your computer day. There's no need to put bread into your computer.

- ✔ Make sure that you're seated, with a nice, upright, firm posture as you write. They tell me that your wrists should be even with your elbows and that you shouldn't have to tilt your head forward. Shoulders are back and relaxed.

- ✔ Don't freak out because you're using a computer. You are in charge! Keep that in mind. Chant silently, over and over: "I am the master."

✔ If you need help starting your computer, refer to my book *PCs For Dummies* for quick and accurate turning-on-the-computer instructions.

✔ You can stop chanting "I am the master" now.

Starting Word the boring way

Without fail, the place to start any program in Windows is at the fabled Start button or, in Windows 8, on the Start screen.

In Windows 8, look for the Word 2013 tile on the Start screen. You may have to scroll the screen to the left to find the tile, as shown in the margin. Click or touch the tile to start the Word program.

In Windows 7, click the Start button, which is often found on the left side of the taskbar and at the bottom of the screen, adorned with the Windows logo. Choose Microsoft Word 2013 from the Start menu's list of programs.

When Word isn't found on the Start menu's list of programs, choose the All Programs menu to look for it. Sometimes, it may be lurking on a Microsoft Office or Microsoft Office 2013 submenu.

After choosing the tile or icon to start Word, you can watch in amazement as the program unfurls its sails on your computer's monitor.

✔ Don't let Word's appearance overwhelm you! Later in this chapter, I describe what you're looking at, in the section "Examining Word's main screen."

✔ If you can't find Word's tile or icon, it may not be installed on your computer. This book is specific to Microsoft Word, not to the Microsoft Works word processor or any other word processor. (See the section "Foolish Assumptions" in this book's Introduction.)

✔ I refer to the program as *Word,* though its icon may be labeled *Microsoft Word, Microsoft Office Word, Microsoft Word 2013,* or another variation.

Starting Word the best way

The *best* way to start Word, and the way I do it every day, is to pin the Word icon to the taskbar. That way, you can start Word directly from the Desktop.

What is a word processor?

At its core, a word processor is computer software —a program — that lets you create documents. That's really the key word — *documents*. A document includes formatted text, margins, maybe even a bit of artwork. The word processor contains all the tools to make that happen; this book explains how those tools work.

In Windows 8, you can pin the icon to the taskbar by following these steps:

1. **Right-click the Word tile on the Start screen.**

2. **Choose the command Pin to Taskbar.**

   The Pin to Taskbar command is found at the bottom of the screen.

To confirm that the icon is properly pinned, press the Win+D keyboard shortcut to see the desktop.

In Windows 7, follow these steps to pin the Word icon to the taskbar:

1. **Find the Word icon on the Start button's All Programs menu.**

   Don't click the Word icon — just find it!

2. **Right-click the Word icon on the All Programs menu.**

3. **Choose the command Pin to Taskbar.**

   The Word icon is *pinned* (permanently added) to the taskbar.

To start Word, you merely click the Word icon that's placed on the taskbar. *Click!* And then Word starts. That's the fastest and bestest way to begin your word processing day.

Opening a document to start Word

You use the Word program to create *documents,* which are stored on your computer in much the same way as people pile junk into boxes and store them in their garages. But that's not important. What is important is that you can use those documents to start Word: Opening a Word document causes Word to start *and* to display that document for editing, printing, or giving others the impression that you're doing something.

What's your point, Dan?

My point is that you can also start Word by opening a Word document. Simply locate the Word document icon (shown in the margin) in a folder window. Double-click to open the document, and Word starts up on the screen, instantly (more or less) displaying the document for editing, reading, modifying, perusing, cussing, mangling, and potentially fouling up beyond all recognition.

- ✔ The Word document you open can be on the desktop, in the My Documents folder, or in any other folder or location where a Word document icon can lurk.

- ✔ The document name appears beneath or to the right of the icon. You can use the name to determine the document's contents — as long as the document was properly named when it was saved to disk. (More on that elsewhere in this book.)

- ✔ You can see a Jump List of recently opened documents by right-clicking the Word icon on the taskbar. Choose a document from the list to start Word and open that document.

- ✔ Word is capable of opening other types of documents, including documents from previous versions of Word, Rich Text Format documents, and others. Each of these documents has its own icon, though the icon looks similar to the standard Word document icon. See Chapter 24 for more information on opening alien documents in Word.

Behold the Word Program

Like all programs in Windows, Word offers its visage in a program window. It's the place where you get your word processing work done.

Using the Word Start screen

The first thing you may see after starting Word is something called the Word Start screen, as shown in Figure 1-1. This screen appears only when you initially start Word and it works to help you get started by opening a recent document, browsing for a document file to open, or choosing a new type of document to start.

Select an option, as illustrated in Figure 1-1, to get working. Or if you're waiting for your muse, choose the Blank Document item and you'll be on your way.

Choose a previous document.   Start a new blank document.

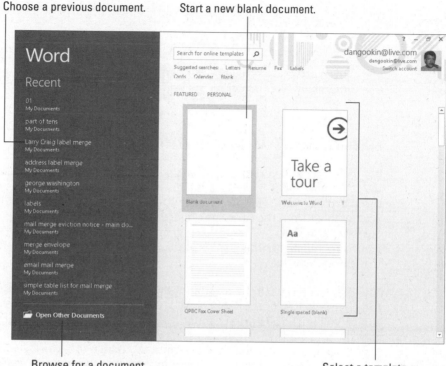

Figure 1-1:
The Word
Start
screen.

Browse for a document.   Select a template.

If you're an old hand at Word, you probably desire to get rid of the Word Start screen. Follow these blessed steps:

1. **In Word, click the File tab on the Ribbon.**

   If you're still staring at the Word Start screen, choose the Blank Document item to get into Word. The File tab is the blue button that says *File,* found near the upper-left corner of the screen.

2. **Choose Options from the list of menu items on the left side of the screen.**

3. **Ensure that the General category is chosen from the left side of the Word Options window.**

4. **Remove the check mark by the item Show the Start Screen When This Application Starts.**

5. **Click the OK button.**

You can repeat these steps and restore the check mark in Step 4 if you want to resurrect the Word Start screen.

✔ The Word Start screen appears only when you first start Word.

✔ The Word Start screen doesn't appear if you start Word by opening a document. See the earlier section, "Opening a document to start Word."

Examining Word's main screen

It's the electronic version of a blank sheet of paper — and more. It's the *more* part that you might find daunting. The dee-dads and goo-bobs that surround the Word program window all have specific names that you need to know to get the most from the program. Figure 1-2 shows the big picture.

Figure 1-3 highlights the gizmos at the top of the Word window, showcasing the Ribbon interface.

The details of how all the dee-dads and goo-bobs in the Word window work are covered elsewhere in this book. Use this book's index to help you find topics you might be curious about.

✔ To get the most from Word's window, change the window size: As with any window, you can use the mouse to drag the window's edges in or out or click the window's Maximize button (the middle button in the window's upper right corner) to have the window fill the screen.

✔ Word's window size affects what you see in the Ribbon command groups. When the Word window is smaller, fewer buttons show up, or they may show up in three rows. When the window is larger, you see more buttons, usually in two rows.

✔ The largest portion of Word's screen is for composing text. It's blank and white, just like a fresh sheet of paper. (Refer to Figure 1-2.) That's where you compose and format your text, and I cover that area specifically in the next section.

✔ Clicking the File tab replaces the contents of the Word window with a screen full of commands and their descriptions. To return to the Word window, click the Back button (shown in the margin) or press the Esc key.

✔ The Ribbon contains all Word commands, which appear as buttons, input boxes, and menus. The Ribbon is divided into tabs (refer to Figure 1-3). The commands on the Ribbon are separated into groups. Some tabs may appear and disappear, depending on what you're doing in Word. And the commands in groups change as you change the window's size.

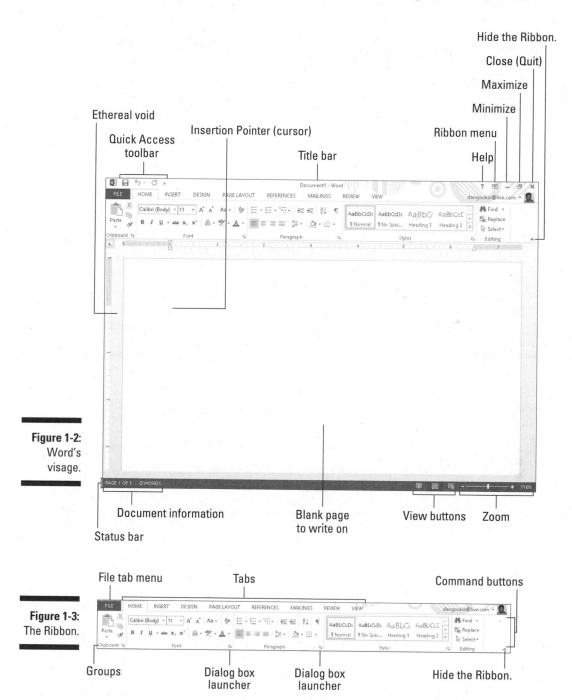

Hide the Ribbon.

Close (Quit)

Maximize

Minimize

Ribbon menu

Help

Ethereal void

Quick Access toolbar

Insertion Pointer (cursor)

Title bar

Figure 1-2:
Word's
visage.

Document information

Blank page
to write on

View buttons

Zoom

Status bar

File tab menu

Tabs

Command buttons

Figure 1-3:
The Ribbon.

Groups

Dialog box
launcher

Dialog box
launcher

Hide the Ribbon.

- ✔ The Ribbon can be shown or hidden by using commands on the Ribbon menu in the upper-right corner of the Word window (refer to Figure 1-2). You can also hide the Ribbon by clicking the Hide Ribbon button shown in Figure 1-3. This book assumes that the Ribbon is visible, and I recommend that you keep it that way as you discover the wonders of Word.

- ✔ The Windows taskbar, located at the bottom of the screen, is a part of Windows itself and not Word. However, as you open documents in Word, buttons representing those documents appear on the Windows taskbar.

- ✔ You can customize the Quick Access Toolbar (refer to Figure 1-2) to add your own commands, groups, and tabs. It's a topic I cover in Chapter 29.

Working with Word on a tablet

If you're using Word on a tablet, you can adjust the spacing between buttons on the Ribbon by activating Touch mode. Follow these steps:

1. **Click or touch the Customize Quick Access Toolbar button.**

   The button is shown in the margin and found near the upper-left corner of the screen.

2. **Choose Touch/Mouse Mode.**

   The Touch/Mouse Mode button appears on the Quick Access toolbar, as shown in the margin.

3. **Touch the Touch/Mouse Mode button and choose the command Touch.**

   The space between items on the Ribbon increases.

Hopefully, the extra space helps forgive how large your fingers are as you attempt to use Word on your mobile computing device or on a computer with a touchscreen monitor.

- ✔ Choose the Mouse command from the Touch/Mouse mode button to diminish (restore) the space between the buttons on the Ribbon.

- ✔ To remove the Touch Mode button, repeat Steps 1 and 2 in this section.

Writing in Word

Word's equivalent of the mind-numbing, writer's-block-inducing blank page can be found in the center part of the Word program window (refer to Figure 1-2). That's where the text you write, edit, and format appears. Unlike with a sheet of paper, however, the text you create in Word can be viewed in a number of different ways.

The most common way to view your document is to use Print Layout view, as shown in Figure 1-2. In this view, the entire page of text is displayed on the screen, looking just the way it prints. Print Layout view shows graphical images, columns, and all sorts of other fancy effects. You even see the blank space between pages, described as the ethereal void in the figure.

The other views are:

Read Mode: Use this mode to read a document like an eBook.

Web Layout: Use this mode when you undertake the dreadful possibility of using Word as a web page editor or to examine web pages you've saved.

Outline: This mode helps you organize your thoughts, as covered in Chapter 25.

Draft. I prefer using Word in Draft view, which shows only basic text and not all the fancy features and formatting. Without that stuff on the screen, I can more easily concentrate on writing.

Switch between Read Mode, Print Layout, and Web Layout views by using the View buttons, found in the lower-right corner of the Word program window (refer to Figure 1-2). Clicking a button with the mouse changes the view.

To get to Outline and Draft views, click the Views tab and choose those views from the Views group.

Understanding the mouse pointer

Though word processing is a keyboard thing, you'll find that the computer mouse comes in handy. You use the mouse to choose commands, move around the document you're editing, and select text. This book explains all these topics elsewhere. For now, it helps to understand how the mouse pointer changes its look as you work in Word:

For editing text, the mouse pointer becomes the I-beam.

For choosing items, the standard 11 o'clock mouse pointer is used.

For selecting lines of text, a 1 o'clock mouse pointer is used.

The mouse pointer may change its look when *click-and-type* mode is active: Lines appear to the left and right of, and below, the I-beam mouse pointer. Refer to Chapter 32 for more information on using click-and-type.

You can use the mouse to see what some of the little buttons and items with pictures on them do in Word. Just hover the mouse pointer over the button, and — voilà! — it's like Folgers instant information crystals.

Cajoling Word to help you

Like most programs in Windows, a Help system is available in Word. You can summon it by pressing the F1 key, which displays the Word Help window. There you can type a topic, a command name, or even a question into the box to search for help.

The F1 key also works any time you're deep in the bowels of Word and doing something specific. The Help information that's displayed tends to be specific to whatever you're doing in Word. Little buttons that look like question marks also summon Word Help.

End Your Word Processing Day

It's the pinnacle of etiquette to know when and how to excuse oneself. Leaving can be done well or poorly. For example, the phrase "Well, I must be off," works lots better than "Something more interesting must be happening somewhere else" — especially at Thanksgiving.

It's entirely possible to quit Word without hurting its feelings or bothering with etiquette. This section covers the many ways to end your word processing day.

Quitting Word

When you're done word processing and you don't expect to return to it anytime soon, you quit the Word program. Quitting a computer program is like putting away a book on a shelf. In the electronic world of the computer, you click the X button in the upper-right corner of the Word program window (refer to Figure 1-2).

The catch? You have to close each and every Word document window that's open before you can say that you've completely quit Word.

The other catch? Word won't quit during that shameful circumstance when you have unsaved documents. If so, you're prompted to save the document, as shown in Figure 1-4. My advice is to click the Save button to save your work.

Figure 1-4: Better click that Save button!

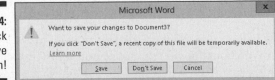

If you click the Don't Save button, your work isn't saved and Word quits. If you click the Cancel button, Word doesn't quit and you can continue working.

- ✔ See Chapter 8 for more information on saving documents.

- ✔ Also see Chapter 8 on how to recover drafts of documents you failed to save.

- ✔ You don't have to quit Word just to start editing another document. Refer to the next couple of sections for helpful, timesaving information!

- ✔ After quitting Word, you can continue to use Windows by starting up any other program, such as Spider Solitaire or perhaps something more calming, like *Call Of Duty*.

Closing a document without quitting Word

You don't always have to quit Word. For example, if you're merely stopping work on one document to work on another, quitting Word is a waste of time. Instead, you can *close* the document.

To close a document in Word, click the File tab and choose the Close command. Word banishes the document from its window, but then the program sits there and waits for you to do something else, such as start working on a new document or open a document you previously saved.

Bottom line: There's no point in quitting Word when all you want to do is start editing a new document.

- ✔ When you try to close a document before it has been saved, Word displays a warning dialog box (refer to Figure 1-4). Click the Save button to save your document. If you want to continue editing, click the Cancel button and get back to work.

- ✔ There's no need to close a document, really. In fact, I work on a document over a period of days and keep it open (and my PC turned on) the entire time — doesn't hurt a thing. (I occasionally save it to disk, which *is* important.)

- ✔ See Chapter 8 for more information about starting a new document.

- ✔ The keyboard shortcut for the Close command is Ctrl+W. This command may seem weird, but it's used to close documents in many programs.

- ✔ To swiftly start up a new, blank document in Word, press Ctrl+N.

Setting Word aside

There's no need to quit Word if you know that you will use it again soon. In fact, I've been known to keep Word open and running on my computer for *weeks* at a time. The secret is to use the Minimize button, found in the upper-right corner of the screen (refer to Figure 1-2).

Clicking the Minimize button shrinks the Word window to the taskbar, where it exists as a button. With the Word program window out of the way, you can do other things with your computer. Then when you're ready to word-process again, click the Word button on the taskbar to restore the Word window to the screen.

Chapter 2

The Typing Chapter

Word processing is about using a keyboard. It's typing. That's the way computers were used for years, long before the mouse and all the fancy graphics became popular. Yep — ask a grizzled old-timer and you'll hear tales of ugly text screens and keyboard commands that would tie your fingers in knots. Though things aren't that bad today, I highly recommend that you bone up on your keyboard skills to get the most from your word processing duties. This chapter tells you what you need to know.

Behold the Keyboard!

Typing happens on a keyboard. At this point in the history of technology, the keyboard can be a physical keyboard or a touchscreen keyboard. This section explores the possibilities.

Using the PC keyboard

Though I'm sure you can easily recognize a computer keyboard, you should know how to refer to its various keys. To assist you, I illustrate a typical computer keyboard in Figure 2-1.

Function keys   Numeric keypad

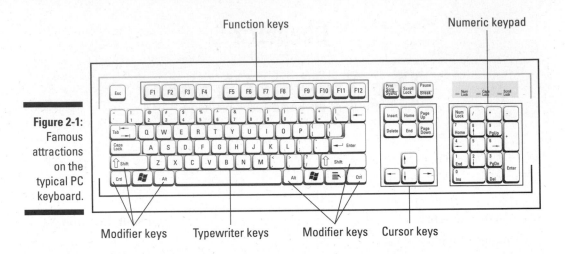

Figure 2-1:
Famous
attractions
on the
typical PC
keyboard.

Modifier keys   Typewriter keys   Modifier keys   Cursor keys

Generic terms are given to clusters of keys found on the PC keyboard. Know where the function keys are, the typewriter keys, cursor keys, and modifier keys, as illustrated in the figure.

Here are some individual keys worth noting:

✔ **Enter:** Marked with the word *Enter* and sometimes a cryptic, bent-arrow thing, this key is used to end a paragraph of text. See the later section, "Pressing the Enter key."

✔ **Spacebar:** The only key with no symbol, it inserts spaces between words. Only one space! See the later section, "Whacking the spacebar."

✔ **Tab:** This key inserts the tab "character," which shoves the next text you type over to the next tab stop. It's an interesting and potentially frustrating formatting key. Using this key properly in Word requires a whole chapter; see Chapter 12.

✔ **Backspace and Delete:** These keys are used to back up and erase text, which is a function many writers find handy. Read more about these keys in Chapter 4.

Every character key you press on the keyboard produces a character on the screen, on the blank part where you write. Typing those character keys over and over is how you write text on a word processor.

✔ The Shift key is used to produce capital letters; otherwise, the text you type is in lowercase.

✔ The Caps Lock key lets you type text in UPPERCASE letters. After you press Caps Lock, the Caps Lock light on your keyboard comes on, indicating that you're entering ALL CAPS mode. Press the Caps Lock key again to return to normal.

✔ Keys on the numeric keypad serve sometimes as cursor keys and sometimes as number keys. The split personality is evident on each key cap,
which displays two symbols. The Num Lock key and its corresponding
light are on if the numeric keypad (1, 2, 3) is active. If the cursor keys
(arrows, Home) are active, Num Lock is off.

✔ Cursor keys are also called *arrow keys;* they control the cursor. Also
included are the non-arrow keys: Home, End, PgUp (or Page Up), PgDn
(or Page Down), Insert, and Delete.

✔ Ctrl is pronounced "control." The variety of names that people give to
the Ctrl key before they know it as *the control key* is amazing.

✔ The Delete key may also be labeled Del on your keyboard.

✔ Modifier keys do nothing by themselves. Instead, the Shift, Ctrl, and Alt
keys work in combination with other keys.

Working a touchscreen keyboard

It's possible, and I'm not thrilled about it, but you can use Word 2013 in an
environment where you type on the monitor, not on a keyboard. In this case,
typing takes place on a virtual keyboard, similar to the one shown in Figure 2-2.

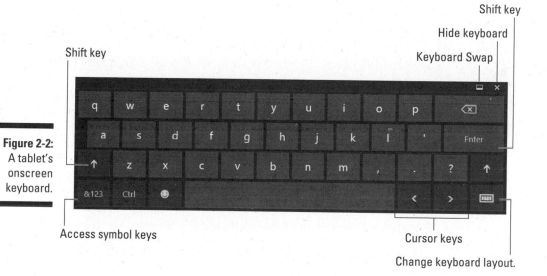

Figure 2-2:
A tablet's
onscreen
keyboard.

Shift key

Hide keyboard

Keyboard Swap

Shift key

Access symbol keys

Cursor keys

Change keyboard layout.

"Do I need to learn to type?"

No one needs to learn to type to use a word processor, but you do yourself a favor when you learn. My advice is to get a computer program that teaches you to type. I can recommend the *Mavis Beacon Teaches Typing* program, even though I don't get any money from her and none of her children resembles me. I just like the name Mavis, I suppose.

Knowing how to type makes a painful experience like using Word a wee bit more enjoyable.

The onscreen keyboard's operation works basically the same as a real keyboard: You type text with your fingers, albeit probably not as fast as on a physical keyboard. Accessing some of the specialized keys (function keys, cursor keys, and so on) is problematic. Still, the idea of using Word on a touchscreen seems to be more of a quick-and-dirty thing than something you would seriously spend time doing.

Then again, I don't know how tolerant you are for pain.

✔ Using the Ctrl key on the onscreen keyboard is a two-step process: Touch the Ctrl key and then touch another key.

✔ Not all Ctrl-key combinations in Word can be produced by using the onscreen keyboard.

✔ Refer to Chapter 1 for information on activating Touch mode, which makes it easier to use Word on a tablet.

✔ You need a computer to create a document. It's possible to edit a document, or even create small documents, using a tablet, but it's not the best tool for a job.

The Old Hunt-and-Peck

After starting Word, you'll most likely type these words next:

Clackity-clack-clack-clack.

Or on a tablet:

Smudge-smear-poke-poke-poke.

The text you type on the keyboard appears on the screen — even the typos and mistakes and bad grammar: It all falls into place regardless of your intent, posture, or good looks. This section offers some basic typing tips, suggestions, and advice.

Following the cursor

The key to writing in Word is to look for the *insertion pointer* in your text. It's a flashing vertical bar:

On a touchscreen, the vertical bar occasionally grows a circle, like an upside-down lollipop:

Use the circle to help move the cursor around; refer to Chapter 3.

Text you type appears *before* the insertion pointer, one character at a time. After a character appears, the insertion pointer hops to the right, making room for more text.

For example, type this line:

```
I want a helping of beets!
```

The insertion pointer moves to the right, marching along as you type. It's called an *insertion* pointer for a reason: Press the left-arrow key a few times to move the insertion pointer back before the word *helping*.

Type the word *second* and a space. The word (and the space) is inserted into your text. The text to the right is pushed off to make room for the new text. Now the sentence should read:

```
I want a second helping of beets!
```

Chapter 3 covers moving the insertion pointer around in more detail.

- When using a multi-touch monitor and the onscreen keyboard, you may occasionally see word suggestions appear as you type. Touch the suggestion to have that word automatically inserted into the text.

- Touching the lollipop insertion pointer's circle displays a pop-up palette of shortcut commands. See Chapter 6 for more information.

Whacking the spacebar

Pressing the spacebar inserts a *space character* into the text. Spaces are important between words and sentences. Withoutthemreadingwouldbedifficult.

The most important thing to remember about the spacebar is that you need to whack it only once. In word processing, as in all typing done on a computer, only *one* space appears between words and after punctuation. That's it!

- I'm serious! If you're an old-timer, you're probably used to putting two spaces after a period, which is what they once taught in typing class, back in the last century. This extra space is wrong on a computer; typing it doesn't add more room between words or sentences in a word processor. Trust me on that.

- Anytime you feel like using two or more spaces, what you need is a tab. Tabs are best for indenting text as well as for lining up text in columns. See Chapter 12 for more information.

- The reason that only one space is needed between sentences is that computers use proportionally spaced type. Old-fashioned typewriters used monospace type, so pressing the spacebar twice after a sentence was supposed to aid in readability (though it's debatable). Computer type is more like professionally typeset material, and both typesetters and professional-document folks know to put only one space after a period or a colon.

- If you want to type two spaces after a period and actually see them, choose a monospace font, such as Courier.

Backing up and erasing

When you make a typo or another type of typing error, press the Backspace key on the keyboard. The Backspace key is used to back up and erase. The Delete key can also be used to erase text, though it gobbles up characters to the *right* of the insertion pointer. See Chapter 4 for more information on deleting text.

Pressing the Enter key

In word processing, you press the Enter key only when you reach the end of a paragraph. Though pressing Enter at the end of a line of text might seem logical, there's no need: Word takes the text that hangs over the end of a line and wraps it down to the next line. Therefore, you press Enter only to end a paragraph.

To practice pressing the Enter key at the end of a paragraph, type the following text:

```
Cindy was very convincing. She explained to her 4-year-old
brother that snails were a delicacy in France, so the
moist, slow-moving monopods were completely safe. Yet
Zach was dubious. Sure, he loved his big sister. And while
he didn't mind occasionally popping a snail's delicate
shell between his toes, he most definitely wasn't going to
put one in his mouth.
```

Now that you're done typing the paragraph, press the Enter key. There. You did it right.

- ✔ There's no need to use the Enter key when you want to double-space your text. Double-spacing uses a text formatting command in Word. See Chapter 11 for more information.

- ✔ Neither do you need to press the Enter key twice to add extra space between your paragraphs. Word can automatically add space before or after paragraphs, which is also covered in Chapter 11.

- ✔ If you want to indent a paragraph, press the Tab key after pressing Enter. This can also be done automatically; refer to (you guessed it) Chapter 11.

- ✔ The process of taking text from the end of one line and placing it at the start of the next line is named *word wrap*.

Curse you, Sticky Keys!

As your mind wanders, your fingers absently press and release the Shift key. Suddenly, you see the warning: Sticky Keys! By pressing the Shift, Ctrl, or Alt key five times in a row, you activate the Windows Sticky Keys function, a tool designed to make a computer keyboard more accessible to people. If you don't need the help, you'll probably find the intrusion annoying.

Don't panic! You can easily turn off the Sticky Keys feature: In the Sticky Keys warning dialog box, click the link titled Go to the Ease of Access Center to Disable the Keyboard Shortcut. In the dialog box that appears, remove the check marks by any and all Sticky Keys options and settings. Click OK and you'll never be bothered again!

Stuff That Happens While You Type

As you madly compose your text, fingers energetically jabbing the buttons on the keyboard, you may notice a few things happening on the screen. You might see spots. You might see lines and boxes. You may even see lightning! All are side effects of typing in Word. They're normal, and they're explained in this section.

Watching the status bar

The reason it's the *status* bar is that it can show you the status of your document, updating information as you type, as shown in Figure 2-3.

Current page

Total pages

Word count

Document proofing

Other stuff may appear here.

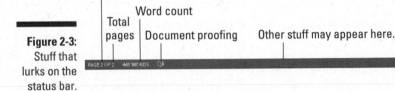

Figure 2-3: Stuff that lurks on the status bar.

PAGE 2 OF 2   445 WORDS   100%

The type of information that's displayed, as well as how much information is displayed, depends on how you configured Word. Chapter 29 explains which features the status bar can display.

To better view the status bar when typing with the onscreen keyboard, touch the Keyboard Swap button, shown in the margin. After you touch the button, the status bar jumps up, above the keyboard.

Observing page breaks

Word tries its best to show you where one page ends and another page begins. This feature is most helpful because oftentimes you want to keep elements on one page, or maybe folks just like to know when the text they're writing flows from one page to the next.

The status bar helps you discover which page you're working on. For example, the page-number indicator changes from 6 to 7 when you start a new page. Word also shows you graphically where one page ends and another begins.

In Print Layout view, which is the way Word normally shows your document, you see virtual pages and a space between them, as shown in Figure 2-4.

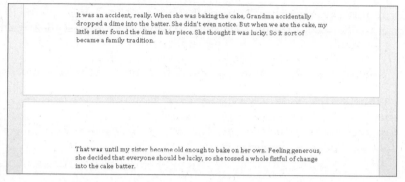

It was an accident, really. When she was baking the cake, Grandma accidentally dropped a dime into the batter. She didn't even notice. But when we ate the cake, my little sister found the dime in her piece. She thought it was lucky. So it sort of became a family tradition.

That was until my sister became old enough to bake on her own. Feeling generous, she decided that everyone should be lucky, so she tossed a whole fistful of change into the cake batter.

Figure 2-4:
The page break in Print Layout view.

Text appearing above the ethereal void is on one page, and text below the void is on the next page. Yes, it looks just like real sheets of paper.

- ✔ In Word, only the Print Layout and Draft views show page breaks. In Draft view, the page break appears as a line of dots marching across the screen. Refer to Chapter 1 for more information on Print Layout and Draft views.

- ✔ You can change the gap between pages in Print Layout view. Point the mouse at the gap. When the mouse pointer changes, as shown in the margin, double-click to either close or open the gap.

- ✔ See Chapter 13 for information on forcing page breaks in Word. My advice: Don't force a page break by pressing the Enter key a gazillion times. You'll regret it.

Working collapsible headers

You may see a tiny triangle to the left of various headings in your documents. These triangles allow you to expand or collapse all text in the header's section. Click once to collapse the text; click again to expand it. Also see Chapter 25, which covers using collapsible headers in detail, as well as using Word's outlining abilities.

Dealing with spots and clutter in the text

There's no cause for alarm if you see spots — or dots — amid the text you type, such as

`This·can·be·very·annoying.¶`

What you're seeing are *nonprinting characters*. Word uses various symbols to represent things you normally don't see: spaces, tabs, the Enter key, and more.

 To turn these items on or off, click the Show/Hide button on the Home tab in the Paragraph group. Click once to show the goobers; click again to hide them.

The keyboard shortcut for the Show/Hide command is Ctrl+Shift+8.

Why bother with showing the goobers? Sometimes, it's useful to check out what's up with formatting, find stray tabs visually, or locate missing paragraphs, for example. (*WordPerfect users:* It's as close as you can get to the Reveal Codes command in Word.)

Understanding colored underlines

Adding underlining to your text in Word is cinchy; Chapter 10 tells you all about that character format. Yet sometimes Word may do some underlining and add strange-colored text on its own.

Red zigzag: Spelling errors in Word are underlined with red zigzags. See Chapter 7.

Blue zigzag: Grammatical and word-choice errors are flagged with a special blue zigzag. The blue underlined text is most likely not the best choice for you to use. Again, see Chapter 7.

Blue underlines: Word courteously highlights web page addresses by using blue, underlined text in your document. You can Ctrl+click the blue underlined text to visit the web page.

Red lines: You may see red lines in the margin, underneath or through text. If so, it means that you're using Word's Track Changes feature. It can drive you nuts when you don't know what's going on, so see Chapter 26 to keep your sanity.

Part II
Your Basic Word

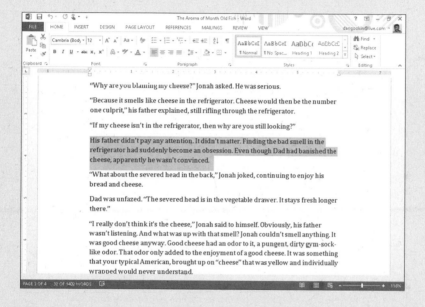

In this part . . .

✔ Discover how to use the scroll bars, move the insertion pointer, and get around with keyboard shortcuts.

✔ Find out how to delete characters, lines, sentences, paragraphs, and pages. You'll also be introduced to the life-saving Undo command.

✔ Learn how to find and replace text in your Word 2013 documents.

✔ Work with blocks of text and see how you can mark, select, copy, move, and paste blocks.

✔ Customize Word 2013's spell checker and AutoCorrect settings.

✔ Get familiar with how to preview and print your Word 2013 documents. You'll also learn how to send a Word 2013 document as an attachment.

✔ Find out how to make Word 2013 spell-check foreign words in your documents at www.dummies.com/extras/word2013.

Chapter 3

To and Fro in a Document

1 like the word *fro.* I like the word *yon.* They're archaic in the English language, referring to a direction and a location, respectively. *Fro* makes no sense by itself, so it's used in the phrase *to and fro,* which refers to going somewhere and then back again. *Yon* is often seen with its friends *hither* and *thither,* meaning "here" and "there." In that context, *yon* is a place beyond *there* (wherever *there* is). It's also short for *yonder,* which is another cool word that most people no longer use.

As you work in Word, you find yourself moving to and fro and hither, thither, and yon. That's because writing text isn't always a linear task. You need to move that little insertion-pointer guy around the document. It's basic movement. It's the topic of this chapter.

Scroll Through a Document

It's ironic that the word *scroll* is used to refer to an electronic document. The scroll was the first form of portable recorded text, existing long before bound books. On a computer, scrolling is the process by which you view a little bit of a big document in a tiny window. This section explains how scrolling is relevant in Word.

Using the vertical scroll bar

On the right side of the Word program window, you find the vertical scroll bar, illustrated in Figure 3-1. The bar can disappear at times; move the mouse over your text, and it shows up again.

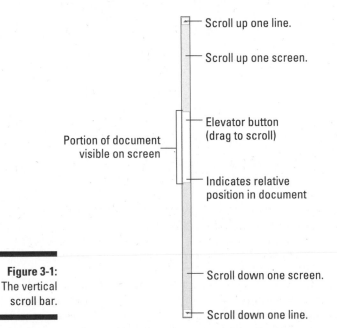

Scroll up one line.

Scroll up one screen.

Elevator button
(drag to scroll)

Portion of document
visible on screen

Indicates relative
position in document

Figure 3-1:
The vertical
scroll bar.

Scroll down one screen.

Scroll down one line.

The vertical scroll bar's operation is similar to the scroll bar in any Windows program:

✔ Click the up- or down-arrow buttons at the top and bottom of the vertical scroll bar to scroll your document up or down. The document scrolls one line of text for each time you click those up- or down-arrow buttons.

✔ An *elevator button* appears inside the scroll bar. You can drag this button with the mouse, up or down, to scroll the document.

✔ You can click above or below the elevator button to scroll up or down one screen of text at a time.

The elevator button's size reflects how much of your document you can see at a time. When the button doesn't show up, or is dimmed, the whole document appears onscreen. Otherwise, the elevator button becomes smaller as your document grows longer.

The elevator button's position also helps show you which part of your document is visible. When the elevator button is at the top of the scroll bar, you're viewing text near the start of the document. When the elevator button is toward the bottom of the scroll bar, you're seeing text near the document's end.

Special bonuses are involved when you drag the elevator button to scroll through your document. As you drag the button up or down, you see a page number displayed, as shown in Figure 3-2. When a document is formatted with heading styles, you also see the heading title below the page number.

Figure 3-2:
Scroll bar
page-
number info.

Page: 9
Martin Kills Brenda because ...

Scrolling through your document doesn't move the insertion pointer. If you start typing, don't be surprised when Word jumps back to where the insertion pointer lurks.

Scrolling a document doesn't move the insertion pointer!

Using the horizontal scroll bar

The horizontal scroll bar appears just above the status bar, at the bottom of the Word window — but only when your document is wider than the window. When that happens, you can use the horizontal scroll bar to shift the page back and forth, left and right.

When the horizontal (left-right) shifting bugs you, consider using Word's Zoom tool to adjust the size of your document on the screen. See Chapter 29.

Scrolling your document with the mouse

Aside from manipulating the scroll bars, you can use your computer mouse to scurry and scamper about your document. Sadly, this suggestions works only when you have one of those wheel mice. Coincidentally, you do all these tricks by manipulating that unique wheel button:

✔ Roll the wheel up or down to scroll your document up or down.

✔ Press and hold the wheel button to activate scrolling mode. With the wheel button down, you can move the mouse up or down to *pan* your document in that direction.

✔ If the mouse's wheel button also tilts from side to side, you can use it to pan left and right.

For computers and tablets with a touchscreen, scroll your document by using your finger: Swipe the screen up to scroll down; swipe the screen down to scroll up. Don't worry! It makes sense when you do it.

Move the Insertion Pointer

The beauty of the word processor is that you can edit any part of your document; you don't always have to work at "the end." The key to pulling off this trick is to know how to move the insertion pointer to the exact spot you want.

Moving the insertion pointer is important! Scientific studies have shown that merely looking at the computer screen does no good. As hard as you wish, new text appears only at the insertion pointer. And, the text you edit or delete? Yup, the insertion pointer's location is important there as well. Obviously, knowing how to move the insertion pointer is a big deal.

Commanding the insertion pointer

The easiest way to put the insertion pointer exactly where you want it is to point the mouse at that spot in your text and then click the mouse button. Point, click, move insertion pointer. Simple.

If you have a touchscreen monitor or are using a tablet, you can move the insertion pointer to any specific location by touching the text with your finger. Use the circle that appears below the insertion pointer for precise positioning.

Moving in small increments (basic arrow keys)

For short hops, nothing beats using the keyboard's arrow keys to quickly move the insertion pointer around a document. The four basic arrow keys move the insertion pointer up, down, right, and left:

Press This Key	To Move the Insertion Pointer
↑	Up to the preceding line of text
↓	Down to the next line of text
→	Right to the next character
←	Left to the preceding character

Moving the cursor doesn't erase characters. See Chapter 4 for information on deleting stuff.

If you press and hold the Ctrl (Control) key and then press an arrow key, you enter Jump mode. The invigorated insertion pointer leaps desperately in all four directions:

Press This Key Combo	To Move the Insertion Pointer
Ctrl+↑	Up to the start of the previous paragraph
Ctrl+↓	Down to the start of the next paragraph
Ctrl+→	Right to the start (first letter) of the next word
Ctrl+←	Left to the start (first letter) of the previous word

You can use either set of arrow keys on the computer keyboard, but when using the numeric keypad, ensure that the Num Lock light is off. Do this by pressing the Num Lock key. If you don't, you see numbers in your text rather than the insertion pointer dancing all over — like444this.

Moving from beginning to end

The insertion pointer also bows to pressure from those cursor keys without arrows on them. The first couple consists of End and Home, which move the insertion pointer to the start or end of something, depending on how End and Home are used:

Press This Key or Combination	To Whisk the Insertion Pointer
End	To the end of a line of text
Home	To the start of a line of text
Ctrl+End	To the end of the document
Ctrl+Home	To the tippy-top of the document

The remaining cursor keys are the Page Up or PgUp key and the Page Down or PgDn key. As you might guess, using these keys doesn't move up or down a page in your document. Nope. Instead, they slide through your document one screen at a time. Here's the roundup:

Press This Key or Combination	To Whisk the Insertion Pointer
PgUp	Up one screen or to the tippy-top of your document, if you happen to be near it
PgDn	Down one screen or to the end of the document, if you happen to be near it
Ctrl+Alt+PgUp	To the top of the current screen
Ctrl+Alt+PgDn	To the bottom of the current screen

The key combinations to move to the top or bottom of the current screen are Ctrl+Alt+PgUp and Ctrl+Alt+PgDn. That's Ctrl+Alt, not just the Ctrl key. And yes, few people use these commands.

You may be tempted to use Ctrl+PgUp and Ctrl+PgDn, but don't: These keyboard shortcuts work with the Find command. See Chapter 5.

Go Back to Where You Once Edited

Considering all the various commands for moving the insertion pointer, it's quite possible to make a mistake and not know where you are in a document. Yea, verily, the insertion pointer has gone where no insertion pointer has gone before.

Rather than click your heels together three times and try to get back the wishful way, just remember this keyboard combination:

Shift+F5

Pressing the Shift+F5 keys forces Word to return you to the last spot you edited. You can do this as many as three times before the cycle repeats. But the first time should get you back to where you were before you got lost.

Sadly, the Shift+F5 keyboard shortcut works only in Word; you can't use this command in real life.

Go to Wherever with the Go To Command

Word's Go To command allows you to send the insertion pointer to a specific page or line or to the location of a number of interesting elements that Word can potentially cram into your document. The Go To command is your word processing teleporter to anywhere.

To use the Go To command, click the Find button in the Home tab's editing group. Choose the Go To command from the menu. Or you can use the Ctrl+G keyboard shortcut. Either way, the Go To tab portion of the Find and Replace dialog box appears, as shown in Figure 3-3.

Figure 3-3:
Telling
Word to
Go To
you-know-
where.

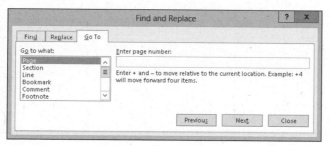

Choose which element to go to, such as a page, from the scrolling list on the left side of the dialog box. Then type the relevant information, such as a page number, in the box on the right side of the dialog box. Click the Go To button to go to that location.

For example, type **14** in the box and press Enter, and you go to page 14 — if you have a page 14 to go to.

Note that you can go to a page *relative* to the current page. For example, to go three pages forward, choose Page and type **+3**. To go 12 pages backward, type **-12** in the box.

Chapter 4

Text Editing

1 believe that writing involves two parts of your brain: The wild, creative-burst part is the typing part. Then there's the tame, controlled-editing part. You need both parts in order to write anything good. In fact, I'd wager that people who become frustrated with writing are too quick to enter the controlled-editing part. Don't fall into that trap: Write! Spew forth your words! Editing your text is easier when you have lots of words than when you have only a scant few.

When you're ready to edit, you'll use Word's text editing commands. They all basically delete the stuff you've written. That's right: Editing text is basically the same task as ruthlessly slashing away words from your text. Word comes with ample tools to make that happen. Use them freely, as described in this chapter. But get your abundance of words down on paper before you enter the vicious slashing mode.

Remove Text You Don't Want

Credit the guy who put the eraser on the end of the pencil: It's a given that human beings make mistakes. The round, soft eraser counterbalances the sharp point of the pencil in more ways than one.

The ability to erase text is just as valuable and necessary as the ability to create text. Deleting text is part of writing text, part of thinking and rethinking, and part of self-editing. Writing. Deleting. Rewriting. Redeleting. That's how it goes!

Both creating and destroying text are accomplished by using the keyboard. The majority of keys are used to create text. Only two keys delete text: Backspace and Delete. How these keys work, and how much of your text they can delete, depends on how the keys are used, as described in this section.

Deleting single characters

Use the Backspace and Delete keys by themselves to delete single characters:

✓ **Backspace key:** Deletes the character to the left of the insertion pointer

✓ **Delete key:** Deletes the character to the right of the insertion pointer

In the following example, the insertion pointer is "flashing" (okay, it *would* be flashing on a computer screen) between the *z* and the *e* in *dozens*. Pressing the Backspace key deletes the *z;* pressing the Delete key deletes the *e:*

```
Duane made doz|ens of delightful things in his
woodshop yet still managed to retain all his
fingers.
```

The touchscreen keyboard features only the Backspace key, which, ironically, supports the universal symbol for the Delete key. Touching this key backs up and erases. There's no Delete key equivalent on the touchscreen keyboard to delete the character to the right of the insertion pointer.

✓ After you delete a character, any text to the right or below the character shuffles over to fill the void.

✓ You can press and hold Backspace or Delete to continuously "machine-gun-delete" characters. Release the key to halt such wanton destruction, although I recommend using other delete commands (covered in this chapter) rather than the machine-gun approach.

✓ Special types of text in Word cannot easily be deleted using either the Backspace key or Delete key. An example is an updating text *field,* which holds special text that always shows, say, today's date. This type of text appears shaded in a light gray color when you try to delete it. That's Word reminding you of the unusualness of the text. Press the Delete or Backspace key a second time to delete such text. See Chapter 23 for more information on fields.

Deleting a word

To gobble up an entire word, add the Ctrl key to the Backspace or Delete key's destructive power:

- ✔ Ctrl+Backspace deletes the word in front (to the left) of the insertion pointer.
- ✔ Ctrl+Delete deletes the word behind (to the right) of the insertion pointer.

These keyboard shortcuts work best when the insertion pointer is at the start or end of a word. When you're in the middle of the word, the commands delete only from that middle point to the start or end of the word.

After you delete a word, the insertion pointer sits at the end of the preceding word (or paragraph) when you use Ctrl+Backspace. Deleting a word by using Ctrl+Delete puts the cursor at the beginning of the next word. This is done to facilitate the rapid deletion of several words in a row.

After deleting the text, Word neatly wraps up the remaining text, snuggling it together in a grammatically proper way; deleting a word doesn't leave a "hole" in your text.

No mere pencil eraser can match Ctrl+Delete or Ctrl+Backspace for sheer speed and terror!

Deleting more than a word

Word lacks keyboard-specific commands to delete more than a word or character of text. Larger chunks of your document can be deleted, swiftly and effectively. It's just that those ways are not that obvious.

Delete a line of text

A line of text is merely a line across the page (not really a grammatical issue). The easiest way to delete a line of text is to use the mouse:

1. **Move the mouse into the left margin of your document.**

   You know you've found the sweet spot when the mouse pointer changes into a northeast arrow.

2. **Point the mouse pointer arrow at the line of text you want to obliterate.**

3. **Click the mouse.**

   The line of text is highlighted, or *selected.*

4. **Press the Delete key to send that line into oblivion.**

Delete a sentence

A sentence is a grammatical thing. You know: Start with a capital letter and end with a period, a question mark, or an exclamation point. You probably mastered this concept in grammar school, which is why they call it grammar school anyway.

Making a sentence go bye-bye is cinchy:

1. **Hover the mouse over the offending sentence.**

2. **Press and hold the Ctrl key and click the mouse.**

   The sentence is selected.

3. **Press the Delete key.**

   Oomph! It's gone.

Delete a paragraph

A paragraph is one or more sentences, or a heading, ending with a press of the Enter key. Here's the fastest way to delete a full paragraph:

1. **Point the mouse at the paragraph.**

2. **Click the mouse button thrice.**

   Thrice means "three times."

3. **Press the Delete key.**

If clicking thrice befuddles you, move the mouse pointer into the left margin, next to the offending paragraph. When the mouse pointer changes to a north-easterly pointing arrow, click twice to select the entire paragraph.

Delete a page

A page of text is just that — all the text from where the page starts to where the page ends. It's a physical thing.

Pages are a formatting issue, not something Word deals directly with regard to editing. Even so, to delete a page, mind these steps:

1. **Press Ctrl+G to summon the Go To tab in the Find and Replace dialog box.**

   See Chapter 3 for more information on the Go To command.

2. **Choose Page from the Go to What list.**

3. **Type the number of the page you want to delete.**

4. **Click the Go To button and then click the Close button.**

   The insertion pointer is positioned at the top of the page you chose in Step 3.

5. **Press the F8 key.**

   The F8 key is used to enter a special selection mode in Word, which I cover in detail in Chapter 6.

6. **Press Ctrl+PgDn (the Page Down key).**

   The entire page is now selected.

7. **Press the Delete key.**

   The page is gone.

Refer to Chapter 9 for special information on deleting that annoying extra, blank page at the end of your document.

Delete an odd-size chunk of text

Word lets you delete any old odd-size chunk of text anywhere in your document. The key is to mark that text as a block. After the block is marked, you can press the Delete key to zap it to Kingdom Come. Refer to Chapter 6 for more information on blocks of text.

Split and Join Paragraphs

For some people, a paragraph in a word processor is a strange thing. It's basically a chunk of text. Like most things that come in chunks — cheese, meat, large men named Floyd — it's often necessary to split or combine them. Well, maybe not for Floyd.

Making two paragraphs from one

To split a single paragraph in twain, locate the point where you want it to break — say, between two sentences. Move the insertion pointer to that location and then press the Enter key. Word splits the paragraph in two; the text above the insertion pointer becomes its own paragraph, and the text following it then becomes the next paragraph.

Depending on how the paragraph was torn asunder, you may need to delete an extra space at the beginning of the second paragraph or at the end of the first paragraph.

Making one paragraph from two

To join two paragraphs and turn them into one, you delete the Enter character between the paragraphs. To do that, move the insertion pointer to the start of the second paragraph and then press the Backspace key. Removing the Enter character joins two paragraphs.

Depending on how neatly the paragraphs were joined, you may need to add a space between the sentences at the spot where the paragraphs were glued together.

The Soft and Hard Returns

Pressing the Enter key in Word ends a paragraph. It's officially known as typing a *hard return*. Yes, it's *return* even though the key is known as Enter on a PC. Don't blame me for this odd nomenclature. I only write the books — not the programs.

The problem with the hard return is that it adds a bit of "air" after a paragraph. That's a good thing; as I explain in Chapter 11, you should have air around paragraphs in a document. Those times when you don't want air, when you need to put lines of text close together, you use a soft return.

The *soft return,* or *line break,* is used primarily in titles and headings; when you have a long title and need to split it up between two lines, you press Shift+Enter to insert the soft return. For example, type this line:

```
Enjoying the Ballet
```

Press Shift+Enter. A new line starts. Continue typing:

```
A Guide for Husbands and Boyfriends
```

The soft return keeps the title text together (in the same paragraph), but on separate lines.

You should also use the soft return when typing an address, either on an envelope or in a letter. Press Shift+Enter after typing each of these lines:

```
Mr. President
1600 Pennsylvania Ave.
Washington, DC 20500
```

If you try typing the same text and press Enter instead, you see more space between the lines, which isn't what you want. Nope, that soft return can sure come in handy.

Undo Mistakes with Undo Haste

That quaffing and drinking will undo you.

— Richard II, William Shakespeare

The Undo command undoes anything you do in Word, which includes formatting text, moving blocks, typing and deleting text, formatting — the whole enchilada. You have two handy ways to unleash the Undo command:

- ✔ Press Ctrl+Z.
- ✔ Click the Undo command button on the Quick Access Toolbar.

 I prefer using the Ctrl+Z key combination, but an advantage of the Undo command button is that it sports a drop-down menu that helps you review the past several things you've done, or that can be undone.

- ✔ Word's Undo command is handy, but don't use it as an excuse to be sloppy!

- ✔ Regrettably, you cannot pick and choose from the Undo command button's drop-down menu; you can merely undo multiple instances of things all at one time.

- ✔ The Undo command works sporadically sometimes. Before this happens, Word warns you. For example, you may see a message such as "There is not enough memory to undo this operation, Continue?" Proceed at your own peril.

- ✔ The Undo command doesn't work when there's nothing to undo or if something simply cannot be undone. For example, you cannot undo a save-to-disk operation.

- ✔ To undo an Undo, choose Redo. See the next section.

Undoing the Undo command with Redo

If you undo something and — whoops! — you didn't mean to, you must use the Redo command to set things back to the way they were. For example, you may type some text and then use Undo to "untype" the text. You can use the Redo command to restore the typing. You have two choices:

- Press Ctrl+Y.
- Click the Redo command button on the Quick Access Toolbar.

The Redo command does exactly the opposite of whatever the Undo command does. So, if you type text, Undo untypes the text and Redo recovers the text. If you use Undo to recover deleted text, Redo deletes the text again.

Using the Repeat command

When the Redo command has nothing left to redo, it changes functions and becomes the Repeat command. Its function is to repeat the last thing you did in Word, whether it's typing text, applying a format, or doing a variety of other things.

Lamentably, you can't use the Repeat command to ease your typing chores. That's because it repeats only the last single character you typed.

- The keyboard shortcut for the Repeat command is Ctrl+Y, the same as the Redo command.

- See Part III of this book for information on formatting.

- In older versions of Word, the Repeat command could be used to replicate vast swaths of text. In Word 2013, however, it repeats only the last character you typed.

Chapter 5

Search for This, Replace It with That

*L*ittle Bo Peep has lost her sheep. Too bad she doesn't know about Word's Find and Replace commands. She could find the misplaced ruminants in a matter of nanoseconds. Not only that, she could use search-and-replace to, say, replace all the sheep with real estate. It's all cinchy after you understand and use the various Find and Replace commands. Sadly it's only words that are replaced. True, if Word could search and replace real things, there'd be a lot less sheep in the world.

Text Happily Found

Finding text is the domain of the Editing group, found on the far right end of the Home tab on Word's Ribbon interface. The Editing command button group may appear in its full glory, shown in Figure 5-1, or, when Word's window is too narrow, simply as an Editing button. When it's a button, you must click the button first to see the palette of commands, which (surprisingly) looks like the one shown in Figure 5-1.

Figure 5-1:
The Editing
group.

Finding a tidbit o' text

Word can quickly and graphically locate text in your document, from the smallest iota to the world's longest run-on sentence. It's handled by the Find command. Abide by these steps:

1. On the Home tab, click the Find button in the Editing group.

You can also use the keyboard shortcut, Ctrl+F, which is one of the few keyboard shortcuts that makes sense.

Clicking the Find button or pressing Ctrl+F summons the Navigation pane, illustrated in Figure 5-2.

View page previews. Close Navigation pane.

Search text Clear search text. Search document up/down.

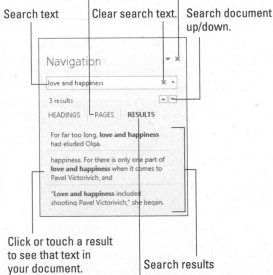

Figure 5-2:
The
Navigation
pane helps
you locate
text.

Click or touch a result to see that text in your document.

Search results

View in-context previews.

2. Type the text you want to find.

As you type, matching text is highlighted in the document. Depending on which tab is chosen in the Navigation pane, you see a summary of matching results beneath the text box (refer to Figure 5-2).

Be exact. For example, if you want to find love and happiness, type **love and happiness** — no period or spaces or quotes. Type only the text you're looking for.

3. **Click the up or down arrows (refer to Figure 5-2) to page through the search results until you find the exact chunk of text you want.**

   As you page, the document scrolls to find the next matching bit of text. Text is highlighted in your document, which makes visually searching easier.

4. **Close the Navigation pane when you're done hunting down text.**

When text can't be found, the Navigation pane tells you that it can't find the text. It uses the pronoun *we,* which I find disturbing.

✔ The Navigation pane may already display text in the Find What box. If so, you can delete the text by pressing the Backspace key.

✔ Do not end the text with a period unless you want to find the period, too.

✔ The Find command can find elements that you can't readily type, such as the Tab key or Enter key. See the section "Finding stuff you can't type," later in this chapter.

✔ If you're not sure whether the text is typed in uppercase or lowercase letters, use lowercase.

✔ If the text isn't found and you're *certain* that it's in there, check your spelling. If it's correct, try searching for a single word rather than two or more words or a sentence.

✔ Word finds text only in the current document (the one you see on the screen). To find text in another document, switch to that document's window and try searching again.

Scouring your document with Advanced Find

The Navigation pane is sweet, like the ideal prom date. But you don't really want the ideal prom date. No, you desire a date that you don't necessarily want to show Mom and Dad. In Word, the prom date you really want for finding text is the traditional Find dialog box, the one that lived in the neighborhood before the Navigation pane rolled into town.

To unleash the Advanced Find command, obey these steps:

1. **Ensure that your parents don't know what you're up to.**

   Good.

2. **Click the Home tab on the Ribbon, if necessary.**

   You need to access the Editing group, which is found on the Home tab.

3. **Click the menu arrow by the Find command in the Editing group.**

   The arrow is that down-pointing triangle next to the Find command button.

4. **Choose Advanced Find.**

   What you see is the traditional Find dialog box, which I find more powerful and precise than the Navigation pane. Shhh!

5. **Click the More button.**

   Upon success, the Find and Replace dialog box grows taller, with a bunch of options and doodads showing at the bottom — its über-abilities — as illustrated in Figure 5-3.

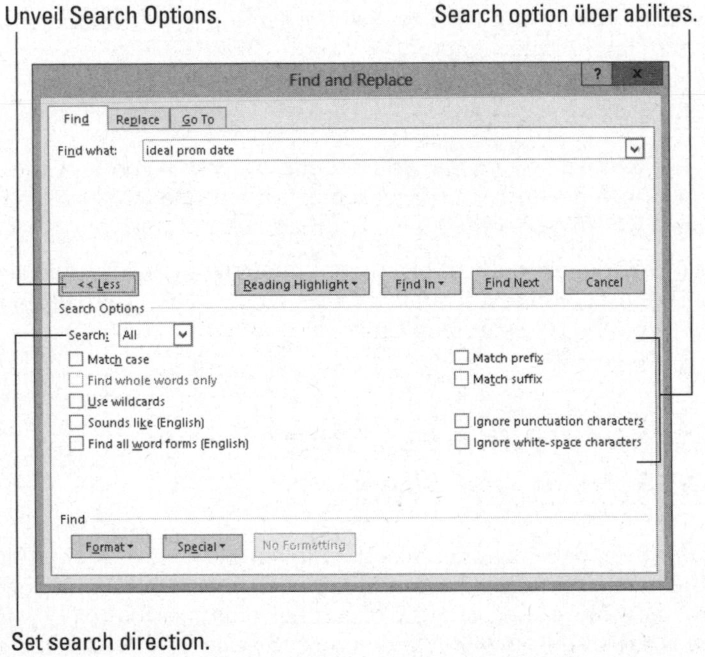

Unveil Search Options.   Search option über abilites.

Figure 5-3: The Advanced Find dialog box.

Set search direction.

The following sections explain how you can use the Advanced Find command.

✔ It's possible to reassign the keyboard shortcut Ctrl+F from the Navigation pane to the Advanced Find dialog box, the way things used to work, back in older versions of Word. This bit of Word wizardry is divulged in Chapter 31.

✔ Options set for the Advanced Find command remain set until you turn them off. If you can't seem to locate text that you *know* is in your document, review the settings in the Advanced Find dialog box. Turn off the ones you no longer need.

Find an exact bit of text

There's a difference between *Pat* and *pat.* One is a name, and the other is to lightly touch something. To use the Find command to find one and not the other, select the Match Case option under Search Options. That way, *Pat* matches only words that start with an uppercase *P* and have lowercase *at* in them.

Find a whole word

Use the Find Whole Words Only option to look for words such as *elf* and *ogre* without also finding words like *shelf* and *progress.*

Find text that sounds like something else

The Sounds Like (English) option allows you to search for *homonyms,* or words that sound the same as the search word. You know: *their* and *there,* or *deer* and *dear,* or *hear* and *here.* How this is useful, I'll never know.

Oh! This isn't a rhyming search command. If you try to use it to find everything that rhymes with *Doris,* for example, it doesn't find *Boris, chorus, pylorus,* or anything of the like.

Find variations of a word

Your editor informs you that no one will believe how the protagonist in your novel uses a pogo stick to travel the South. So you make him a biker. That involves changing every variation of the word *hop* (*hopping* and *hopped,* for example) to *ride.* In Word, you put a check mark by the option Find All Word Forms (English) in the Advanced Find command's dialog box (refer to Figure 5-3) and type the word **hop** in the Find What box. Click the Find Next button and you're on your way.

Search this way or that

Word normally searches from the insertion pointer's position to the end of a document and then back 'round the top again. You can override this stubbornness by placing your hand on the Find command's tiller in the Search drop-down list (refer to Figure 5-3). You have three options:

- **Down:** When this option is chosen, Word searches from the insertion pointer's location to the end of your document, and then it stops.

- **Up:** Word searches — backward — from the insertion pointer's location to the start of your document. Then it stops.

- **All:** Word searches the entire document, from the insertion pointer's location down to the end of the document, back up to the beginning, and then back to where you started searching.

You can use keyboard shortcuts to search up or down. The Ctrl+PgDn key combination repeats the last search downward; the Ctrl+PgUp key combination repeats the most recent search upward.

Finding stuff you can't type

You can search for certain items in a document that you just cannot type at the keyboard. No, I'm not talking about nasty things — this isn't a censorship issue. Instead, I'm referring to items such as tabs, Enter keys (paragraphs), page breaks, graphics, and other, similar nontypeable things.

The techniques described in the sections that follow use the Advanced Find dialog box, described in the earlier section, "Scouring your document with Advanced Find." Also refer to Figure 5-3.

Find special characters

To hunt down untypeable characters in your document, click the Special button in the Advanced Find dialog box. Up pops a list of 22 items that Word can search for but that you would have a dickens of a time typing.

Despite the exhaustive list, there are probably only a half dozen items you'll eventually (if ever) use. They include

- **Any Character, Any Digit,** and **Any Letter** are special characters that represent, well, just about anything. These items can be used as wild cards for matching lots of stuff.

- **Caret Character** allows you to search for a caret (^) symbol, which may not seem like a big deal, but it is: Word uses the ^ symbol in a special way for finding text; see the next section.

- **Paragraph Mark** (¶) is a special character that's the same as the Enter character — the one you press to end a paragraph.

- **Tab Character** moves the cursor to the next tab mark.

- **White Space** is any number of blank characters: one or more spaces, tabs, empty lines, or a combination of each one.

Use ^ to find special characters

It's possible, although nerdy, to manually type the special characters into the Find What text box. Although this method avoids using the Special menu, which can be big and baffling, it means that you need to memorize the character codes. Each one starts with the caret character, ^, and some of them are logical, such as ^p for Paragraph Mark (Enter) or ^t for Tab. Here are a few other handy shortcuts, for reference:

Paragraph mark	^p
Tab character	^t
Any character	^?
Any digit	^#
Any letter	^$

Caret character	^^
Em-dash	^+
En-dash	^=
Manual line break	^1
Manual page break	^m
White space	^w

You can mix special characters with plain text. For example, to find a tab character followed by *Hunter,* you use the Special button to insert the tab character (^t on the screen) and then type **Hunter**. It looks like this:

```
^tHunter
```

Choose an item from the list to search for that special character. When you do, a special, funky shorthand representation for that character (such as ^t for Tab) appears in the Find What box. Click the Find Next button to find that character.

Find formatting

In its most powerful superhero mode, the Find command can scour your document for formatting information. For example, if you want to find only those instances of the word *lie* in boldface type, you can do that. Before you attempt this task, I recommend that you understand Word's formatting abilities and commands, which are covered in Part III of this book.

The formatting options you can search for are revealed to you after a click of the Format button, which appears in the Advanced Find dialog box when the More button is clicked (refer to Figure 5-3). Clicking the Format button displays a pop-up menu of Word's primary formatting commands. Choosing any item from that list displays a corresponding dialog box, from which you can choose the formatting attributes to search for.

Suppose that you want to find a *red herring* in your document. Follow these steps:

1. **Summon the Advanced Find dialog box.**

   Refer to the earlier section, "Scouring your document with Advanced Find."

2. **Type** red herring **in the Find What box.**

3. **If needed, click the More button to display the bottom part of the Find and Replace dialog box.**

4. **If the No Formatting button is available, click it.**

   This button is used to clear any previous formatting attributes you may have searched for. If the button can be clicked, click it to clear out those attributes and start afresh.

5. **Click the Format button.**

6. **Choose Font from the pop-up list.**

   The Find Font dialog box appears, which is where you set or control various text attributes. Say that the red herring you're searching for is 24 points tall.

7. **Choose 24 from the Size list.**

   Look in the upper-right corner of the Find Font dialog box.

8. **Click OK.**

   The Font dialog box goes away and you return to the Find and Replace dialog box.

   Notice the text just beneath the Find What box: `Format: Font: 24 pt`. This bit of text is telling you that Word is now geared up to find only text that's 24 points tall — about twice the normal size.

9. **Click the Find Next button to find your formatted text.**

If you want to search only for a format, leave the Find What text box blank (refer to Step 2). That way, you can search for formatting attributes without caring what the text reads.

You can use this technique to look for specific occurrences of a font, such as Courier or Times New Roman, by selecting the font from the selection list. Scroll through the font menu to see what you can choose.

You can also search for paragraph formatting, such as an indented paragraph, by choosing Paragraph rather than Font from the Format pop-up list in the Find and Replace dialog box.

Yes, you can search for more than one formatting attribute at a time. Just keep choosing format options from the Format button.

The Find command remembers your formatting options! The next time you want to search for plain text, click the No Formatting button. Doing so removes the formatting attributes and allows you to search for text in any format.

Replace Found Text

The Find command is good only for finding stuff. When you want to find something and replace it with something else, you use the Find and Replace command. This section describes the details.

Replacing one thing with another

Suppose that you may want to change all instances of *ungulates* in your document to *ruminants*. Here's how that's done:

1. **On the Home tab, click the Replace command button, found nestled in the Editing group on the far right side of the Ribbon.**

    When the Replace command button isn't visible in the Editing group (refer to Figure 5-1), click the Editing button, and then choose the Replace command button from the pop-up group of command buttons that appears.

    Choosing the Replace command button displays the Find and Replace dialog box, as shown in Figure 5-4. It should be familiar if you've often used the Advanced Find command. After all, finding stuff is the first part of using Find and Replace.

Figure 5-4: The Replace part of the Find and Replace dialog box.

Find and Replace	?	X

Find | Replace | Go To

Find what: one thing

Replace with: another

More >>   Replace   Replace All   Find Next   Cancel

2. **In the Find What box, type the text you want to find.**

    You want to replace this text with something else. So, if you're finding *coffee* and replacing it with *tea*, type **coffee**.

    Press the Tab key when you're done typing.

3. **In the Replace With box, type the text you want to use to replace the original text.**

   To continue from the example in Step 2, you type **tea** here.

4. **Click the Find Next button.**

   At this point, the Replace command works just like the Find command: Word scours your document for the text you typed in the Find What dialog box. When that text is found, you move on to Step 5; otherwise, the Replace command fails because there's nothing to replace.

5. **Click the Replace button.**

   Word replaces the found text, highlighted onscreen, with the text typed in the Replace With box.

6. **Continue replacing.**

   After you click the Replace button, Word immediately searches for the next instance of the text, at which point you repeat Step 5 until the entire document has been searched.

7. **Read the summary that's displayed.**

   After the last bit of text is replaced, a dialog box appears and tells you that the operation is complete.

8. **Click the Close button.**

You're done!

- ✔ All the restrictions, options, and rules for the Find command also apply to finding and replacing text. Refer to the section "Text Happily Found," at the start of this chapter.

- ✔ The keyboard shortcut for the Replace command is Ctrl+H. The only way I can figure that one out is that Ctrl+F is the Find command and Ctrl+G is the Go To command. F, G, and H are found together on the computer keyboard, and Find, Replace, and Go To are found together in the Find and Replace dialog box. Go figure.

- ✔ The Replace command's dialog box also sports a More button, which can be used exactly as the More button for the Find command. See the section "Scouring your document with Advanced Find," earlier in this chapter.

- ✔ Word may find and replace your text in the middle of another word, such as *use* in *causes*. Oops! Click the More button and select the Find Whole Words Only option to prevent such a thing from happening.

- ✔ If you don't type anything in the Replace With box, Word replaces your text with *nothing!* It's wanton destruction!

✔ Speaking of wanton destruction, the Undo command restores your document to its preceding condition if you foul up the Replace operation. See Chapter 4 for more information.

Replacing it all at once

The steps in the previous section work well to find and replace tidbits of text around your document. But it can often be tedious to keep pressing that Replace button over and over. That's why the Replace command's dialog box sports the handy Replace All button.

The Replace All button directs the Replace command to find all instances of the Find What text and — without question — replace it with the Replace With text. To use this button, simply click the Replace All button in Step 5 in the preceding section. Then skip to Step 8.

Be doubly certain that you made the proper settings in the Find and Replace dialog box before you click that Replace All button! You can still undo any mistakes, but for a large document, a lot of text can be found and replaced in a manner most merciless.

Finding and replacing formatting

Just as the Find command can search for text with specific formatting, you can use the Replace command to replace text and apply formatting or to replace one type of formatting with another. Needless to say, this process can be tricky: Not only do I recommend that you be familiar with Word's formatting commands, but you should also be well practiced in using the Find and Replace command.

Suppose that you want to replace all instances of underlined text with italic. Underlined text reeks so much of typewriter, and that's just too 20th century for these modern times. By replacing underline with italic, you're searching for one text format and replacing it with another; you're not even searching for text. So be careful. Do this:

1. **Press Ctrl+H to summon the Find and Replace dialog box.**

2. **Click the mouse in the Find What text box and press the Delete key.**

   All text must be removed from the Find What text box.

3. **Click the More button, if necessary, to display the full dialog box.**

4. **Click the Format button and choose Font from the pop-up menu that appears.**

   The Find Font dialog box appears.

5. **In the Find Font dialog box, choose the single underline graphic from the Underline style drop-down list, and then click the OK button.**

   Back in the Find and Replace dialog box, the text `Format: Underline` appears below the Find What box.

6. **Click the Replace With text box and press Backspace to delete that text.**

   Any text in the Replace With text box must be erased.

7. **Choose Font from the Format button's pop-up list.**

8. **In the Replace Font dialog box, choose (None) as the underline style.**

   This step is necessary because, otherwise, Word wouldn't remove the first style; it would merely add to that style. Likewise, text attributes such as Not Bold and Not Italic are found in the Replace Font dialog box.

9. **Choose Italic from the Font Style list, and then click OK to close the Replace Font dialog box.**

   Below the Replace With box, it should say `Format: Font: Italic, No underline`. That means Word will search for underlined text and replace it with italic text *and* remove the underline.

10. **Click the Replace All button.**

    Word scours your document and replaces any underlined text with italic.

11. **Click OK when the find-and-replace is done.**

As long as you set things up carefully, searching and replacing text formatting is a quick and easy way to spiff up a boring document.

✔ To replace one format with another, such as underline with italic, be sure to leave the Find What and Replace With text boxes empty. That way, only the text formatting is replaced.

✔ An easier way to update formatting in a document is to use and apply *styles*. Refer to Chapter 15 for details.

✔ Don't forget about the No Formatting button! You need to click it if you want to change the formats or replace text without paying attention to formats.

Chapter 6

Blocks o' Text

● ●

● ●

You'll find plenty of interesting blocks when it comes to writing. First are those moveable blocks used by the ancient Chinese for printing. Then comes the inevitable writer's block. In Word, you can take advantage of blocks of text in a document, which is probably far more useful than the other types of blocks. That's because working with blocks in Word is like playing with blocks as a kid: Mix in some, cut, copy, and paste, and you have this engaging chapter on working with blocks of text.

The Tao of Text Blocks

A *block* is simply a portion of text in your document, from a single character to the entire document. The block has a beginning and an end, and the block itself consists of all the text between them.

You create a block by selecting text. You *select* text by using the keyboard or the mouse or one of various other text-selection techniques covered in this chapter.

On the screen, the block appears highlighted, as shown in Figure 6-1.

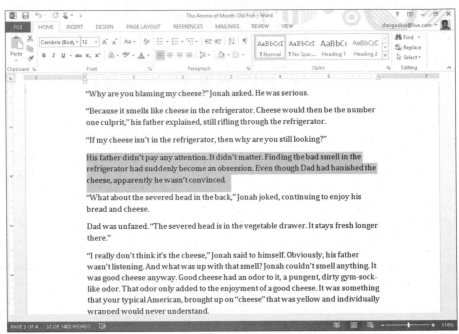

Figure 6-1:
A block
of text is
selected.

By marking off text as a block, you can perform certain actions, or use various Word commands, that affect only the text in that block. Or you can copy, move, or delete the block of text.

- ✔ A block of text in Word includes all letters and characters *and* the text formatting.

- ✔ Graphics and other nontext elements can also be selected as a block. In fact, you can select graphics along with text in the same block.

- ✔ When the status bar is displaying a word count, the number of words selected in the block of text is displayed, next to the total number of words in the document. (Refer to Figure 6-1.)

- ✔ When the Find command locates text, the text is selected as a block. Refer to Chapter 5 for more information on the Find command.

- ✔ Selecting text also means selecting characters such as tabs and the Enter keypress that marks the end of a paragraph. Fortunately, Word shows the Enter "character" as an extra blank space at the right end of a paragraph. When you select that blank, you select the whole paragraph as a paragraph. To avoid selecting the Enter character, don't select the blank space at the end of a paragraph.

Mark a Block of Text

Word offers you many ways to *mark* text as a block in your document. This section mulls over the possibilities.

Using the keyboard to select text

The secret to using the keyboard to select text is the Shift key. By holding down the Shift key, you can use the standard keyboard commands that move the insertion pointer to select blocks of text. Table 6-1 has some suggestions for you.

Table 6-1	Shifty Selection Wizardry
To Select This	*Press This*
A character at a time to the right of the insertion pointer	Shift+→
A character at a time to the left of the insertion pointer	Shift+←
A block of text from the insertion pointer to the end of the line	Shift+End
A block of text from the insertion pointer to the beginning of the line	Shift+Home
A block of text from the insertion pointer to a line above	Shift+↑
A block of text from the insertion pointer to a line below	Shift+↓

You can use any keyboard cursor-movement command (I list them in Chapter 3), but I recommend using this Shift key method for selecting only small chunks of text. Otherwise, you may end up tying your fingers into knots!

Either Shift key works, although I prefer to use the left Shift key and then work the arrow keys on the right side of the keyboard.

Selecting text on a touchscreen

It's cinchy to mark a block of text on a multi-touch monitor: Simply drag your finger over the text. Because this procedure may also scroll the document, a better option is to long-press a word:

Touch and hold the screen to select a single word. The word becomes selected, but also grows two lollipop insertion pointers on each end. You can then drag each of the insertion pointers to extend the selection.

Out, damn Mini toolbar!

When the mouse is used to select text, Word displays the Mini toolbar, looking like this:

The *Mini toolbar* is a palette of common formatting commands that Word supposes you need for a quick format on that selected text. After initially disliking the Mini toolbar, I've grown to enjoy it. But I recognize that you may find it more annoying than useful. If so, you can suppress its display. Follow these steps:

1. **Choose the Options command from the File tab's menu.**

2. **If necessary, choose General from the list on the left side of the Word Options window.**

3. **Remove the check mark by the item Show Mini Toolbar on Selection.**

4. **Click OK.**

If you would rather not eternally banish the Mini toolbar, note that it hides itself whenever you move the mouse beyond the selected chunk of text.

To work with a selected block on a touchscreen, touch the block. You see the touchscreen version of the Mini toolbar, referenced in the earlier sidebar, "Out, damn Mini toolbar!," and shown in Figure 6-2. The commands on that toolbar help manipulate the block.

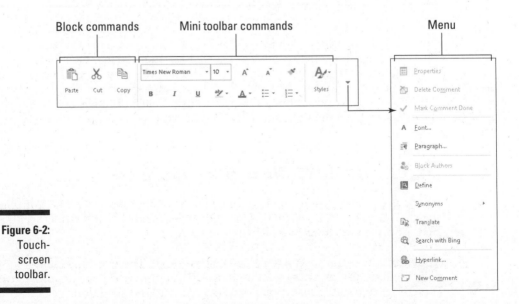

Figure 6-2:
Touch-
screen
toolbar.

Marking a block with the mouse

Forget cheese. The computer mouse was born to mark text, by selecting vast swaths of words with a wide sweep of your hand, by clicking a number of times, or by using the old click-and-drag routine. Mickey may rule a kingdom, but your computer mouse rules over text selection in your computer.

Drag over text to select it

The most common way to select text is by using the computer mouse. Point the mouse at the start of the text block, and then drag the mouse over the text you want to select. As you drag, the text becomes highlighted or selected. (Refer to Figure 6-1.) Release the mouse — stop the dragging — to mark the end of the block.

✔ You can use this simple technique to select any old block size in your document, though it works best when you use the mouse to drag over only the text you can see on the screen. When you try to select text beyond what you see on the screen, you have to select and scroll — which can be unwieldy; the mouse scrolls the text up and down quickly and, well, things get out of hand.

✔ When you find yourself becoming frustrated over not selecting all or part of a word, refer to the nearby sidebar, "Would you rather select text by letter or by word?"

Click the mouse to select text

A speedy way to select specific sizes of chunks of text is to match the power of the mouse with the dexterity of your index finger. Table 6-2 explains some clicking-and-selecting techniques worth noting.

Would you rather select text by letter or by word?

When you're selecting more than a single word, the mouse tends to grab text a full word at a time. If you want Word to select text by characters rather than by words (which is what I prefer), follow these steps:

1. **Choose the Options command from the File tab's menu.**

2. **Choose Advanced from the list on the left side of the Word Options window.**

3. **Under the Editing Options heading, remove the check mark by the item labeled When Selecting Automatically Select Entire Word.**

4. **Click OK.**

Table 6-2	Mouse-Selection Arcana
To Select This Chunk of Text	*Click the Mouse Thusly*
A single word	Point at the word with your mouse and double-click.
A line	Move the mouse pointer into the left margin beside the line you want to select. The mouse pointer changes to an arrow pointing northeastward. Click the mouse to select a line of text, or drag the mouse up or down to select several lines.
A sentence	Position the insertion pointer over the sentence and Ctrl+click. (Press the Ctrl key and click the mouse.)
A paragraph	Point the mouse somewhere in the paragraph's midst and triple-click.

Select text with the old poke-and-point

TIP

Here's the best way to select a chunk of text of any size, especially when that chunk of text is larger than what you can see on the screen at one time:

1. **Click the mouse to set the insertion pointer wherever you want the block to start — the anchor point.**

2. **Scroll through your document.**

   You must use the scroll bar or the mouse wheel to scroll through your document. If you use the cursor-movement keys, you reposition the insertion pointer, which isn't what you want.

3. **To mark the end of the block, press and hold the Shift key and click the mouse where you want the block to end.**

   The text from the insertion pointer to wherever you clicked the mouse is selected as a block.

Using the F8 key to mark a block

If you can remember that the F8 key on the computer's keyboard can be used to mark text, you can exploit one of the most powerful but seldom used text-marking tools that Word has to offer.

Yes, wacky as it sounds, the F8 key is used to mark a block of text. Pressing F8 once enters *Extended Selection* mode. That's where Word drops anchor at the insertion pointer's location, and then lets you use either the mouse or the cursor keys to select text. In fact, you cannot do anything but select text in Extended Selection mode.

As an example, follow these steps to use the F8 key to mark a block of text:

1. **Position the insertion pointer at the start of the block of text.**

2. **Press the F8 key.**

   The F8 key drops anchor and marks one end of the block.

3. **Use the keyboard's cursor keys to select the block of text.**

   The cursor-navigation keys are discussed in Chapter 3.

   Press a letter key to select text up to and including that letter. If you press N, you select all text up to and including the next *N* in your document. Nice. Nifty. Neat-o.

   Word highlights text from the point where you dropped anchor with F8 to wherever you move the insertion pointer.

4. **Do something with the selected block of text.**

   Word remains in Extended Selection mode until you do something with the block or you press the Esc key to cancel Extended Selection mode.

Doing something with a block of text is covered in the second half of this chapter.

To cancel the extended selection, press the Esc key. This action ends Extended Selection mode and keeps the block of text marked.

- ✔ You can use the mouse and the F8 key to get fancy. Position the cursor at either end of the block you want to mark, and press the F8 key. Then position the mouse cursor at the other end of the block, and press the left mouse button. Everything from there to there is marked.

- ✔ After pressing the F8 key, you can use the Find command to locate a specific bit of text. Word marks all text between the spot where F8 was pressed (the anchor) and the text that the Find command locates.

- ✔ Press the F8 key twice to select the current word (the one the insertion pointer is blinking inside of).

- ✔ Press the F8 key thrice (three times) to select the current sentence.

- ✔ Press the F8 key four times to select the current paragraph as a block of text.

✔ Press the F8 key five times to select the entire document, from top to bottom.

✔ No matter how many times you press F8, be aware that it always drops anchor. So pressing F8 once or five times means that Word is still in Extended Selection mode. Do something with the block or press Esc to cancel that mode.

Blocking the whole dang-doodle document

The biggest block you can mark is an entire document. Word has a specific command to do it, to select all text in a document: From the Home tab, locate the Editing area. (Click the Editing button when the entire Editing area isn't visible.) Then choose Select⇨Select All. Instantly, the entire document is marked as a single block o' text.

From the keyboard, you can use Ctrl+A to select an entire document or press the F8 key five times. Or you can even use the obscure Ctrl+5 (the 5 on the numeric keypad) key combo.

Deselecting a block

When you mark a block of text and change your mind, you must unmark, or *deselect,* the text. Here are a few handy ways to do it:

✔ **Move the insertion pointer.** It doesn't matter how you move the insertion pointer, with the keyboard or with the mouse — doing so unhighlights the block. Note that this trick doesn't exit the F8 key's Extended Selection mode.

✔ **Press the Esc key and then the ← key.** This method works to end Extended Selection mode.

✔ **Press Shift+F5.** The Shift+F5 key combo is the "go back" command (see Chapter 3), but it also deselects a block of text *and* returns you to the text you were editing before making the selection.

Manipulate the Block of Text

You can block punches, block hats, block and tackle, play with building blocks and engine blocks, take nerve blocks, suffer from mental blocks, jog for blocks, and, naturally, block text. But what can you do with those marked blocks of text?

Why, plenty of things! You can apply a format to all text in the block, copy a block, move a block, search through a block, proof a block, print a block, and even delete a block. The information in this section explains those tricks.

- ✔ Blocks must be selected before you can manipulate them. See the first half of this chapter.

- ✔ When a block of text is marked, various Word commands affect only the text in that block.

- ✔ To replace a block, type some text. The new text (actually, the initial character) replaces the entire block.

- ✔ Delete a block by pressing the Delete or Backspace key. Thwoop! The block is gone.

- ✔ Formatting commands can be applied to any marked block of text — specifically, character and paragraph formatting. See Part III of this book.

- ✔ Also see Chapter 32 for information on Word's bizarre yet potentially useful Collect and Paste feature.

Copying a block

After a block is marked, you can copy it into another part of your document to duplicate the text. The original block remains untouched by this operation. Follow these steps to copy a block of text from one place to another:

1. **Mark the block.**

   Detailed instructions about doing this task are offered in the first part of this chapter.

2. **From the Home tab, choose the Copy tool from the Clipboard group.**

   Or you can use the common Ctrl+C keyboard shortcut for the Copy command.

   You get no visual clue that the text has been copied; it remains selected.

3. **Move the insertion pointer to the position where you want to place the block's copy.**

   Don't worry if there's no room! Word inserts the block into your text.

4. **Choose the Paste tool from the Clipboard area.**

   Or you can use the common Ctrl+V keyboard shortcut for the Paste command.

The block of text you copy is inserted into your text just as though you had typed it there by yourself.

 ✔ See the later section, "Setting the pasted text format," to find out what to do about the wee li'l Clipboard icon that appears by the pasted text.

 ✔ After you copy a block, you can paste it into your document a second time. That's because whenever a block of text is cut or copied, Word remembers it. You can yank that block into your document again at any time — sort of like pasting text again after it has already been pasted. You use Ctrl+V, the Paste shortcut. Pasting text again simply pastes down a second copy of the block, spit-spot (as Mary Poppins would say).

 ✔ You can paste the block into another document you're working on or even into another application. (This is a Windows trick, which most good books on Windows discuss.)

Moving a block

To move a block of text, you select the text and then *cut* and paste. This process is almost exactly the same as copying a block, described in the preceding section, although in Step 2 you choose the Cut tool rather than the Copy tool or press the Ctrl+X keyboard shortcut for the Cut command. Otherwise, all steps are the same.

Don't be alarmed when the block of text vanishes! That's cutting in action; the block of text is being *moved,* not copied. You see the block of text again when you paste it in place.

If you screw up, the Ctrl+Z Undo shortcut undoes a block move.

Setting the pasted text format

When you paste text in Word, the Paste Options icon appears near the pasted block of text, as shown in the margin. Don't let it annoy you! That button allows you to select formatting for the pasted block because occasionally the block may contain formatting that, well, looks quite ugly after it's pasted in.

To work the Paste Options button, click it with the mouse or press and release the Ctrl key on the keyboard. You see a menu of options, illustrated in Figure 6-3.

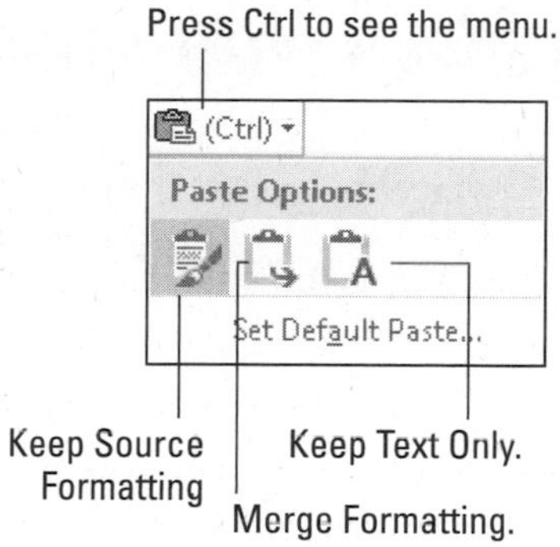

Press Ctrl to see the menu.

Figure 6-3:
Pasting
options.

Keep Source
Formatting

Merge Formatting.

Keep Text Only.

Table 6-3 summarizes the available paste options.

Table 6-3	**Paste Option Options**		
Icon	*Keyboard Shortcut*	*Name*	*Description*
	K	Keep Source Formatting	The formatting is fine; don't do a thing.
	M	Merge Formatting	Reformat the pasted block so that it looks like the text it's being pasted into.
	T	Keep Text Only	Just paste in the text — no formatting.

To keep only text with a copied or cut block (no formatting), you can press the Ctrl key and then the T key after pasting. That's two separate keys, not Ctrl+T.

Using the Paste Options icon is utterly optional. In fact, you can continue typing or working in Word and the icon bows out, fading away like some nebbish who boldly asked a power blonde to go out with him and she utterly failed to recognize his existence. Like that.

You can choose the Set Default Paste command after clicking the Paste Options icon to direct Word on how to permanently deal with pasted text. It's a handy trick, especially when you find yourself repeatedly choosing the same Paste Options format.

Copying or moving a block with the mouse

When you have to move a block only a short distance, you can use the mouse to drag-move or drag-copy the block. This feature works best when you're moving or copying a block to a location that you can see right on the screen. Otherwise, you're scrolling your document with the mouse while you're playing with blocks, which is like trying to grab an angry snake.

 To move any selected block of text with the mouse, just drag the block: Point the mouse cursor anywhere in the blocked text, and then drag the block to its new location. Notice how the mouse pointer changes, as shown in the margin. That means you're moving the block of text.

 Copying a block with the mouse works just like moving the block, except that you press the Ctrl key as you drag. When you do that, a plus sign appears in the mouse pointer (see the margin). It's your sign that the block is being copied and not just moved.

✔ The Paste Options icon appears after you "drop" the chunk of text. Refer to the preceding section for more information on the Paste Options icon.

✔ When you drag a block of text with the mouse, you're not copying it to the Clipboard. You cannot use the Paste (Ctrl+V) command to paste in the block again.

 ✔ A *linked copy* is created by dragging a selected block of text with the mouse and holding down *both* the Shift and Ctrl keys. When you release the mouse button, the copied block plops down into your document with a dark highlight. It's your clue that the copy is linked to the original; changes in the original are reflected in the copy and vice versa. If not, right-click the linked copy and choose the Update Link command.

Chapter 7

Spell It Write

There's no such thing as spelling in English. Spelling in English evolved over time. Even the venerable Bard, William Shakespeare, spelled his own name several different ways. It wasn't until the notion of the "dictionary" appeared that spelling became more or less standardized.

The same feeling of randomness can be applied to English grammar. Despite all those schoolteachers and editors out there, English is *not* Latin. English grammar has more exceptions than it has rules. That makes English a remarkably flexible and poetic language, but also makes it frustrating to discern meaning or ply some type of consistency from our mother tongue.

Word tries its best to remedy the situation: It comes with document-proofing tools. They include on-the-fly and in-your-face spelling and grammatical checkers. This chapter describes how they work, when to use them, and how to disregard them.

Check Your Spelling

Spell checking in Word works the second you start typing. Offending or unknown words are immediately underlined with the red zigzag of shame.

Word can also be employed to scan the entire document, word by word, for your attempts at mangling the English language. Word can be trained to use the AutoCorrect feature to automatically correct your common typos and misspellings. This section describes the details.

Checking words as you type

Word has an internal library stocked with zillions of words, all spelled correctly. Every time you type a word, it's checked against that dictionary. When the word isn't found, it's marked as suspect in your document. The mark is a red zigzag underline. I'm sure you've seen it.

My advice: Keep typing. Don't let the "red zigzag of a failed elementary education" perturb you. Focus on getting your thoughts up on the screen rather than on stopping and fussing over inevitable typos.

When you're ready, say, during one of those inevitable pauses that takes place as you write, go back and fix your spelling errors. Here's what to do:

1. **Locate the misspelled word.**

   Look for the red zigzag underline.

2. **Right-click the misspelled word.**

   Up pops a shortcut menu, as shown in Figure 7-1.

Figure 7-1:
Deal with
that typo.

3. **Choose from the list the word you intended to type.**

   In Figure 7-1, the word *fancy* fits the bill. Click that word and it's automatically inserted into your document, to replace the spurious word.

If the word you intended to type isn't on the list, don't fret. You may have to use a traditional dictionary (the paper kind) or take another stab at spelling the word phonetically and then correct it again.

Hue right grate

Word's document-proofing tools are as tech-nologically advanced as the programmers at Microsoft can make them. As the title of this sidebar suggests, however, there's something to be said about context.

Just because your document appears to contain no errors doesn't mean that everything is perfect. You have no better way to proof a document than to read it with human eyes.

✔ When the word is spelled correctly and Word is just too stupid to recognize it, you can add the word to its dictionary. See the next section.

✔ Word turns off automatic proofing when your document grows larger than a specific size. For example, on my computer, when the document is more than 100 pages long, automatic spell-checking is disabled. A warning appears, to alert you when this happens. Note that you can still manually spell-check, which is covered in the section "All-at-Once Document Proofing," later in this chapter.

Dealing with words incorrectly flagged as being misspelled

Occasionally, Word's spell checker bumps into a word it doesn't recognize, such as your last name or perhaps your city. Word dutifully casts doubt on the word, by underlining it with the notorious red zigzag. Yes, this case is one of those where the computer is wrong.

Two commands are on the spell checker's right-click menu (refer to Figure 7-1) to deal with those false negatives: Ignore All and Add to Dictionary.

Ignore All: Select this command when the word is properly spelled and you don't want Word to keep flagging it as misspelled in the current document.

For example, your science fiction short story has a character named Zadlux. Word believes it to be a spelling error, but you (and all the people of the soon-to-be-conquered planet Drebulon) know better. After you choose the Ignore All command, all instances of the suspect word are cheerfully ignored, but only in that document.

Add to Dictionary: This command adds words to Word's custom dictionary, which is a supplemental list of correctly spelled words that are used to proof a document.

For example, I once lived on Pilchuck Avenue, which Word thinks is a mis-spelling of the word *Paycheck*. If only. So, when I right-click the incorrectly flagged word, I choose the Add to Dictionary command. Presto — the word *Pilchuck* is added to Word's custom dictionary. I'll never have to spell-check that word again.

- ✔ If the word looks correct but is red-wiggly-underlined anyway, it could be a repeated word. They're flagged as misspelled by Word, so you can choose to either delete the repeated word or just ignore it.

- ✔ Word doesn't spell-check certain types of words — for example, words with numbers in them or words written in all capitals, which are usually abbreviations. For example, Pic6 is ignored because it has a 6 in it. The word *NYEP* is ignored because it's in all caps.

- ✔ You can adjust how spell-checking works, especially if you feel that it's being too picky. See the section "Control Word's Proofing Options," later in this chapter.

Undoing the Ignore All command

Choosing the Ignore All command means that all instances of a given mis-spelled word or typo are considered correctly spelled in your document. This statement holds true even when you save that document and open it again later. So, if you make a mistake and would rather have the ignored word regarded once more, do this:

1. **Choose the Options command from the File tab's menu.**

   The Word Options window appears.

2. **Choose Proofing on the left side of the window.**

3. **Click the Recheck Document button.**

   A warning dialog box appears, reminding you of what you're about to do.

4. **Click the Yes button.**

   Everything you've told Word to ignore while proofing your document is now ignored. It's the ignore-ignore command!

5. **Click the OK button to return to your document.**

By following these steps, you direct Word to un-ignore not only all previously ignored words but also any grammatical errors you've chosen to ignore. You have no way to undo this command.

The steps for undoing the Ignore All command affect only the current docu-ment. The Ignore All command affects only the current document.

Removing words from the custom dictionary

When you choose the Add to Dictionary command, the given word is placed into the custom dictionary. Recognizing that people may change their minds, Word allows you to edit its custom dictionary, to remove words you may have added accidentally.

To remove unwanted words from the custom dictionary, follow these steps:

1. **Click the Word Options button on the File tab's menu.**

   The Word Options window shows up.

2. **From the left side of the window, choose Proofing.**

3. **Click the button labeled Custom Dictionaries.**

   The Custom Dictionaries dialog box appears.

4. **Select the item RoamingCustom.dic (Default).**

   It's probably the only item in the list.

5. **Click the button labeled Edit Word List.**

   You see a scrolling list of words you've added to the custom dictionary.

6. **Find and select the word you want to remove from the dictionary.**

   The word is selected by clicking it once.

7. **Click the Delete button.**

8. **Repeat Steps 6 and 7 if you want to remove more words.**

9. **Click the OK button when you're done editing the dictionary.**

   Close any other open windows.

The 25 most frequently misspelled words

a lot	atheist	grammar	maneuver	ridiculous
accidentally	collectible	gauge	no one	separate
acquire	consensus	independent	occurrence	supersede
amateur	definite	kernel	realize	their
argument	embarrass	liaison	receive	weird

AutoCorrect Your Common Typos

Some typos and spelling errors are never graced by the red zigzag. That's because Word quickly fixes hundreds of common typos and spelling errors on the fly. The AutoCorrect feature does it, and you have to be quick to see it.

Understanding AutoCorrect

There's nothing to using AutoCorrect; it happens automatically. In Word, try to type the word *mispell.* You can't! Word uses AutoCorrect and suddenly you see *misspell.*

Most commonly misspelled words can be found in AutoCorrect's repertoire: *acomodate, suposed, recieve,* and so on. Try a few. See whether you can baffle Word!

In addition to fixing spelling errors, AutoCorrect helps you enter special characters. For example, type **(C)** and AutoCorrect properly inserts the © copyright symbol. Ditto for **(TM)** for the trademark. Typing –> is translated into an arrow, and even **:)** becomes a happy face.

Beyond spelling, AutoCorrect fixes certain common punctuation. It automatically capitalizes the first letter of a sentence. AutoCorrect capitalizes *I* when you forget to, properly capitalizes the names of days, fixes the iNVERSE cAPS lOCK pROBLEM, plus other common typos.

Undoing an AutoCorrect correction

You can reverse AutoCorrect instant changes, but only when you're quick. The secret is to press Ctrl+Z (the Undo command) immediately after AutoCorrect makes its correction. The change is gone.

When AutoCorrect fixes a word, a blue rectangle appears under the first letter. That's your key to access AutoCorrect options and change the way AutoCorrect behaves: Point the mouse at the rectangle to see a button, which you can then click to see various AutoCorrect options, as shown in Figure 7-2.

Figure 7-2:
Adjusting an
Auto-
Correction.

I'll be brief, chief

↩   Change back to "cheif"
     Stop Automatically Correcting "cheif"
⚙   Control AutoCorrect Options...

Here are your options:

- **Change Back to "*whatever*":** Undo the AutoCorrection.

- **Stop Automatically Correcting "*whatever*":** Remove the word from the AutoCorrect dictionary so that it's not corrected automatically again. (But it may still be flagged as incorrect by the spell checker.)

- **Control AutoCorrect Options:** Display the AutoCorrect dialog box, which is used to customize various AutoCorrect settings and to edit or create new entries in the AutoCorrect library. Refer to the section "Control Word's Proofing Options," later in this chapter.

Grammar Be Good

Mark Twain once referred to spelling in the English language as "drunken." If that's true, English grammar must be a hallucination. To help you to detox, Word comes with a grammar checker. It's just like having your eighth grade English teacher inside your computer — only it's all the time and not just third period.

Word's grammar checker works on the fly, just like the spelling checker. The main difference is that words are underlined with a blue, not red, zigzag underline. That's your hint of Word's sense of grammatical justice, which, as I've written elsewhere, is merely a suggestion, given the illusionary nature of English grammar in the first place.

As with a spelling error, right-click the blue-underlined text. The pop-up menu that appears either explains what's wrong or offers an alternative suggestion. You also have the option to ignore the error, which I find myself using quite often.

- Sometimes, you may be puzzled about a word that the grammar checker flags as wrong. Don't give up! Always check the entire sentence for a potential error. For example, the grammar checker may suggest *had* in place of *have*. Chances are good that *have* is correct but another word in the sentence has an unwanted *s* attached.

- You can customize or even turn off grammar checking. Refer to the section "Control Word's Proofing Options," later in this chapter.

All-at-Once Document Proofing

You can cheerfully ignore all of Word's on-the-fly document proofing, and instead opt to make a once-over scan for spelling and grammatical errors. This process can take place when you're done writing, just before printing or publishing your document. I consider it a final scan, kind of like ironing out the wrinkles in a freshly laundered shirt. Here's how it works:

1. **Click the Review tab on the Ribbon.**

2. **In the Proofing group, click the Spelling & Grammar button.**

   The Spelling pane or Grammar pane box appears, depending on how you've offended Word's grammatical sensibilities. Errors are shown one at a time as they occur in your document. You may even be regaled with an explanation of what's wrong and other comments that may or may not affect you emotionally.

3. **Deal with the offense.**

   Here's what you can do for spelling errors:

   - To keep your typo, click the Ignore button.

   - To avoid Word pestering you again and again for the same spelling sin, click the Ignore All button.

   - Click the Add button to dispatch the word to the custom dictionary.

   - Choose a replacement word from the listed suggestions, and then click the Change button to have Word fix it. Or you can click the Change All button, and each instance is repaired throughout your document.

   Here are my suggestions for dealing with grammatical boo-boos:

   - To fix the error, edit the highlighted text in your document. Click the Resume button when you're done.

   - Use the Ignore button to skip the error.

   - Click the Change button to replace the text with what Word believes to be something more proper.

4. **Continue checking your document until Word says that it's done.**

   On my computer, Word tells me that I'm "good to go." Whatever.

If you find this all-at-once method of document checking easier and more gentle to your ego, you can turn off on-the-fly spelling and grammar checking. The next section explains how to do it. If you choose that option, don't forget to proof your document before you finish your work.

- For spelling errors, the Spelling pane appears. For grammatical transgressions, the Grammar pane appears.

- You can easily enter a trancelike state while you're document proofing. You might find yourself clicking the Ignore button too quickly. My advice: Use the Undo command, Ctrl+Z. It lets you go back and change text that you may not have paid attention to.

- You can click the Proofing button on the status bar to direct Word to take you to the next mangled chunk of English in your document. Using this button is another way to hop through and proof your document.

Control Word's Proofing Options

All document-proofing options and settings are kept in one place, buried deep in Word's bosom. Here's how to get there:

1. **Click the File tab.**

2. **Choose Options from the File tab's menu.**

3. **In the Word Options window, choose Proofing from the left side.**

The right side of the window contains options and settings for document proofing. The following sections describe what you can do there.

When you're done working in the Word Options window, click the OK button to lock in whichever changes you've made.

Changing spell-check and grammar settings

After you find yourself in the Word Options window, in the Proofing corner, you can peruse and change the way Word reacts to your mangling of the planet's number-one language. Here are some highlights:

- To turn off on-the-fly spell checking, remove the check mark by the item Check Spelling As You Type.

- To disable grammar checking, remove the check mark by the item Mark Grammar Errors As You Type.

- Click the Settings button by the Writing Style drop-down list to customize and hone the grammatical disobedience that Word marks. (I typically disable the Contractions warning.)

Perusing AutoCorrect options

You can click the AutoCorrect Options button in the Word Options window to view the AutoCorrect dialog box and its slew of automatic word-correcting and typo-fixing options, as shown in Figure 7-3.

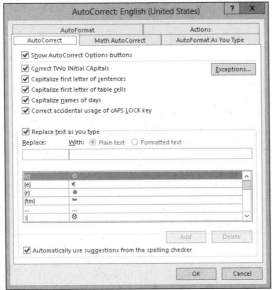

Figure 7-3:
Oodles of
AutoCorrect
options.

Here are some things you can do:

TIP

- ✔ The AutoCorrect tab lists all problems that AutoCorrect fixes for you, plus common typo corrections. That's also where you can remove the AutoCorrect entries you detest.

- ✔ If you don't like how Word changes web page addresses in your document into real hyperlinks, remove the check mark by the option Internet and Network Paths with Hyperlinks on the AutoFormat tab.

- ✔ The AutoFormat tab also harbors those insidious options that automatically create bulleted lists and heading styles in Word; remove the appropriate check marks to disable those unwanted features.

- ✔ Also refer to the AutoFormat As You Type tab to kill off additional automatic numbering and bulleted list features in Word.

Chapter 8

Document Calisthenics: New, Open, Save, and Close

I like the word *document*. It's elegant. It's much better than saying "a file" or "that thing I created with my word processor." A document could include everything from a shopping list to a note excusing little Jimmy's absence because you thought he might have impetigo but it turned out to be jelly stuck to his chin from the night before — it makes all that trivial text somehow seem more important.

Regardless of size or importance, it's called a *document*. It's the goal of your using Word. You'll create new documents, conjure up old documents to work on them again, save documents, and close documents. This chapter covers document basics.

What is a file?

A Word document is a *file*. This notion is vital to grasp if you ever want your computer experience to be a pleasant one. In fact, most of the trouble people have with computers comes from not understanding the concept of a file.

Your computer stores all kinds of information: word processing documents, graphics, music, video, and all sorts of things. Those items are all stored in a digital container known as a *file*.

As files, Word documents exist as unique and separate from other items on the computer,

including the word processor itself. Word is merely the device you use to create the document or file; Word itself is not the document.

Think of the relationship this way: A pianist uses sheet music to play a tune, but the sheet music isn't part of the piano. Just as you can store sheet music in the piano bench, you can store a Word document file on your computer. The Word document is its own, unique file.

Behold! A New Document

All documents begin life plucked from the electronic ether. The empty document is presented on the screen like a blank sheet of paper, ready for you to compose your thoughts.

You can summon a new document from the Word Start screen by clicking the Blank Document item. Or, after you've started your Word session, you can bring forth a new document by obeying these steps:

1. **Click the File tab.**

   The Word window changes to display the File screen.

2. **Choose the New command from the left side of the window.**

   The New screen appears. It lists a slew of options for starting a new document, many of which may appear confusing to you, which is, I believe, the program's intent.

3. **Click the Blank Document item.**

   The Word window returns to normal and you see a blank page, ready for typing.

You can repeat these steps as often as you need new documents; Word lets you work with several documents at a time. See Chapter 24 for information on multiple-document mania.

- ✔ Refer to Chapter 1 for information on the Word Start screen.

- ✔ Ah, the shortcut: Press Ctrl+N to quickly summon a new, blank document in Word.

- ✔ The New screen contains numerous options for starting something new in Word. Rather than use the Blank Document choice, you can choose a template or task from the list. *Templates* help save time by predefining document layout and formatting (and sometimes even text). See Chapter 16 for more information.

Save Your Stuff!

It doesn't matter whether you've written a masterpiece or are jotting down notes for tonight's PTA meeting, the most important thing you can do to a document is *save it.*

Saving creates a permanent copy of your document, encoding your text as a file on the computer's storage system. That way, you can work on the document again, publish it electronically, or have a copy ready in case the power goes *poof.* All these tasks require saving.

Saving a document the first time

Don't think that you have to wait until you finish a document to save it. In fact, you should save almost immediately — as soon as you have a few sentences or paragraphs. Save! Save! Save!

How big can a Word document be?

There's no upper limit on how many pages you can have in a Word document. Theoretically, a document can be thousands of pages long. Even so, I don't recommend that you make your documents that big.

The longer a document is in Word, the more apt the computer is to screw things up. So, rather than advise you to make a single long document, I recommend that you split your work into smaller, chapter-size documents. Those documents can then be organized into a single *master document* in Word, where page numbers and references can be used as though the smaller documents were one larger document.

See Chapter 25 for more information on managing several smaller documents into a single large document.

To save a document for the first time, follow these steps:

1. **Click the File tab and choose the Save As command.**

   The Save As screen appears, similar to the one shown in Figure 8-1. This screen is an intermediate step before the traditional Save As dialog box. It allows you to choose a location for your document, either locally or on the Internet.

2. **Choose a location for the document.**

   Chose the Computer item to create and save the document on your own computer, which is what I recommend.

   The SkyDrive item saves the file on your Windows SkyDrive, if you've set up and configured that feature. The advantage is that your document will be available anywhere you have an Internet access. The disadvantage is that the document is not available when you don't have Internet access.

Locations to save your document   Choose a recent folder.

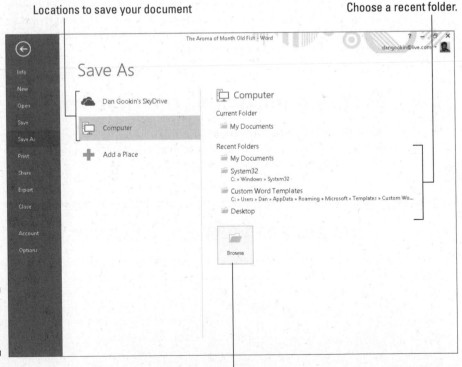

Figure 8-1:
The Save As
screen.

Summon the traditional Save As dialog box.

3. Click the Browse button, or choose an item from the Recent Folders list.

Ah, the familiar Save As dialog box appears.

4. Type a name for your document in the File Name box.

Word automatically selects the first line or first several words of your document as a filename and puts it in the Save As dialog box. If that's okay, you can move to Step 5. Otherwise, type a name in the File Name box.

Be descriptive! The more concisely you name your document, the easier it is to recognize it by that name in the future.

5. Work the options in the Save As dialog box (optional).

Use the various gizmos in the Save As dialog box to choose a specific folder for your document — though if you chose a specific folder in Step 3, this step is unnecessary.

6. Click the Save button.

The file is now safely stored in the computer's storage system.

At this point, you can keep working. As you work, continue to save; refer to the section "Saving or updating a document," later in this chapter.

✔ From the And-Now-He-Tells-Us Department, you don't really need to work through Step 1 the first time you save a document. Instead, you can click the Save button on the Quick Access Toolbar. Because the document hasn't yet been saved, the Save As screen appears automatically.

✔ There's no need to quit after you save a document. Indeed, the idea is to save as you go.

✔ After initially saving, you use the Save command to update your document. See the section "Saving or updating a document."

✔ Your clue that the file has been successfully saved is that the name you gave it (the *filename*) now appears on the document's title bar, at the top center of the Word window.

✔ Always save your document, even after you type only a few lines of text.

✔ The Save As command can also be used to save a document with a new name or to a different location on disk or in a different format. See Chapter 24.

✔ Do not save a document to removable media, such as an optical disc or memory card. Instead, save the document to the computer's main storage device, the hard drive or SSD. After saving the document, and quitting Word, you can use Windows to copy that document to the removable media. Otherwise, Word may lose your document, or the computer may crash if you remove the media before you're done working on the document.

Complicated — but important — information about filenames

Word lets you be creative in your writing, but your creativity is limited in naming a document as it's saved to disk. Here are the rules:

- A filename can be longer than 200 ridiculous-something characters; even so, keep your filenames short but descriptive.

- A filename can include letters, numbers, and spaces, and can start with a letter or number.

- A filename can contain periods, commas, hyphens, and even underlines.

- A filename cannot contain any of these characters: \ / : * ? " < > |.

Word automatically appends a *filename extension* to all documents you save — like a last name. You may or may not see this extension, depending on how you've configured Windows. No matter: You don't need to manually type the extension yourself; just concern yourself with giving the document a proper and descriptive filename.

Dealing with document-save errors

Saving a document involves working with both Word and the Windows operating system. This process doubles the chances of something going wrong, so it's high time for an error message. A potential message you may see is

```
The file whatever already exists
```

You have three choices:

- **Replace Existing File:** Nope.
- **Save Changes with a Different Name:** Yep.
- **Merge Changes into Existing File:** Nope.

After choosing the middle option, type a different file name in the Save As dialog box.

Another common problem occurs when a message that's displayed reads something like this:

```
The file name is not valid
```

That's Word's less-than-cheerful way of telling you that the filename contains a boo-boo character. To be safe, stick to letters, numbers, and spaces when you're naming a file. Check the nearby sidebar, "Complicated — but important — information about filenames." Then click OK and try again.

Saving or updating a document

Every so often as you continue to work on your document, you should save again. That way, any changes you've made since the last time you saved are remembered and recorded on the computer's storage system permanently. I generally save my documents dozens of times a day — usually, when the phone rings or when I need to step away and the cat is lurking too closely to the keyboard or, often, when I'm just bored.

To resave a document that has already been saved to disk, click the File tab and choose the Save command from the File screen. You get no feedback, and the Save As dialog box doesn't show up. That's because you already gave the file a name; the Save command merely updates the existing file.

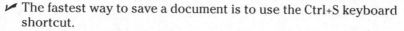

 ✔ The fastest way to save a document is to use the Ctrl+S keyboard shortcut.

 ✔ You can also click the Save icon on the Quick Access Toolbar to save a document to disk.

 ✔ The most bizarre command for saving a document? Shift+F12. Weird.

Forgetting to save before you quit

When you're done writing in Word, you close the document, close the window, or quit Word outright. No matter how you call it quits, when the document hasn't yet been saved or was changed since the last save, you're asked to save one last time. Here are your options:

Save: The document is saved. If you've been bad and haven't saved the document even once, the Save As screen appears. See the earlier section, "Saving a document the first time."

Don't Save: The document isn't officially saved, but it may be available for later recovery. See the later section, "Recover a Draft," to see how that works.

Cancel: Word returns you to your document for more editing and stuff.

I recommend choosing the Save option.

Open a Document

Saving a document means nothing unless you have a way to retrieve it. You have several ways to *open* a document that was previously saved as a file. This section mulls the possibilities.

Using the Open command

Open is the standard computer command used to fetch a document that already exists on the computer's storage system. You use Open to hunt down documents that were previously saved and open them like you're unwrapping a present. The document is then displayed in Word's window as though it has always been there.

To grab a document you already worked on — to *open* it — follow these steps:

1. **Click the File tab to display the File screen.**

2. **Choose the Open command.**

   The Open screen materializes, as shown in Figure 8-2.

3. **Choose a location where the document may lurk.**

   Your choices are Recent Documents (refer to Figure 8-2), the SkyDrive, or your computer.

   If you can find your document in the Recent Documents list, click it. The document opens on the screen. Congratulations — you're done. If you don't see your document, you have to continue hunting for it on the SkyDrive or your computer.

4. **Choose a recent folder from the list or click the Browse button when the recent folders displayed do not please you.**

   Finally, the familiar Open dialog box appears. Your job is to use the Open dialog box to find the document you want to open.

5. **In the Open dialog box, click to highlight the file you want to open.**

6. **Click the Open button.**

   Word opens the highlighted file and slaps it down on the screen. You may even see displayed the last location where you were working, along with a "Welcome back" message.

Places to look for a document

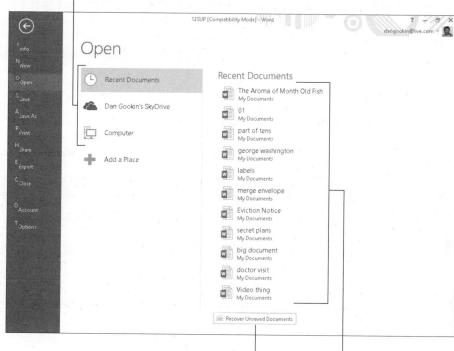

Figure 8-2:
The Open
screen.

Rescue an unsaved document.　　　　Choose a recent document.

After the document is open, you can edit it, look at it, print it, or do whatever you want.

- Opening a document doesn't erase it from storage. In fact, the original copy of the file stays on the storage system until you use the Save command to save the document again.

- When you open a document, there's no need to use the Save As command to save it again. Simply use the Save command (shortcut: Ctrl+S). That's because the document already has a filename.

- The shortcut key to get to the Open screen is Ctrl+O.

- Right-click the Word icon on the taskbar, and you see the jump list pop up; choose a recently opened file from that list.

- Pushpins appear when you hover the mouse over a recently opened document's. They allow you to permanently pin a document to the Open screen. Click a pushpin to "push it in." That makes the document stick around in the list. Clicking the pushpin again allows the document to fade away after a while.

- To permanently remove a document from the Recent Documents list, right-click the document's icon. Choose the Remove from List command.

✔ Avoid opening a file on any removable media, such as a digital memory card or an optical disc. Although it's possible, it can lead to headaches later if you remove the media before Word is done with the document. Because of that, I recommend that you use Windows to copy the document from the removable media to the computer's storage system. Then open it in Word.

Opening a document icon

One way to work on a document is to find its icon in Windows and double-click to open the document. Merely locate a Word document icon in any folder window, from the desktop, or on the Start button's Recent Documents list and then double-click, and Word loads that document for editing.

Opening one document inside another

It's possible in Word to open one document inside of another. Doing so isn't as rare as you'd think. For example, you may have your biography, résumé, or curriculum vitae in a file on disk and want to add that information to the end of a letter begging for a job. If so, or in any other circumstances that I can't think of right now, follow these steps:

1. **Position the insertion pointer where you want the other document's text to appear.**

   The text is inserted at that spot.

2. **Click the Ribbon's Insert tab.**

3. **From the Text group, choose Object⇨Text from File.**

   The Object button is depicted in the margin. It lurks in the lower-right corner of the Text group. Ensure that you click the menu button (the down-pointing rectangle). If you see the Object dialog box, try again.

   Upon success, you see the Insert File dialog box.

4. **Choose the icon representing the document you want to insert.**

   You can also use the gadgets and gizmos in the dialog box to locate a file in another folder or on another disk drive or even on someone else's computer on the network. Such power!

5. **Click the Insert button.**

The document you selected is inserted into the current document, just as though you had typed (and formatted) the whole thing right there with your stubby little fingers.

- ✔ The resulting combined document still has the same name as the first document; the document you inserted remains unchanged.

- ✔ You can insert any number of documents into another document, one at a time. There's no limit.

- ✔ Inserting text from one document into another is often called *boilerplating*. For example, you can save a commonly used piece of text in a document and then insert it into other documents as necessary. This process is also the way that sleazy romance novels are written.

- ✔ Biography. Résumé. *Curriculum vitae.* The more important you think you are, the more alien the language used to describe what you've done.

Close a Document

When you're done writing a document, you need to do the electronic equivalent of putting it away. That electronic equivalent is the Close command: Choose the Close command from the File screen, or use the handy Ctrl+W keyboard shortcut.

If you haven't saved your document recently, Word prompts you to save before you close; click the S button and the document is saved. (If it hasn't yet been saved — shame on you! — you see the Save As dialog box, as described earlier in this chapter).

When the document has been saved, closing it simply removes it from view. At that point, you can quit Word, start up a new document, open a document on disk, or put away Word and hit another game of Spider Solitaire.

- ✔ Refer to Chapter 1 for more quitting options.

- ✔ You don't have to choose the Close command. You can click the X (Close) button in the upper-right corner of the Word window, which is almost the same thing: You're prompted to save your document if it needs saving. But when you click the X button, you also quit Word.

Recover a Draft

Computers crash. Users forget to save in a pinch. Or perhaps another type of disaster has befallen your unsaved Word document. When the planets are properly aligned and the word processing gods are smiling, it's possible to recover those lost documents, the ones that Word calls *drafts*. Here's how:

1. **Click the File tab to view the File screen.**

2. **Choose the Open command.**

3. **Choose Recent Documents.**

   You see the list of recent documents (refer to Figure 8-2). When unsaved drafts are available, you see a button at the bottom of the list: Recover Unsaved Documents.

4. **Click the Recover Unsaved Documents button.**

   The Open dialog box appears.

5. **Choose from the list a document to recover.**

   The document may have an unusual name, especially when it has never been saved.

6. **Click the Open button to open and recover the document.**

The document you recover might not be the one you wanted it to be. If so, try again and choose another document. You might also find that the document doesn't contain all the text you typed or thought would be there. You can't do anything about it, other than *remember to save everything* in the first place!

The recovery of drafts is possible because of Word's AutoRecover feature. Refer to Chapter 31 for more information on AutoRecover.

Chapter 9

Publish Your Document

A long time ago, the final step in document creation was printing. After writing, editing, formatting, and proofing (with lots of document-saving along the way), you printed your masterpiece to show the world. The process was called simply *printing* because you could do little else with the document. Times have changed.

Today, the final step in the word processing saga is *publishing*. No, it doesn't mean that you need to get an agent or shop your book to big-time New York publishers and face a slew of rejection letters. Publishing a Word document means printing, but it also includes other electronic ways to share your document: Send it by e-mail, post it to a website, stick it on a blog somewhere, or engage in other electronic adventures. It's all publishing.

Your Document on Paper

Getting it down on paper has been the goal of writers ever since paper was invented. The word processor, the best writing tool ever invented, is also the first writing tool to utterly avoid paper. You can change that situation, however, by using the most traditional method to publish your document: Print it. You use a printer, either attached directly to your computer or available on a network, to create a *hard copy* of your document.

Preparing the printer

Before you print a document, I recommend following these steps to ensure that the printer is ready to print:

1. **Make sure that your printer is plugged in and properly connected to your computer.**

   Refer to my book *PCs For Dummies* for more information on connecting and using a printer and using various printer tips and stuff like that.

2. **Ensure that your laser printer has plenty of toner or that your ink printer's cartridges are brimming with ink.**

   Whenever the printer is low on ink or toner, replace it at once!

3. **Check the printer for paper.**

   The paper can feed from the back or top or enter from a paper tray, or it can be manually fed one sheet at a time. However your printer eats paper, be sure that it's properly stocked before you print.

4. **Turn on the printer.**

   You can try to print with the printer turned off, but it takes quite a long time.

5. **Your printer must be *online* or *selected* before you can print.**

   This is weird: Some printers can be on but not ready to print. The power is on, but unless the printer is online or selected, it ignores the computer. To force these types of printers to listen to the computer, you must press the Online, Ready, or Select (or similar) button.

When you're certain that the printer is up to the task, proceed with the printing operation in Word.

Previewing before printing

Before you print, preview the look of the final document. Yeah, even though your document is supposed to look the same on the screen as it does on paper, you may still see surprises: missing page numbers, blank pages, screwy headers, and other jaw-dropping blunders, for example.

Fortunately, a print preview of your document appears as part of the Print screen, as shown in Figure 9-1.

You only need to remember to peruse your document before printing it. Follow these steps:

1. Save your document.

Yep — always save. Saving before printing is a good idea.

2. Click the File tab.

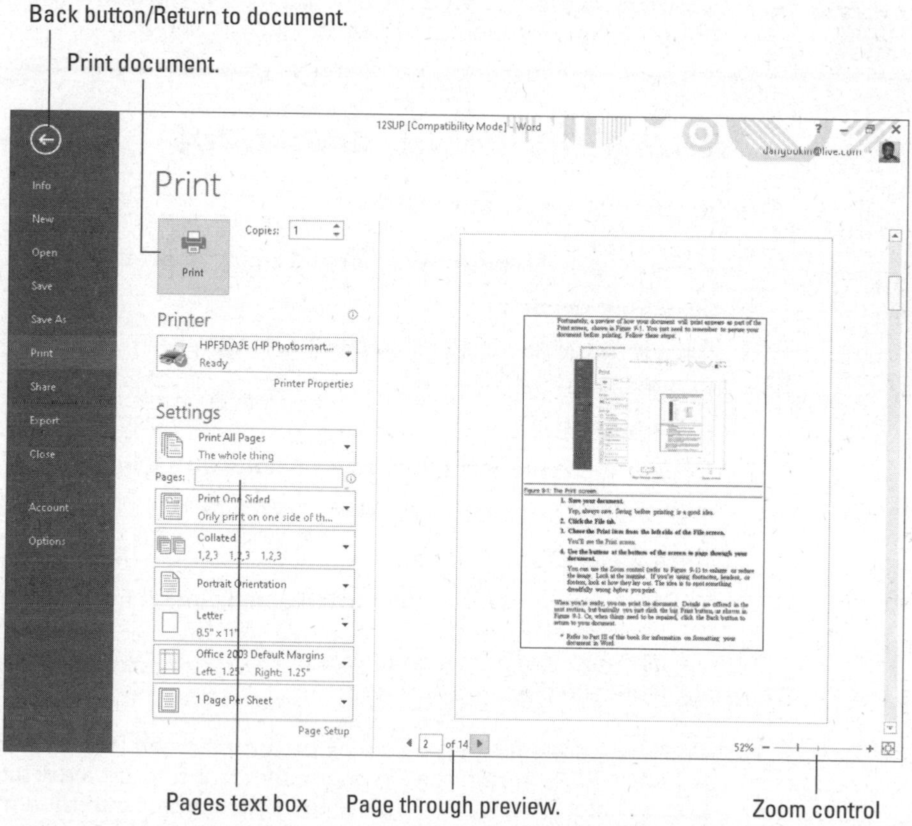

Back button/Return to document.

Print document.

Figure 9-1: The Print screen.

Pages text box   Page through preview.   Zoom control

3. **Chose the Print item from the left side of the File screen.**

   You see the Print screen.

4. **Use the buttons at the bottom of the screen to page through your document.**

   You can use the Zoom control (refer to Figure 9-1) to enlarge or reduce the image. Look at the margins. If you're using footnotes, headers, or footers, look at how they lay out. The idea is to spot anything that's dreadfully wrong *before* you print.

When you're ready, you can print the document. Details are offered in the next section, but basically you click the big Print button, as shown in Figure 9-1. Or when things need to be repaired, click the Back button to return to your document.

> ✔ Refer to Part III of this book for information on formatting your document in Word.

> ✔ Sideways printing, paper sizes, and other document-related options are set when you format your document's pages. These are Word functions, not ones you set when you print. Refer to Chapter 13.

Printing the whole document

Printing the document is easy to do:

1. **Make sure that the printer is on and ready to print.**

2. **Save your document.**

   Click the little Save button on the Quick Access Toolbar for a quickie save.

3. **Click the File tab.**

4. **Choose the Print command from the File tab's window.**

   The Print screen appears, as shown in Figure 9-1.

5. **Click the big Print button.**

   The Print screen closes, and the document spews forth from the printer.

Printing may take some time — a *long* time. Fortunately, you can continue working while the document prints.

> ✔ The keyboard shortcut to display the Print screen (refer to Figure 9-1) is Ctrl+P. Even better, the keyboard shortcut to print a document is Ctrl+P, Enter. Press Ctrl+P to see the Print screen, and then press Enter to "click" the Print button.

✔ If nothing prints, don't use the Print command again! There's probably nothing awry; the computer is still thinking or sending information to the printer. If you don't see an error message, everything will probably print, eventually.

✔ The computer prints one copy of your document for every Print command you incant. If the printer is just being slow and you impatiently click the Print button ten times, you print ten copies of your document. (See the section "Canceling a print job," later in this chapter.)

✔ When your document is formatted using a unique paper size, the printer may prompt you to load that paper size. Printing on paper of different sizes is a printer-specific function, not something that Word does. But you set the paper size in Word as part of the page formatting. Refer to Chapter 13.

✔ Manual-feed printers beg for paper before they can print. The printer may say "Feed me paper!" or the ever-popular "PC Load Letter." Like a dutiful mother, you must comply: Stand by the printer, line up the paper, and shove it into the printer's gaping maw until your document has finished printing. Fortunately, there's no need to burp the printer after manually feeding it paper.

✔ In addition to saving your document, you may consider proofreading it before you print. See Chapter 7.

Printing a specific page

Follow these steps to print only one page of your document:

1. **Move the insertion pointer so that it's sitting somewhere on the page you want to print.**

   Check the page number on the status bar to ensure that you're on the right page.

2. **Choose the Print command from the File screen, or press Ctrl+P.**

3. **Click the button beneath the Settings heading and choose Print Current Page from the menu.**

   The button is illustrated in Figure 9-1.

4. **Click the Print button.**

The single page prints with all the formatting you applied, including footnotes and page numbers and everything else, just as though you plucked that page from a complete printing of the entire document.

Delete that extra blank page at the end of a document

Occasionally, you may be surprised when your document prints and has one extra page — a blank page. And it bothers you because you cannot get rid of it! Until now:

To remove the ugly, blank page that often roots at the end of your document, press Ctrl+End.

With the insertion pointer at the end of your document, press the Backspace key repeatedly until the extra page is gone. How can you tell? Keep an eye on the total page count on the status bar. When the page count decreases by one, you know that the extra page is gone.

Printing a single page in this manner is useful for when you goof up (or the printer goofs up) one page in a document and you need to reprint only that page. Printing only a single page doesn't waste paper.

Printing a range of pages

Word enables you to print a range of pages, odd pages, even pages, or a hodgepodge combination of random pages from within your document. To print a range or group of pages, summon the Print screen, as described earlier in this chapter.

Your key to printing a hodgepodge of pages is to use the Pages text box (refer to Figure 9-1). Here are some suggestions for what to type in that text box:

To print pages 3 through 5, for example, type **3-5**.

To print pages 1 through 7, type **1-7**.

To print pages 2 and 6, type **2,6**.

To print page 3, pages 5 through 9, pages 15 through 17, and page 19 (boy, that coffee went everywhere, didn't it?), type **3, 5-9, 15-17, 19**.

Click the big Print button when you're ready to print. Only the pages you specify churn from the printer.

Printing odd and even pages

To print all odd pages, click the Print All Pages button on the Print screen. Choose the command Only Print Odd Pages from the menu. To print only even pages, choose the command Only Print Even Pages. Click the big Print button, and only those pages you've chosen print.

Remove the Document Properties sheet

A printing problem that can potentially vex you is finding the Document Properties sheet printing with your document. This extra sheet of paper prints first, listing information about the document. The Document Properties sheet isn't printed unless its option is set, but for some reason the option gets set on some folks' computers.

To prevent the Document Properties sheet from printing, click the File tab and choose the Options command. In the Word Options dialog box, click the Display item on the left side of the window. In the Printing Options area on the Display screen, remove the check mark by the item Print Document Properties. Click OK.

A reason to print all odd or even pages is that you want to print on both sides of the page on a printer that doesn't have *duplex* (two-sided) printing. First print the odd pages. Then reinsert the paper into the printer, flipped over, and then print the even pages.

Printing a block

After you mark a block of text onscreen, you can beg the Print command to print only that block. Here's how:

1. **Mark the block of text you want to print.**

   See Chapter 6 for all the block-marking instructions in the world.

2. **Summon the Print screen.**

3. **From the button beneath the Settings heading, choose the item Print Selection.**

   The Print Selection item is available only when a block is selected in your document.

4. **Click the Print button.**

The block you selected prints at the same position, with the same formatting (headers and footers) as though you had printed the entire document.

Printing more than one copy of something

Imagine how silly it would be to send your résumé to a company but add that you need your résumé returned because you have only one copy. No, I'm not trying to convince you that buying a photocopier is necessary. Why do that when Word can easily print multiple copies of any document? Here's how:

1. **Press Ctrl+P on the keyboard to summon the Print screen.**

2. **Enter the number of copies in the Copies text box.**

   To print three copies, for example, click the box and type **3**.

3. **Click the big Print button to print your copies.**

Under normal circumstances, Word prints each copy of the document one after the other. This process is known as *collating*. However, if you're printing seven copies of a document and you want Word to print seven copies of page 1 and then seven copies of page 2 (and so on), choose the option Uncollated from the Collated menu button, found under the Settings heading on the Print screen.

Choosing another printer

Your computer can have more than one printer attached. Even small offices and home offices have computers networked and sharing printers. In any case, you can use Word's Print screen to choose which printer to use to print your document.

Choose a different printer on the Print screen by clicking the button beneath the Printer heading. A list of available printers appears; simply choose a printer from the list. Make other settings in the window as well, and then click the big Print button. Your document prints on the chosen printer.

Canceling a print job

The fastest, easiest way to cancel a print job is to rush up to the printer and touch the Cancel button. Sometimes, the button has a red X icon on it. Touch that button, and the printer will stop — maybe not at once, but the button cancels the document from printing.

A more awkward way to cancel a print job is to use Windows. This method involves quite a few steps, and it's not always successful. That's because most documents are small and zip off to the printer before you have time to stop them. But if you want to try, obey these steps:

1. **Double-click the li'l printer icon by the current time on the taskbar.**

   If you don't see the li'l printer icon, it's too late to cancel the print job by using this technique. Otherwise, you see the printer's window, which lists any queued printing jobs.

2. **Click the name of your Word document job on the list.**

3. **From the window's menu, choose either the Document⇨Cancel command or the Document⇨Cancel Printing command.**

 4. Click Yes or OK to terminate the job.

 5. Close the printer's window when you're done.

It may take a while for the printer to stop printing. That's because the printer has its own memory, and a few pages of the document may be stored there *and* continue to print even after you tell the printer to stop. (Stupid printer — stupid.)

 ✔ Stopping a print job is a Windows task, not one that Word has control over.

 ✔ If you're using a network printer, you may not be able to cancel printing. Oh, well.

Electronic Publishing

Mr. Bunny likes to live in the forest. It's his home. The forest is full of trees and friendly critters. It's also home to predators who would love to eat Mr. Bunny, but that's not my point. My point is that you can do your part to help save Mr. Bunny's home by publishing your documents electronically. Keep this statement in mind: It's not always necessary to print your documents.

Preparing a document for sharing

Lots of interesting things can be put into your Word document that you don't want published. These items include comments, revision marks, hidden text, and other items useful to you or your collaborators, which would mess up a document you share with others. The solution is to use Word's Check for Issues tool, like this:

 1. Ensure that your document is finished, finalized, and saved.

 2. Click the File tab.

 On the File screen, the Info area should be highlighted. If not, click the word *Info*.

 3. Click the Check for Issues button.

 4. Choose Inspect Document from the Check for Issues button menu.

 The Document Inspector window shows up. All items are checked.

 5. Click the Inspect button.

After a few moments, the Document Inspector window shows up again, listing any issues with your document. The issues shown are explained, which allows you to cancel out of the Document Inspector to fix individual items.

   6. Click the Remove All button next to any issues you want to clear up.

   Remember that this step is entirely optional. Now that you know what the issues are, you can always click the Close button and return to your document to manually inspect them.

   7. Click the Close button, or click Reinspect to give your document another once-over.

   8. Click the Back button to return to your document.

You can go forward with publishing your document or continue working.

Sending a Word document by e-mail

E-mailing your Word document is a snap — as long as you're using Microsoft Outlook as your e-mail program. This opening statement also implies that your organization uses an "Exchange Server." If that's you, great — you can follow these steps to e-mail your document:

   1. Save your document one more time.

   2. Click the File tab.

   3. Choose the Share command.

   4. Choose the E-Mail item found under the Share heading.

   5. Click the Send As Attachment button.

   At this point, Outlook takes over and you compose your e-mail message. When you send the message, your Word document is sent along as well.

If you don't use Outlook (and I don't blame you), you can always send a Word document just as you send any e-mail file attachment. The key is to save the document *and* remember its filename and location so that you can find it later. To attach a Word document to an e-mail message by using just about any e-mail program, follow these general steps:

   1. Compose your e-mail message as you normally do.

   2. Use the Attach command to find the Word document and attach it to the message.

   3. Send the message.

Also see the following section.

Saving a Word document in a sharable format

Not everyone can read Word documents. In fact, users of ancient versions of Word might not be able to read the Word documents you create in Word 2013. To ensure that the files are compatible, you can publish your documents in a more compatible or universal file format. Obey these steps:

1. **Finish your document.**

   Yes, that includes saving it one last time.

2. **Click the File tab.**

3. **Choose the Export command.**

4. **Choose Change File Type.**

   Use the options in the Document File Types list to save your document by using another file type, one that would be more compatible than Word's own document file format. Here are my suggestions:

   Word 97-2003 Document: This is the most compatible Word file format, ideal for sharing your documents with anyone who has Word.

   Rich Text Format: This file format is compatible with every word processing program available. In fact, RTF was created so that documents can be shared between different computers and programs.

   Single File Web Page: You're basically creating a web page document in Word. Almost anyone with a web browser, which is just about everyone who uses a computer, can read documents saved in this format.

5. **Click the Save As button.**

   This button is found at the bottom of the Document File Types list. The Save As dialog box appears.

   If you want, you can change the document's filename and location by using the Save As dialog box.

6. **Click the Save button to save your document.**

The document is now saved, using the new file type. It's ready for sharing on the Internet, as a file attachment or however else you need to get it out there.

✔ You can save the document in plain-text format in Step 4: Choose the option Plain Text. Even so, rarely does anyone use the plain-text format any more. This format stores no formatting, no fonts, no images. It's just plain old text, but the option is there in case you're requested to save a document that way.

✔ To save a document as a PDF, or Adobe Acrobat, document, in Step 4 click the Create PDF/XPS Document button. Click the Create PDF/XPS button again (which is kind of redundant). Use the Publish As PDF or XPS Document dialog box to complete the exporting process.

✔ After saving a document in the new file format, you will have changed the document's filename in Word. Check the window's title bar to confirm. To continue editing the original document, you need to close the current document and then reopen that original document.

✔ Yes, it's okay to save the document by using the same filename as Word originally chose. That's because the file *type* is different; two files can share the same name as long as they are of different types.

✔ Unlike saving your document in another file format, saving it as a PDF doesn't change the document's name in Word.

✔ You need a copy of the Adobe Reader program to view PDF files. Don't worry: It's free. Go to www.adobe.com/acrobat.

✔ Also see Chapter 24 for more information on using and sharing documents with unusual file formats.

Part III
Fun with Formatting

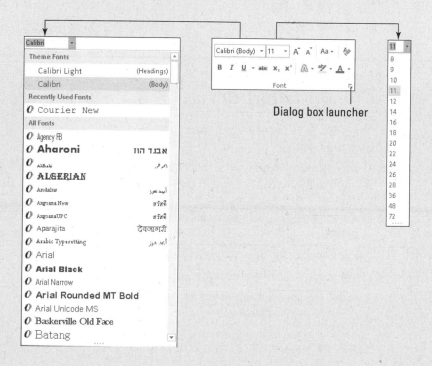

Dialog box launcher

In this part . . .

- ✔ Learn how to format your characters by choosing a font, text size, and color.
- ✔ Discover the various ways you can format paragraphs in Word 2013, including how to control line spacing, space before and after, and indenting.
- ✔ Get to know the ruler and all the ways you can use tabs to align your text.
- ✔ Find out how to change page size, orientation, and margins.
- ✔ Get familiar with adding headers, footers, and cover pages.
- ✔ Learn all you need to know about creating and applying styles and how to use templates.
- ✔ Learn how to add your own styles to the Word 2013 Style Gallery at www.dummies.com/extras/word2013.

Chapter 10

Character Formatting

*J*ust as your body is composed of millions of cells, documents are composed of thousands of characters. Like a cell, a *character* is the basic building block of the document. Characters include letters, symbols, and Aunt Eunice, who claims to talk with squirrels and even knits sweaters for them.

The most basic element you can format in a document is text — the letters, numbers, and characters you type. You can format text to be bold, underlined, italicized, little, or big or in different fonts or colors — all sorts of pretty and distracting attributes. Word gives you a magnificent amount of control over the appearance of your text. This chapter contains the details.

Text Formatting 101

You can change the format of your text in two ways:

✔ **Choose a text-formatting command first, and then type the text.** All the text you type is formatted as chosen.

✔ **Type the text first, and then select the text as a block and apply the formatting.** This technique works best when you're busy with a thought and need to return to format the text later.

You use both methods as you compose text in your document. Sometimes, it's easier to use a formatting command and type the text in that format. For example:

1. **Type this line:**

   ```
   The cake was
   ```

2. **Press Ctrl+I to activate *italic text*.**

3. **Type this word:**

   ```
   really
   ```

4. **Press Ctrl+I again, which turns off italic.**

5. **Continue typing:**

   ```
   salty.
   ```

The final sentence looks like this:

```
The cake was really salty.
```

For more complex formatting, type the text first, go back, mark the text as a block, and then apply the formatting: Type the sentence **The cake was really salty**, and then double-click the word *really* to select it. Press Ctrl+I.

See Chapter 6 for more information on marking blocks of text.

Basic Text Formatting

Word stores some of the most common text-formatting commands on the Home tab, in the Font group, as shown in Figure 10-1. The command buttons in this group carry out most of the basic text formatting you use in Word. This section mulls over the possibilities.

✔ Text can also be formatted by using the Mini toolbar, which appears whenever you select text. Refer to Chapter 6.

✔ The Font group can help you quickly determine which type of formatting is applied to your text. For example, in Figure 10-1, the text where the insertion pointer is blinking is formatted in the Calibri font. The number 11 tells you that the text is 11 points tall. If the B button were highlighted, you would also know that the text was formatted in bold. (These text formats are discussed throughout this section.)

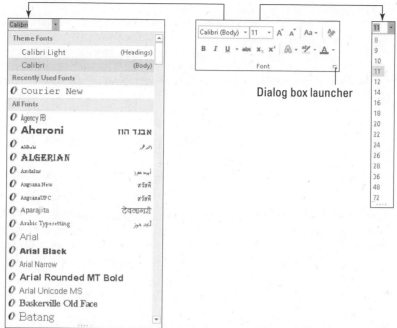

Dialog box launcher

Changing the font

The most basic attribute of text is its *typeface,* or *font.* The font sets up the
way your text looks — its overall text style. Although deciding on a proper
font may be agonizing (and, indeed, many graphic artists are paid well to
choose just the right font), the task of selecting a font in Word is quite easy. It
generally goes like this:

1. **On the Home tab, in the Font group, click the down arrow to display
    the Font Face list.**

    A menu of font options appears, as shown on the left in Figure 10-1.

    The top part of the menu shows fonts associated with the document
    theme. The next section contains fonts you've chosen recently, which
    is handy for reusing fonts. The rest of the list, which can be quite long,
    shows all fonts in Windows that are available to Word.

2. **Scroll to the font you want.**

    The fonts in the All Fonts part of the list are displayed in alphabetical
    order as well as in context (as they appear when printed).

3. Click to select a font.

You can also use the Font menu to preview the look of fonts. Scroll through the list to see which fonts are available and how they may look. As you move the mouse over a font, any selected text in your document is visually updated to show how that text would look in that font. The text isn't changed until you select the new font.

✔ When no font is displayed in the Font group (the listing is blank), it means that more than one font is being used in the selected block of text.

✔ You can quickly scroll to a specific part of the menu by typing the first letter of the font you need, such as T for Times New Roman.

✔ Graphic designers prefer to use two fonts in a document — one for the text and one for headings and titles. Word is configured this way as well. The font you see with Body after its name is the current text, or *body*, font. The font marked as Heading is used for headings. These two fonts are part of the document theme.

✔ Refer to Chapter 16 for more information on document themes.

✔ Fonts are the responsibility of Windows, not Word. Thousands of fonts are available for Windows, and they work in all Windows applications.

Applying character formats

The Font group lists some of the most common character formats. They're applied in addition to the font. In fact, they enhance the font. Use them as you see fit:

To make text bold, press Ctrl+B or click the Bold command button.

Use **bold** to make text stand out on a page — for titles and captions or when you're uncontrollably angry.

To make text italic, press Ctrl+I or click the Italic command button.

Italic has replaced underlining as the preferred text-emphasis format. Italicized text is light and wispy, poetic and free.

Underline text by pressing Ctrl+U or clicking the Underline command button. You can click the down arrow next to the Underline command button to choose from a variety of underline styles or set an underline color.

<u>Underline</u> is what they use at the DMV when they're feeling saucy.

 Strike through text by clicking the Strikethrough command button. (There's no keyboard shortcut for this one.)

I don't know why strikethrough text made it to the Font group. If I were king of Microsoft, I would have put small caps up there instead. But who am I? Strikethrough is commonly used in legal documents, when you mean to say something but then ~~change your mind~~ think of something better to say.

 Make text subscript by pressing Ctrl+= (equal sign) or clicking the Subscript command button.

Subscript text appears below the baseline, such as the 2 in H_2O. Again, I'm puzzled about how this formatting command ranks up there with bold and italic. I suppose that there's a lot of subscripting going on somewhere.

X^2 Make text superscript by pressing Ctrl+Shift+= (equal sign) or clicking the Superscript command button.

Superscript text appears above the line, such as the 10 in 2^{10}.

More text formats are available in Word, such as small caps, outline, and shadow. You can access them from the Font dialog box. Refer to the section "Fun with the Font Dialog Box," later in this chapter.

> REMEMBER

- ✔ Basic character formatting affects only selected text or any new text you type.

- ✔ To turn off a text attribute, use the command again. For example, press Ctrl+I to type in *italic.* Then press Ctrl+I again to return to normal text.

- ✔ You can mix and match character formats. For example, press Ctrl+B and then Ctrl+I to apply bold and italic text. You press Ctrl+B and Ctrl+I, or the command buttons, to turn off these attributes again.

> TIP

- ✔ The best way to use superscript or subscript is to write text first. Then go back, mark as a block the text you want to superscript or subscript, and *then* use these commands. So 42 becomes 4^2 and CnH2n+1OH becomes $C_nH_{2n+1}OH$. Otherwise, when you apply super- or subscript, the text you modify tends to be rather teensy and hard to edit. Better to write it first and then format.

- ✔ If you can remember that Ctrl+= adds subscript, just press the Shift key to apply Ctrl+Shift+= for superscript — if you can remember.

- ✔ When will the Underline text attribute die? I'm baffled. Honestly, I think we're waiting for the last typewriter-clutching librarian from the 1950s to pass on before underlining is officially gone as a text attribute. And please don't fall prey to the old rule about underlining book titles. It's *Crime and Punishment,* not <u>Crime and Punishment.</u>

Using less-common character attributes

Here are a few more text attributes — call them second-string players. You may not use these as often as bold or italic, but Word makes them available to you just as well:

To switch to all caps text, press Ctrl+Shift+A. This is a text format, not applied by pressing the Shift or Caps Lock key. In fact, like other formats, it can be removed. (Also see the later section, "Change Text Case.")

To set double-underlined text, press Ctrl+Shift+D. <u>This text is double-underlined.</u>

To produce small caps, press Ctrl+Shift+K. Small caps formatting is ideal for headings. I use it for character names when I write a script or play:

BILL. That's a clever way to smuggle a live grenade into prison.

To underline words only, and not the spaces between words, press Ctrl+Shift+W. <u>Word underlining looks like this.</u>

You create hidden text by pressing Ctrl+Shift+H. Hidden text is good for what it says — hiding text in a document. Of course, you don't see the text onscreen, either. To show hidden text, click the Show/Hide command button (in the Paragraph group on the Home tab) as described in Chapter 2, in the section about dealing with spots and clutter in the text. The hidden text shows up in the document with a dotted underline.

Text Transcending Teeny to Titanic

In Word, you can choose the size of your text, from indecipherably small to monstrously huge. Of course, more common is the subtle text-size adjustment; rare is the student who hasn't fudged the length of a term paper by inching up the text size a notch or two.

Understanding points

Word (and Windows) deals with text size as measured in *points*. It's a typesetting term. One point is equal to $\frac{1}{72}$ inch. Don't bother memorizing it. Instead, here are some point pointers:

- ✔ The bigger the point size, the larger the text.

- ✔ Most printed text is either 10 or 12 points tall.

- ✔ Headings are typically 14 to 24 points tall.

- ✔ Most fonts can be sized from 1 point to 1,638 points. Point sizes smaller than 6 are generally too small for a human to read.

- ✔ Seventy-two points is equal (roughly) to 1-inch-high letters.

- ✔ The point size of text is a measure from the bottom of the descender to the top of the ascender — from the bottom of the lowercase *p* to the top of the capital *E*, for example. So the typical letter in a font is smaller than its given font size. In fact, depending on the font design, text formatted at the same size but with different fonts *(typefaces)* may not appear to be the same size. It's just one of those typesetting oddities that causes regular computer users to start binge drinking.

Setting the text size

Text size is set in the Font group on the Home tab. Immediately to the right of the Font box is the Size box. Clicking the down arrow displays a list of font sizes for your text, as shown on the right in Figure 10-1.

The Size menu lists only common text sizes. To set the text size to a value that isn't listed or to a specific value, type the value in the box. For example, to set the font size to 11.5, click in the Size box and type **11.5**.

You can preview the new text size by pointing the mouse at an item on the Size menu. The word under the insertion pointer, or a selected block of text, is updated on the screen to reflect the new size. Click to choose a size or press Esc to cancel.

Nudging text size

Sometimes, choosing text size is like hanging a picture: To make the picture level on the wall, you have to nudge it just a little this way or that. Word has similar tools for nudging the text size larger or smaller, two of which are found in the Font group.

To increase the font size, click the Grow Font command button or press Ctrl+Shift+>.

The Grow Font command nudges the font size up to the next value as listed on the Size menu (refer to Figure 10-1). So if the text is 12 points, the Grow Font command increases its size to 14 points.

 To decrease the font size, click the Shrink Font command button or press Ctrl+Shift+<.

The Shrink Font command works in the opposite direction of the Grow Font command, by reducing the text size to the next-lower value as displayed on the Size menu (refer to Figure 10-1).

I remember the Grow and Shrink keyboard commands easily because the greater-than symbol is > and the less-than symbol is <. Just say, "I'm making my text *greater than* its current size" when you press Ctrl+Shift+> or "I'm making my text *less than* its current size" when you press Ctrl+Shift+<.

 When you want to increase or decrease the font size by smaller increments, use these shortcut keys:

Ctrl+] Makes text one point size larger

Ctrl+[Makes text one point size smaller

More Colorful Characters

Adding color to your text doesn't make your writing more colorful. All it does is make you wish that you had more color ink when it's time to print your document. Regardless, you can splash around color on your text, and there's no need to place a drop cloth in the document's footer.

 Text color is applied by clicking the Font Color command button. The bar below the *A* on the Font Color command button indicates which color is applied to text.

To change the color, you must click the menu arrow to the right of the Font Color command button. A color menu appears, which I don't show in this book because it's not in color and the image would bore you. Even so, as you move the mouse pointer over various colors on the menu, selected text in your document is updated to reflect that color. When you find the color you like, click it. That color then becomes the new text color associated with the Font Color command button.

- Theme colors are associated with the document theme. Refer to Chapter 16.

- Select the More Colors item from the Font Color menu to display the special Colors dialog box. Use the dialog box to craft your own, custom colors.

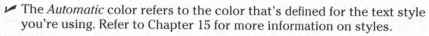

✔ The *Automatic* color refers to the color that's defined for the text style you're using. Refer to Chapter 15 for more information on styles.

✔ The Font Color command affects only the text color, not the background. To color the background, you use the Shading command, covered in Chapter 18.

✔ Colored text prints in color only when a color printer is available and readily stocked with color ink.

✔ Be careful with the colors you use! Faint colors can make text extremely difficult to read. If you want to hide text in your document, use the Hidden text attribute, described elsewhere in this chapter.

✔ Be careful not to confuse the Font Color command button with the Text Highlight Color command button, to its left. Text highlighting is a text attribute, but it's best used for document markup. See Chapter 26.

Change Text Case

Believe it or not, upper- and lowercase have something to do with a font. Back in the old days of mechanical type, a font came in a case, like a briefcase. The top part of the case, the upper case, held the capital letters. The bottom part of the case held the noncapital letters. So, in a way, changing the case of text is a font-formatting trick.

Aa ▾   To change the case of text in Word, use the Change Case command button in the Font group. Choosing this button displays a menu of options, each showing a different way to capitalize words in a sentence. Select the text you want to change, and then choose the proper item from the Change Case command button. Your text is modified to match the menu item that's selected.

✔ You can also use the Shift+F3 command to change the case of selected text. But this keyboard shortcut cycles between only three of the menu options shown in the figure: ALL CAPS, lowercase, and Capitalize Each Word.

✔ The Change Case command is not really a formatting command; even so, it overrides the All Caps text format.

Remove Character Formatting

So many Word formatting commands are available that it's possible for your text to look more like a pile of formatting remnants than anything that's readable in any human language. Word understands this problem, so it created the Clear Formatting command to let you peel away all formats from your text, just like you peel the skin from a banana:

To blow away formatting from a block of selected text or the text the insertion pointer is on or future text you type, use the Clear Formatting command button in the Font group. The keyboard shortcut for this command is Ctrl+spacebar.

The Clear Formatting command removes any formats you've applied to the text: font, size, text attributes (bold or italic), color, and so on.

✔ The Clear Formatting command removes the ALL CAPS text format but doesn't change the case of text you created by using Shift, Caps Lock, or the Change Case command in Word.

✔ Another key combination for Ctrl+spacebar is Ctrl+Shift+Z. Remember that Ctrl+Z is the Undo command. To undo formatting, all you do is add the Shift key, which may make sense — well, heck, if any of this makes sense.

 ✔ Technically, the Ctrl+spacebar command restores characters to the formatting defined by the *style* you're using. So if the Body style is 12-point Calibri, pressing Ctrl+spacebar restores that font and size. Don't let this information upset or confuse you! Instead, turn to Chapter 15 for more information on Word styles.

Fun with the Font Dialog Box

Word has a place where all your font-formatting delights are kept in a neatly organized fashion. It's the Font dialog box, as shown in Figure 10-2.

Figure 10-2: The neatly organized Font dialog box.

To summon the Font dialog box, click the Dialog Box Launcher button in the lower-right corner of the Font group (refer to Figure 10-1) or press the Ctrl+D keyboard shortcut.

The Font dialog box contains *all* the commands for formatting text, including quite a few that didn't find their way into the Font group on the Ribbon. As with all text formatting, the commands you choose in the Font dialog box affect any new text you type or any selected text in your document.

When you're done setting up your font stuff, click the OK button. Or click Cancel if you're just visiting.

- ✓ The best benefit of the Font dialog box is its Preview window, at the bottom. This window shows you exactly how your choices affect text in your document.

- ✓ The Font names *+Body* and *+Heading* refer to the fonts selected by the current document theme. This is done so that you can use Word's theme commands to quickly change body and heading fonts for an entire document all at one time.

- ✓ Click the Text Effects button in the Font dialog box to access festive attributes such as Shadow, Outline, Emboss, and Engrave. They're useful for titles and headings.

- ✓ You can use the Advanced tab in the Font dialog box to set options for changing the size and position of text on a line.

- ✓ The Set As Default button in the Font dialog box is used to change the font that Word uses for a new document. If you prefer to use a specific font for all your documents, choose the font (plus other text attributes) in the Font dialog box, and then click the Set As Default button. In the dialog box that appears, choose the option All Documents Based on the Normal Template, and then click the OK button. Afterward, all documents start with the font options you selected.

Chapter 11

Paragraph Formatting

- -

In This Chapter

▶ Understanding paragraph formatting

▶ Finding paragraph-formatting commands

▶ Aligning paragraphs left, center, right, and full

▶ Changing line spacing

▶ Adding room between paragraphs

▶ Indenting a paragraph

▶ Making a hanging indent

▶ Double-indenting a paragraph

▶ Using the ruler

- -

Word lets you hang many attributes onto a paragraph, probably more than you realize. Beyond alignment and margins, there are ways to format spacing in and around a paragraph of text. There are also special formatting commands just for the first line of a paragraph. Then there's the agonizing subject of tabs, which is really a paragraph-formatting attribute, but too much of a nut for me to include in this chapter. So I cover only the essentials of paragraph formatting.

How to Format a Paragraph

Question: What is a paragraph?

Answer: A mechanical gizmo that lets you draw pears.

Real Answer: A sentence or collection of sentences expressing a thought.

Word Formatting Answer: A chunk of text that ends when you press the Enter key. So as long as you type a single character, word, or sentence and then press Enter, you have a paragraph in Word.

You can format a paragraph in several ways:

- ✔ With the insertion pointer in a paragraph, use a formatting command to format that paragraph. This trick works because all paragraph-formatting commands affect the paragraph in which the insertion pointer is blinking.

- ✔ Use a paragraph-formatting command, and then type a new paragraph in that format.

- ✔ Use the formatting command on a block of selected paragraphs to format them all at once. To format all paragraphs in a document, press Ctrl+A to select all text in the document.

Some folks like to see the Enter key symbol (¶) in their documents, visually marking the end of every paragraph. You can do this in Word by following these steps:

1. **Click the File tab.**

2. **Choose the Options command from the File screen.**

   The Word Options dialog box appears.

3. **Click Display.**

4. **Place a check mark by Paragraph Marks.**

5. **Click OK.**

Now, every time you press the Enter key, the ¶ symbol appears at the end of the paragraph.

Where the Paragraph Formatting Commands Lurk

In a vain effort to confuse you, Word has placed popular paragraph-formatting commands in not one but *two* locations on the Ribbon. The first place to look is in the Paragraph group, found on the Home tab. The second place is in the Paragraph group found on the Page Layout tab. Both groups are illustrated in Figure 11-1.

But wait! There's more.

The Paragraph dialog box, shown in Figure 11-2, can be conjured up by clicking the dialog box launcher button in either of the Paragraph groups (refer to Figure 11-1). In it, you find some finer controls that the command buttons on the Ribbon just don't offer.

Dialog box launcher   Dialog box launcher

Figure 11-1:
Paragraph
groups.

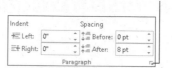

Home Tab
Paragraph Group

Page Layout Tab
Paragraph Group

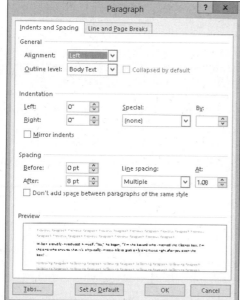

Figure 11-2:
The
Paragraph
dialog box.

The obnoxious keyboard shortcut to summon the Paragraph dialog box is
Alt+H, P, G. Don't mock it! If you can remember the keyboard shortcut, it saves
you time.

Click the Cancel button or press the Esc key to dismiss the Paragraph
dialog box.

The commands in the various paragraph-formatting locations are covered
throughout the rest of this chapter.

The Mini toolbar, which shows up after you select text, also contains a smattering of paragraph-formatting buttons. Refer to Chapter 6 for more information on the Mini toolbar.

Paragraph Justification and Alignment

Paragraph alignment has nothing to do with politics, and justification has nothing to do with the right or wrong of how paragraphs are formatted. Instead, both terms refer to how the left and right edges of the paragraph look on a page. The four options are Left, Center, Right, and Fully Justified, each covered in this section.

Line up on the left!

Much to the pleasure of southpaws the English-speaking world over, left-aligning a paragraph is considered normal: The left side of the paragraph is all even and tidy, and the right side is jagged, not lined up.

 To left-align a paragraph, press Ctrl+L or click the Align Left command button.

✔ This type of alignment is also known as *ragged right*.

✔ Left-aligning a paragraph is how you "undo" the other types of alignment.

Everyone center!

Centering a paragraph places each line in that paragraph in the middle of the page, with an equal amount of space to the line's right or left.

 To center a paragraph, press Ctrl+E or use the Center command button.

✔ Centering is ideal for titles and single lines of text. It's ugly for longer paragraphs and makes reading your text more difficult.

✔ You can center a single word in the middle of a line by using the center tab. Refer to Chapter 12 for the details.

Line up on the right!

A *right-aligned* paragraph has its right margin nice and even. The left margin, however, is jagged. When do you use this type of formatting? I have no idea, but it sure feels funky typing a right-aligned paragraph.

 To flush text along the right side of the page, press Ctrl+R or click the Align Right command button.

> ✔ This type of alignment is also known as *ragged left* or *flush right*.
>
> ✔ You can right-justify text on a single line by using a right-align tab. Refer to Chapter 12 for more info.

Line up on both sides!

Lining up both sides of a paragraph is *full justification:* Both the left and right sides of a paragraph are neat and tidy, flush with the margins.

To give your paragraph full justification, press Ctrl+J or click the Justify command button.

> ✔ Fully justified paragraph formatting is often used in newspapers and magazines, which makes the narrow columns of text easier to read.
>
> ✔ Word makes each side of the paragraph line up by inserting tiny slivers of extra space between words in a paragraph.

Make Room Before, After, or Inside Paragraphs

Word lets you add "air" to the space before or after or in the middle of your paragraphs. In the middle of the paragraph, you have line spacing. Before and after the paragraph comes paragraph spacing. Figure 11-3 shows you where the spacing can be found. The following sections describe how to control that spacing.

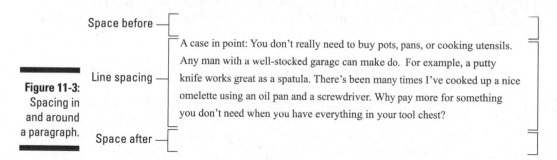

Figure 11-3:
Spacing in and around a paragraph.

Space before

Line spacing

Space after

A case in point: You don't really need to buy pots, pans, or cooking utensils. Any man with a well-stocked garage can make do. For example, a putty knife works great as a spatula. There's been many times I've cooked up a nice omelette using an oil pan and a screwdriver. Why pay more for something you don't need when you have everything in your tool chest?

Setting the line spacing

Changing the line spacing inserts extra space between *all* lines of text in a paragraph. Because Word adds the space *below* each line of text in the paragraph, the last line in the paragraph will also have a little extra space after it.

The Line Spacing command button is found in the Home tab's Paragraph group. Click this button to view a menu listing common line-spacing values. Choose a new line-spacing value from the menu to change the line spacing for the current paragraph or all paragraphs selected as a block.

✔ Word sets line spacing at 1.08 as its standard, or *default.* Supposedly, that extra .08 lines of text makes text more readable than using single spacing, or 1.0.

✔ To double-space your text, choose the value 2.0 from the Line Spacing command button menu. This setting formats the paragraph with one blank line below each line of text. To triple-space, choose the value 3.0, which makes one line of text appear with two blank lines below it.

✔ Ah! The keyboard shortcuts:

• To single-space, press Ctrl+1.

• To double-space, press Ctrl+2.

• To use 1½-space lines, press Ctrl+5.

✔ Yes, Ctrl+5 applies 1½-line spacing, not 5-line spacing. Use the 5 key in the typewriter area of the computer keyboard. Pressing the 5 key on the numeric keypad activates the Select All command.

✔ There's no such thing as having no line spacing. If you want to "remove" fancy line spacing, select some text and press Ctrl+1 for single spacing.

✔ When you want text to stack up one line atop another line, such as when typing a return address, use the *soft return* at the end of a line: Press Shift+Enter. See the section in Chapter 4 about soft and hard returns.

Setting specific line-spacing options

For persnickety line spacing, you summon the Paragraph dialog box (refer to Figure 11-2). In the Spacing area of the dialog box, use the Line Spacing drop-down list to set various line-spacing values: Single, 1.5, and Double, as found on the Line Spacing command button menu.

Some options in the Line Spacing drop-down list require you to also use the At box to sate your specific line-spacing desires. Values set in the At box indicate line spacing, as described in this list:

- ✔ **At least:** The line spacing is set to the specified value, which Word treats as a minimum value. Word can disobey that value and add more space whenever necessary to make room for larger type, different fonts, or graphics on the same line of text.

- ✔ **Exactly:** Word uses the specified line spacing and doesn't adjust the spacing to accommodate larger text or graphics.

- ✔ **Multiple:** This option is used to enter line-spacing values other than those specified in the Line Spacing drop-down list. For example, to set the line spacing to 4, choose Multiple from the Line Spacing drop-down list and type **4** in the At box. Word's default 1.08 line-spacing value is set with the Multiple option.

Values are specified in the At box in increments of 0.01. So, when you want to tighten up text on a page, select all paragraphs on that page, choose Multiple from the Line Spacing drop-down list, and then type **0.99** in the At box. Or, to add more room subtly, type **1.01**.

Click the OK button to confirm your settings and close the Paragraph dialog box.

Making space between paragraphs

It's a silly thing to do: Press Enter twice to end a paragraph. People say that they need the extra space between the paragraphs for readability. That's true, but what they don't realize is that Word can add that space automatically. The secret is to use the Before and After paragraph formatting commands — commands that have nothing to do with losing weight.

To add room after a paragraph, use the After command. It's found in the Page Layout tab's Paragraph group (refer to Figure 11-1).

To add room before a paragraph, use the Before command, also found on the Page Layout tab's Paragraph group.

Both commands are also found in the Paragraph dialog box, in the Spacing area (refer to Figure 11-2).

- ✔ The space you add before or after a paragraph becomes part of its format.

- ✔ Most of the time, space is added after a paragraph.

- ✔ You can add space before a paragraph, for example, to further separate text from a document heading or subhead.

- ✔ To add space inside a paragraph, use the line-spacing commands, described earlier in this chapter.

- ✔ The values used in the After or Before boxes are *points,* not inches or potrzebies. Points are also used in Word to set text size; see Chapter 10.

- ✔ Adding space before or after a paragraph is a great way to spread out a list of bullet points or numbered steps without affecting the line spacing within the bullet points or steps.

- ✔ Graphics designers prefer to insert more space between paragraphs when the first line of a paragraph isn't indented, as in this book. When you indent the first line, it's okay to have less spacing between paragraphs. See the next section.

Paragraph Indentation

Do you suffer from the shame of manual paragraph indenting? It's a hidden secret. Yes, even though computers enjoy doing tasks automatically, too many Word users still begin a paragraph of text by pressing the Tab key. It's ugly, but it's a topic that must be discussed.

Word can indent your paragraphs for you: left side, right side, both sides, or maybe just the first line. It can even outdent the first line, which is truly something to behold. This section discusses various paragraph-indenting and -outdenting options.

Indenting the first line of a paragraph

To have Word automatically indent the first line of every paragraph you type, heed these steps:

1. **Conjure up the Paragraph dialog box.**

   Refer to the section "Where the Paragraph Formatting Commands Lurk," earlier in this chapter, for proper conjuring incantations.

2. **In the Indentation area, locate the Special drop-down list.**

3. **Select First Line from the list.**

4. **Enter an amount in the By box (optional).**

   Unless you've messed with the settings, the box should automatically say 0.5", which means that Word automatically indents the first line of every paragraph a half inch — one tab stop. Type another value if you want your indents to be more or less outrageous. (Items are measured here in inches, not in points.)

5. Click OK.

The selected block, or the current paragraph, automatically has an indented first line.

To remove the first-line indent from a paragraph, repeat these steps and select (none) from the drop-down list in Step 3. Then click the OK button.

Word's AutoCorrect feature can perform these steps for you, but it's tricky. First you must type the paragraph. Then go back to the start of the paragraph and press the Tab key. This action instantly sets the paragraph indentation when AutoCorrect is on. If you see the AutoCorrect icon on the screen (shown in the margin), paragraph indenting is fixed. *Ta-da!*

If you choose to indent the first line of your paragraphs, you don't really need to add space after your paragraphs. Sure, you can do such a thing, but legions of graphics artists will frown at you.

Making a hanging indent (an outdent)

A *hanging indent* isn't in imminent peril, nor can it affect the outcome of an election. Instead, it's a paragraph in which the first line sticks out to the left and the rest of the paragraph is indented. It's a preferred way to present paragraph lists — like this:

Snore putty: It works every time. Just apply a little snore putty to your partner's mouth and nostrils. In just moments, that rattling din is gone and you're back to sleeping comfortably.

To create such a beast, position the insertion pointer in the paragraph you want to hang and indent. Press Ctrl+T, the Hanging Indent keyboard shortcut.

Because you probably won't remember Ctrl+T all the time (who could?), paragraphs can also be hanged and indented in the Paragraph dialog box. Follow the steps from the preceding section, but in Step 3 choose Hanging from the drop-down list.

✔ As a bonus, every time you press Ctrl+T, the paragraph is indented by another half inch.

✔ To undo a hanging indent, press Ctrl+Shift+T. That's the unhang key combination, and it puts the paragraph's neck back in shape.

Indenting a whole paragraph

Just as you can indent the first line of a paragraph, you can indent every line of a paragraph, by moving the paragraph's left margin over to the right a notch, just like Mr. Bunny: Hop, hop, hop. This technique is popular for typing block quotes or *nested* paragraphs.

 To indent a paragraph one tab stop from the left, click the Increase Indent command button in the Home tab's Paragraph group or press Ctrl+M.

 To unindent an indented paragraph, click the Decrease Indent command button in the Home tab's Paragraph group or press Ctrl+Shift+M.

Each time you use the Increase Indent command, the paragraph's left edge hops over one tab stop (typically, one half-inch). To undo this and shuffle the paragraph back to the left, use the Decrease Indent command.

When you want to get specific, you can set the left and right indents for a paragraph by using the Page Layout tab's Paragraph group or the Paragraph dialog box. (Refer to Figure 11-2). The Left item sets the indentation of the paragraph's left edge. The Right item sets the indentation of the paragraph's right edge.

✔ Indenting a paragraph doesn't affect the paragraph's alignment.

✔ To indent both the left and right sides of a paragraph, set both left and right indents to the same value.

✔ To undo any paragraph indenting, set both Left and Right indent values to 0.

✔ Setting positive values for the paragraph's indent in the Page Layout tab's Paragraph group moves the paragraph's edges inward. Setting negative values moves the edges outward. When the values are set to 0, the paragraph's margins match the page's margin.

✔ You cannot decrease the indent beyond the left margin of the page.

 ✔ Refer to Chapter 13 for more information on the page margins.

✔ Do not try to mix left and right indenting with a first-line indent or hanging indent while drowsy or while operating heavy equipment.

Who Died and Made This Thing Ruler?

Paragraph formatting can be confusing. Two places on the Ribbon are for paragraph formatting, or if you opt instead to use the Paragraph dialog box, your mind may go into shock from the abundance of options. A more graphical, and therefore more fun, way to manipulate a paragraph's indentation and margins is to use the ruler.

The ruler is naturally hidden in Word. To show the ruler, click the View tab and place a check mark by the Ruler item, found in the Show group.

In Print Layout view, the ruler appears on the top of the writing part of the Word window, as shown in Figure 11-4. A vertical ruler also shows up and runs down the left side of the window, though that ruler is only for show.

Tab gizmo

First line indent

Figure 11-4:
The ruler.

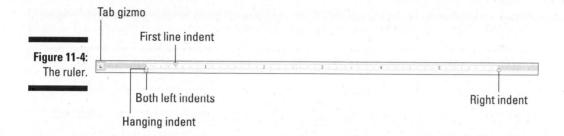

Both left indents

Right indent

Hanging indent

The dark gray part of the ruler (the outer ends) is beyond the page margins. The lighter gray part is inside the page margins, and the ruler measures that space from the left, starting with zero inches.

On the ruler, and illustrated in Figure 11-4, you find four gizmos that control paragraph indenting: one downward-pointing triangle, two upward-pointing triangles, and one block. These gizmos reflect the current paragraph formatting, and they can be manipulated with the mouse to change the paragraph formatting. The next few paragraphs describe the settings they control.

To adjust a paragraph's right margin, grab the Right Indent guy on the ruler and drag him to the right or left.

The first line indent is set independently of the rest of the lines in a paragraph by dragging the First Line Indent doojobbie to the left or right.

To adjust a paragraph's left margin for all lines but the first line — called a hanging indent — grab the Hanging Indent thing on the ruler and slide it to the left or right. Moving this gizmo does not affect the First Line indent.

The Left Indent thing controls both the Hanging Indent and First Line Indent at the same time. It allows you to adjust both the paragraph's left margin as well as the first line indent with one mouse action rather than two.

  ✔ The ruler measures from the page's left margin, not from the left edge of the page.

  ✔ The page's left margin is set when you format a page of text. See Chapter 13.

  ✔ The Tab gizmo is used to set the various tab stops used in Word. This confusing and frustrating subject is covered in Chapter 12.

  ✔ The ruler works fine for visually setting indents, but when you need to be precise, use the Paragraph dialog box.

Paragraph-formatting survival guide

This table contains all the paragraph-formatting commands you can summon by holding down the Ctrl key and pressing a letter or number. By no means should you memorize this list.

Format	Key Combination	Command Button
Center	Ctrl+E	
Fully justify		Ctrl+J
Left-align (flush left)		Ctrl+L
Right-align (flush right)		Ctrl+R
Indent		Ctrl+M
Unindent		Ctrl+Shift+M
Hanging indent		Ctrl+T
Unhanging indent	Ctrl+Shift+T	
Line spacing	Alt+H, K	
Single-space lines		Ctrl+1
1.15 line spacing	Ctrl+0	
Double-space lines	Ctrl+2	
1½-space lines	Ctrl+5	

Chapter 12

Tab Formatting

. . . .

. . . .

The tab is one of the handiest and most overlooked and frustrating things in all of Word. By using tabs, you can quickly line up text and create lists nice and neat. Yet most folks don't bother with tabs because, honestly, Word doesn't handle them in anything approaching a logical, friendly manner. Because of that frustration, and even though the tab is a part of paragraph formatting, I decided to create a special chapter just on the topic of using tabs in Word.

Once Upon a Tab

On my ancient Underwood typewriter, the Tab key is on the right side of the keyboard and is named Tabular Key. Elsewhere, I've seen it named Tabulator. In every case, the root word is *table*. The Tab key is used to help build tables or to organize information in a tabular way.

Pressing the Tab key in Word inserts a tab *character* into your document. The tab character works like a wide space character, where its size is determined by a predefined location marked across a page. That location is called the *tab stop*.

It's the tab stop that makes the Tab key work: Press the Tab key, and the insertion pointer hops over to the next tab stop. That way, you can precisely line up text on multiple lines — definitely much nicer than trying to fudge together columns of text by using the spacebar.

✔ Anytime you press the spacebar more than once, you *need* a tab. Believe me, your documents will look prettier and you'll be happier after you understand and use tabs rather than spaces to line up your text.

✔ Word presets tab stops at every half-inch position across the page — that is, unless you set your own tab stops.

✔ You use Backspace or Delete to remove a tab character, just as you delete any character in a document.

✔ Tabs work best for a single line of text or for only the first line of a paragraph. For anything more complex, use Word's Table command. See Chapter 19.

✔ The diet beverage Tab was named for people who like to keep a tab on how much they consume.

Seeing the tab stops

Tab stops are set in Word by using the Tabs dialog box, which is covered later in this chapter. A more visual way to set tab stops, as well as see all tab stops no matter how they're set, is to use the ruler.

The ruler appears just above the text page in Word's document window. When the ruler isn't visible, click the View tab and place a check mark by the Ruler item in the Show group.

Figure 12-1 shows the ruler with several tab stops appearing as tiny, black symbols. Three tab stops are set in the figure: a left tab stop at the half-inch mark, a center tab stop at the 1½-inch mark, and a right tab stop at the 2½-inch mark.

Figure 12-1:
Tab stops
on the ruler.

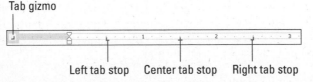

In your document, tabs appear as blank spaces. You can direct Word to display the tab character, if you like. Clicking the Show/Hide button, the one with the ¶ symbol, does the trick. You see the tab character appear as a teensy, right-pointing arrow, as shown in the margin. Click the Show/Hide button again to conceal the tab characters.

✔ The Show/Hide command is found in the Paragraph group on the Ribbon's Home tab.

 ✔ You can also use the Show/Hide command to find two spaces together in your document. They appear as two teensy dots, one after the other.

 ✔ To show only the tab character in your document, and not all the other junk displayed by the Show/Hide command, choose Options from the File screen to display the Word Options dialog box. Click Display from the left side of the dialog box. Then put a check mark by the Tab Characters option. Click OK.

 ✔ When several paragraphs are selected, you may spot a light gray, or *phantom,* tab stop on the ruler. The phantom indicates a tab stop that's set in one paragraph but not in all. To apply the tab stop to all selected paragraphs, click the phantom tab stop once.

 ✔ See the later section, "Tab Stop, Be Gone!" for information on using the ruler to remove, or unset, a tab stop.

Setting tab stops on the ruler

You manipulate tab stops on the ruler by using the mouse: Choose one of five tab-stop types from the Tab gizmo on the left end of the ruler (refer to Figure 12-1). Then click the mouse on the ruler to set the tab stop at a specific position.

For example, to set a left tab stop at the 2-inch position, you follow these steps:

1. **Ensure that the Tab gizmo on the left end of the ruler displays the left tab stop.**

   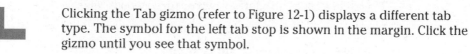

   Clicking the Tab gizmo (refer to Figure 12-1) displays a different tab type. The symbol for the left tab stop is shown in the margin. Click the gizmo until you see that symbol.

2. **Click the ruler at the exact spot where you want the tab stop set.**

   For example, click on the number 2 for the 2-inch spot.

Later sections in this chapter discuss each of the five different types of tab stops, when and how to set them, as well as how to set tabs by using the Tabs dialog box.

Tab stops are paragraph-level formatting. Tab settings affect only the paragraph that the toothpick cursor is blinking in, or for all paragraphs selected as a block. Refer to Chapter 6 for blocky stuff.

The Standard Left Tab Stop

The left tab stop is the traditional type of tab stop. When you press the Tab key, the insertion pointer advances to the left tab stop, where you can continue to type text. This works best for typing lists, organizing information in single-line paragraphs, or indenting the first line of a multiline paragraph. This section provides some examples.

Creating a basic tabbed list

A common use for the left tab stop is to create a simple two-column list, as shown in Figure 12-2.

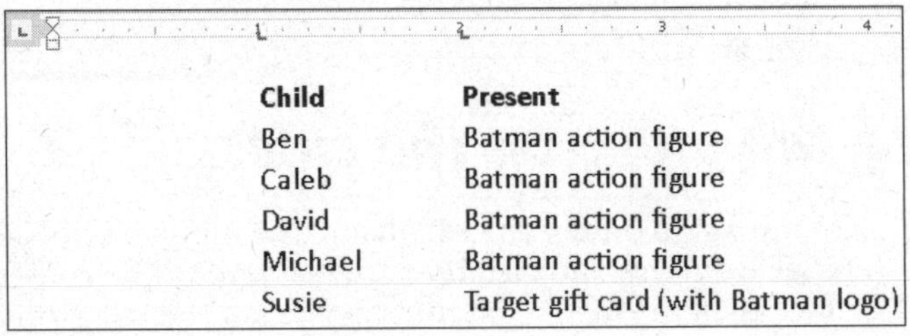

Child	Present
Ben	Batman action figure
Caleb	Batman action figure
David	Batman action figure
Michael	Batman action figure
Susie	Target gift card (with Batman logo)

Figure 12-2: Two-column list.

The following steps describe how to set up this type of list:

1. **On a new line, press Tab.**
2. **Type the item for the first column.**

   This item should be short — two or three words, max.
3. **Press Tab.**
4. **Type the item for the second column.**

   Again, make it short.
5. **Press Enter to end that line and start a new line.**

   Yes, your list looks horrible! Don't worry. Just get the data typed first, and then format it.
6. **Repeat Steps 1 through 5 for each item in the list.**

   After the list is finished, you set the tab stops visually by using the ruler.
7. **Summon the ruler, if necessary.**

   Directions are offered earlier in this chapter.

8. **Select all lines of text that you want to organize into a two-column tabbed list.**

   Refer to Chapter 6 for more information on marking blocks of text.

9. **Choose a left tab stop from the Tab gizmo on the ruler.**

   If necessary, click the Tab gizmo until the Left tab-stop icon shows up.

10. **Click the mouse on the ruler at the number 1, the 1-inch position.**

    This step sets a left tab stop at 1 inch. You see how the selected text falls into place immediately.

11. **Click the mouse to set a second tab stop at the 3-inch mark.**

    The list looks nice and even, in two columns (refer to Figure 12-2).

12. **Adjust the tab stops, if necessary.**

    Slide the tab stops left or right on the ruler as needed to help clean up your list. As you slide the tab stops, notice how a dashed vertical line extends through your text. That line shows you where text lines up.

These steps can also be used to create a three- or even four-column list. The idea is to keep the text on one line and separated by single tabs. Then use the tab stops on the ruler to line up the columns and make them look pretty.

REMEMBER

✔ You need only one tab between items in a column list. That's because it's the *tab stop,* not the tab character, that lines up your text.

✔ For a tabbed list to work, each paragraph must be a line by itself, and the items in each column should be only a word or two long. Any longer, and you need to use Word's Table command, as covered in Chapter 19.

Creating a two-tab paragraph thing

Tabs can also be used to form an item list where the paragraph text remains in the rightmost column. Figure 12-3 shows how the 2-tab paragraph thing works. It combines both paragraph- and tab-formatting skills.

Character	Planet	Description
Norzon	Dinky	Norzon is the chief deputy sub-accountant for Bosco the Magnificent, ruler of planet Dinky. Norzon is in love with Bosco's third mistress, Unno.
Unno	Dinky	Third mistress of Lord Bosco, she is stunningly beautiful save for her extremely long toes. Fortunately, her father is an excellent cobbler.
Qbbs	Thrombo	Queen of the Thrombonians, she finances Norzon's bakery to get revenge upon Lord Bosco. Despite her irritating personality, she is a good clarinet player.

Figure 12-3: A tab-tab-paragraph format for text.

Follow these steps to create a similar list:

1. **On a new line, type the item for the first column.**

   The shorter, the better.

2. **Press Tab.**

3. **Type the second column's text and press Tab.**

   This step is optional; you can create a simpler tab-paragraph list, which looks just like the one shown in Figure 12-3, but without the Planet column (and spaced accordingly).

4. **Type the paragraph text.**

   Unlike with the first two items, you're free to type more text here. That's because this final paragraph column will wrap (refer to Figure 12-3).

5. **Press Enter to end the line and start a new line.**

   Don't let the ugly look of your text deceive you at this point. The text beautifies itself when you add the tab stops.

6. **Repeat Steps 1 through 5 for all items in the tab-paragraph list.**

   When you're done, you can set the tab stops. You need the ruler for Step 7.

7. **Bid the ruler appear, if need be.**

   Directions for beckoning forth the ruler are found earlier in this chapter.

8. **Select all the lines of text you want to organize into a tab-tab-paragraph list.**

   Chapter 6 discusses block-selection techniques.

9. **Slide the Hanging Indent triangle to the 2-inch position on the ruler.**

   As an alternative, you can click the Tab gizmo until the Hanging Indent icon appears. Then click the ruler at the 2-inch position.

10. **Ensure that the Left tab stop is chosen on the Tab gizmo.**

    The margin shows the Left Tab symbol.

11. **Click the mouse to set a tab stop at 1 inch.**

    The second column snaps into place.

12. **Adjust the tab stop and hanging indent triangle as necessary.**

    With the text still selected, you can slide the Left tab stop and the Hanging Indent icons on the ruler to the left or right to adjust the look of your tab-tab-paragraph. Whatever looks best works best.

You can vary these rules to have a tab-paragraph or even a triple-tab-paragraph. The more tabs you have, the tighter the paragraph becomes in the last column, so be careful.

The Center Tab Stop

The *center tab* is a unique critter with a special purpose: Text placed at a center tab is centered on a line. Unlike centering a paragraph, only text placed at the center tab stop is centered. This feature is ideal for centering text in a header or footer, which is about the only time you need the center tab stop.

Figure 12-4 shows an example of a center tab. The text on the left is at the start of the paragraph, which is left-justified. But the text typed after the tab is centered on the line.

Figure 12-4:
Center tab
in action.

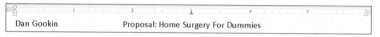

Dan Gookin   Proposal: Home Surgery For Dummies

Here's how to make that happen:

1. **Start a new paragraph, one containing text that you want to center.**

   Center tabs inhabit 1-line paragraphs.

2. **Set a center tab at the 3-inch position on the ruler.**

   If necessary, show the ruler; directions are found earlier in this chapter.

   To pluck a center tab stop, click the Tab gizmo on the ruler until a center tab appears (as shown in the margin). Click on the ruler to set the tab stop.

3. **Type some text to start the line (optional).**

   The text you type should be short; it appears only at the start of the line.

4. **Press the Tab key.**

   The insertion pointer hops over to the center tab stop.

5. **Type the text to center.**

   As you type, the text is centered on the line. Don't type too much; remember that the center tab is a single-line thing.

6. **Press Enter to end the line of text.**

Obviously, if you want only to center text on a line, centering the entire paragraph is a better choice; see Chapter 11. Otherwise, this technique finds itself used mostly in page headers and footers, which are covered in Chapter 14. Look there for an additional example.

The Right Tab Stop

A right tab seems useless until you've seen one in action. You use it to right-justify text at a tab stop, allowing a single line of text to contain both right- and left-justified text. You've probably seen such a thing but never thought you could create it easily. Read this section and discover how it's done.

✔ As with the other unusual tab stops, the right tab stop works best on a single line of text.

✔ The following two sections assume that the ruler is visible. To show the ruler, click the View tab and ensure that a check mark appears by the Ruler item in the Show group.

Making a right-stop, left-stop list

To create a centered, 2-column list with a right tab stop and a left tab stop, shown in Figure 12-5, obey these steps:

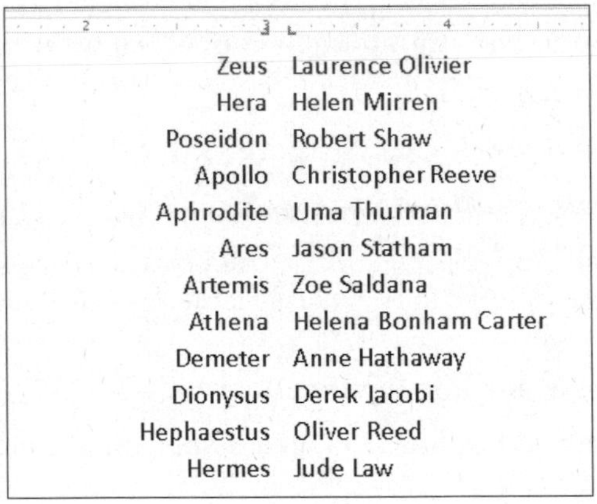

Zeus	Laurence Olivier
Hera	Helen Mirren
Poseidon	Robert Shaw
Apollo	Christopher Reeve
Aphrodite	Uma Thurman
Ares	Jason Statham
Artemis	Zoe Saldana
Athena	Helena Bonham Carter
Demeter	Anne Hathaway
Dionysus	Derek Jacobi
Hephaestus	Oliver Reed
Hermes	Jude Law

Figure 12-5: Right tab stops are used to center-align this list.

1. **Start out on a blank line, the line you want to format.**

2. **Choose the right tab stop from the Tab gizmo.**

   Keep clicking the Tab gizmo with the mouse until the right tab stop appears.

3. **Click the mouse at the 3-inch position on the ruler.**

4. **Choose the left tab stop from the Tab gizmo.**

   Click, click, click until you see the left tab stop.

5. **Click the mouse at the 3⅛-inch position on the ruler.**

   Use Figure 12-5 as your guide. Don't fret — you can change the tab stop positions when you're just about done.

6. **Press the Tab key.**

   The insertion pointer hops over to the 3-inch stop, the right tab stop.

7. **Type your text.**

   The text is right-justified at the right tab stop.

8. **Press the Tab key.**

9. **Type your text.**

   The text is left-justified (normal).

10. **Press Enter to end the line of text.**

11. **Repeat Steps 6 through 10 for each line in the list.**

As long as you limit the text to one line, the list should look great (refer to Figure 12-5).

To make adjustments, select the list as a block (see Chapter 6) and use the mouse to adjust the tab stops on the ruler. As you move the tab stops, a dashed line extends through your text, showing you where the text lines up. Or, to be more precise, you can use the Tabs dialog box, as covered later in this chapter.

Building a 2-column right-stop list

Another type of right-tab stop list is shown in Figure 12-6. This type is commonly found in dramatic programs but works just as well for a variety of purposes. Here's how to concoct such a thing:

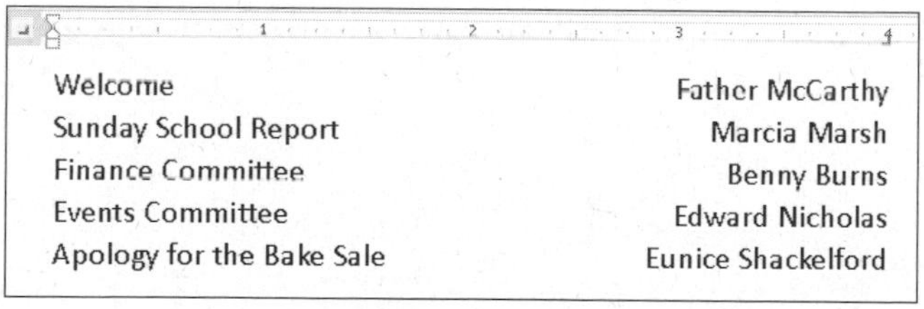

Figure 12-6:
Right tab stops right-align the second column of this list.

Welcome	Father McCarthy
Sunday School Report	Marcia Marsh
Finance Committee	Benny Burns
Events Committee	Edward Nicholas
Apology for the Bake Sale	Eunice Shackelford

1. **Start out with a blank line of text.**

2. **Ensure that the Tab gizmo on the ruler shows the right tab stop.**

3. **Click the mouse at the 4-inch position on the ruler.**

   The position is just a guess at this point. Later, you can adjust the right tab stop setting to a more visually appealing one.

4. **Type the left column text.**

   The text is left-justified, like normal.

5. **Press the Tab key.**

   The insertion pointer hops to the right tab stop.

6. **Type the right column text.**

   The text you type is right-justified, pushing to the left as you type.

7. **Press Enter to end the line of text.**

8. **Repeat Steps 4 through 7 for every line in the list.**

Afterward, you can mark the text as a block and then use the mouse to drag the right tab stop back and forth to whatever looks more visually appealing.

✔ You can drag the left indent (shown in the margin) toward the center of the page to offset the list from the left margin.

✔ Also refer to the section "Setting leader tab stops," later in this chapter, for information about adding a dotted leader, dashed leader, or underline to the right tab stop.

The Decimal Tab

The decimal tab is used to line up columns of numbers. Although you can use a right tab to do this job, the decimal tab is a better choice. Rather than right-align text, as the right tab does (see the preceding section), the decimal tab aligns numbers by their decimal portion — the period in the number, as shown in Figure 12-7.

Figure 12-7:
Lining up
numbers
with the
decimal tab.

Checked Baggage	$30.00
Extra Leg Room	$15.00
Window Seat	$10.00
Onboard Meal	$8.00
Bathroom Visits	Free!

Here's how to work with such a beast:

1. **Start a blank line of text.**

2. **Choose the Decimal tab stop from the Tab gizmo on the ruler.**

   The Decimal tab stop icon is shown in the margin.

3. **Set the tab stop on the ruler by clicking the mouse at the 3-inch position.**

4. **Type the left column text.**

5. **Press the Tab key.**

6. **Type the numerical amount.**

   The number is right-justified until you press the period key. After that, the rest of the number is left-justified. The effect is lined up so that the value is at the decimal tab stop by the period in the number.

7. **End that line of text by pressing Enter.**

8. **Repeat Steps 4 through 7 for each line in the list.**

Text typed without a period is right-justified at the decimal tab stop (refer to Figure 12-7) until you press the period key.

You can adjust your text by selecting all lines as a block and then using the mouse to drag the decimal tab stop on the ruler.

The Bar Tab

Aside from being a most excellent pun, the bar tab isn't a true tab stop in Word. Instead, consider it a text decoration. Setting a bar tab merely inserts a vertical line into a line of text, as shown in Figure 12-8. Using this feature is much better than using the pipe (|) character on the keyboard to create a vertical line in your document.

Figure 12-8:
The mysterious bar tab.

Squid	Kingdom	Animal
	Phylum	Mollusca
	Class	Cephalopoda
	Superorder	Decapodiformes
	Order	Teuthida
	Genus	Squid
	Name	Squidly Diddly

You set a bar tab stop the same way you set any other type of tab stop. But, rather than insert a tab stop, you insert a black, vertical line in the text. The line always appears, even when no text or tab is used on a line.

In Figure 12-8, four tab stops are set, though the tab character works only the left tab stops. The two bar tabs, at positions 1-inch and 2 1/2-inches, merely place a vertical line in the text, as shown in the figure. This is normally how bar tabs are used, although for all practical purposes, it's easier in Word to surrender here and use the Table function instead; see Chapter 19.

The Tabs Dialog Box

If setting tabs on the ruler is the right-brain approach, using the Tabs dialog box is the left-brain method. The Tabs dialog box, which should be called the Tab Stop dialog box, is shown in Figure 12-9. It gives you more precision over using the ruler by itself. The frustrating part is summoning that dialog box.

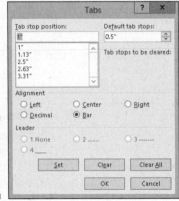

Figure 12-9:
The Tabs
(tab stop)
dialog box.

The simplest way to beckon forth the Tabs dialog box is to double-click the mouse on the bottom edge of the ruler (on the light gray part under the 2 in Figure 12-8). Of course, this technique also *sets* a tab stop, which can be frustrating.

You can also double-click any tab stop icon on the ruler to bring forth the Tabs dialog box.

The adventurous way to open the Tabs dialog box is to summon the Paragraph dialog box: Click the Dialog Box Launcher button in the lower-right corner of the Paragraph group on the Home tab. When the Paragraph dialog box is visible, click the Tabs button in the lower-left corner to see the Tabs dialog box.

Fix the default tab stops

When you don't set tab stops, Word does it for you. They're called default tab stops, and Word places one every half-inch all across the page. That way, when you press the Tab key, it dutifully hops to one of those preset tab stops, even though you haven't set any specific tab stops.

You can use the Tabs dialog box (refer to Figure 12-9) to change the interval of Word's default tab stops. Open the Tabs dialog box, and use the text box beneath the Default Tab Stops heading to set the proper interval. In Figure 12-9, the value is 0.5", which is every half inch.

Setting a tab stop in the Tabs dialog box

When you need for your tab stops to be precise and the ruler is proving unruly, follow these steps to set tabs in the Tab dialog box:

1. **Summon the Tabs dialog box.**

   Refer to the preceding section for delightful details.

2. **Enter the exact tab stop position in the Tab Stop Position box.**

   For example, type **1.1875** to set a tab at exactly that spot.

3. **Choose the type of tab stop from the Alignment area.**

   The standard tab stop is named Left. Other types of tab stops are covered elsewhere in this chapter.

4. **Click the Set button.**

   The Set button — not the OK button — creates the tab stop. After you click Set, the tab stop is placed on the list below the Tab Stop Position box. (You may notice that numbers are rounded to the nearest hundredth; Word interprets 1.1875 as 1.19, for example.)

5. **Continue setting tab stops.**

   Repeat Steps 1 through 3 for as many tab stops as you need to set.

6. **Click OK.**

The tab stops you set affect the current paragraph or a selected group of paragraphs. The tab stops you set are visible on the ruler, if the ruler itself is visible.

You must click the Set button to set a tab stop! I don't know how many times I click OK, thinking that the tab stop is set when it isn't.

Setting leader tab stops

You can do only one task in Word in the Tabs dialog box that you cannot do with the ruler: Set a leader tab stop.

What is a leader tab stop?

A *leader tab stop* produces a row of dots where the tab character appears. This trick is the only way to get a tab character to appear in your document, and it's quite useful.

Three styles are available for leader tab stops:

Fearless dot-leader tabs	158
Zipper-line leader tabs	158
U-boat underline leader tabs	158

You can apply a leader to any tab stop in Word other than the bar tab. To do so, refer to other sections in this chapter that tell you how to set the various types of tab stops — specifically, the right tab stop. To add the dot leader to the tabbed list you created, follow these steps:

1. **Select the text as a block.**

   Refer to Chapter 6 for block-marking directions.

2. **Bring forth the Tabs dialog box.**

3. **Select the tab stop from the Tab Stop Position list.**

   For example, in Figure 12-6, the right tab stop shows up in the Tab Stop Position list as 4". Click to select that item in the list.

4. **In the Leader area, choose the leader style.**

   None means *no leader,* and it's selected already. Choose one of the other three options.

5. **Click the Set button.**

   Don't click OK before you set the tab stop to add the leader. This step is the one you'll screw up most often.

6. **Click OK.**

   After clicking the Set button, you can click OK to close the Tabs dialog box and gawk at your text.

The leader tab that uses the underline character is also the best way to create fill-in-the-blanks forms. Use the Tabs dialog box to set a left tab stop at the far right margin (usually, 6.0 inches). Choose an underline leader for that tab. Click Set and then OK. Back in your document, type the prompt for the fill-in-the-blanks line, such as:

```
Your name: _____
```

Rather than type a zillion underlines, just press the Tab key. Instantly, a line extends from the colon to the right margin.

Tab Stop, Be Gone!

Removing a tab stop is as easy as dragging a tab stop icon from the ruler: Point and click at the tab stop, and drag the mouse downward. The tab stop is gone.

The Tabs dialog box can also be used to remove tab stops. It's especially good for those times when you may have several tab stops close together and plucking one out with the mouse would be exasperating. In the Tabs dialog box, choose the tab stop position in the Tab Stop Position list, and then click the Clear button. Poof! It's gone!

Clicking the Clear All button in the Tabs dialog box removes all tab stops from the paragraph's formatting in one drastic sweep.

To delete a Tab character, of course, simply back up over it with the Backspace key.

Chapter 13

Page Formatting

In This Chapter

▶ Choosing the page size

▶ Switching the page orientation

▶ Setting margins

▶ Automatically numbering your pages

▶ Changing page numbers

▶ Creating a new page

▶ Coloring a page

▶ Including a watermark

You probably don't think about the pages on which you write your document. That's because Word assumes that you want your document to print on a standard sheet of paper. Further, Word guesses that you want a uniform 1-inch margin all around the page. That's pretty much it. Ho-hum. Yawn.

In the real world, things can be different, of course. You can print on any size paper that can be properly fed into a computer printer. You may want narrow margins, or to print sideways or with a watermark. Even though you may never bother with such things, Word is more than capable. This chapter explains the possibilities for page formatting.

Describe That Page

Page formatting starts with the size of the page, which is normally the size of the paper you're printing on. Page and paper are similar concepts, but in Word you can do more with a page than just print on it.

Formatting commands covered in this section use the Page Setup group, found on the Page Layout tab on the Ribbon.

Setting page size

When Word starts out, it assumes that your document is destined to be printed on a sheet of paper and that the paper will be the standard size for your region, such as 8½-by-11 inches in the United States and the A4 size just about everywhere else. As the computer user, you have every right to disagree with Word and choose a different page size for your document, and you're not limited to the standard paper sizes, either.

To set the page size, obey these steps:

1. **Click the Page Layout tab on the Ribbon.**

2. **In the Page Setup group, click the Size button.**

   Size

   The Size button icon is shown in the margin.

   Clicking the Size button displays the Paper Size menu, stocked with a vast assortment of sheets of paper of different sizes.

3. **Choose a page size from the list.**

   For example, if you want to print on that tall, legal-size paper, choose Legal from the list.

Your entire document is updated to reflect the new page size, from first page to last. Well, that is, unless you split your document into sections. Then the page size change is reflected only for the current section. Refer to Chapter 14 for information on sections.

   ✔ To select a size not shown on the menu (refer to Step 3), choose the More Paper Sizes command, found at the bottom of the Size menu. You can then manually set the page size by using the Paper tab in the Page Setup dialog box.

   ✔ Word dutifully sets your document to any paper size imaginable, but can your printer handle that paper size? If you're only publishing the document electronically, page size is no big deal. But if you want to print a document, ensure that the printer can handle whatever paper size you chose.

Setting orientation (landscape or portrait)

Word assumes that you want your document's text to print from left to right on a page that's taller than it is wide. That's what it considers *normal*. It's also called *portrait* orientation because the page is presented vertically, like a portrait.

Word can also be told to print longways, or in *landscape* orientation. To perform this trick, follow these steps:

1. **Click the Page Layout tab on the Ribbon.**

2. **Click the Orientation button to see its menu.**

Orientation

The Orientation button is illustrated in the margin. It has two items on its menu: Portrait and Landscape.

3. **Choose Landscape.**

Word shifts the orientation for every page in your document. This doesn't mean that the text is sideways, but rather that the text prints wide on a page (though I suppose you could look at it as printing sideways).

To change the pages back, choose Portrait in Step 3.

✔ Changing the page orientation may require you to adjust the document's margins; see the next section.

✔ Page-orientation changes affect the entire document unless you split your document into sections. In this case, the change applies to only the current section. Read Chapter 14 for details on sections, including directions on how to stick a landscape page into a document that's otherwise portrait oriented.

TIP

✔ Make the decision to have your document in landscape orientation before you do any extensive formatting. This orientation affects your paragraphs and other "lower-level" formatting, so you should have it done first, before you start composing text.

✔ Scientists who study such things have determined that human reading speed slows drastically when people must scan a long line of text, which happens when you use Landscape orientation. Reserve landscape orientation for printing lists, graphics, and tables for which normal paper is too narrow.

✔ Landscape printing is ideal for using multiple columns of text. See Chapter 20.

✔ If you just want sideways text without turning the page, use a text box. See Chapter 23 for information on text boxes.

Configuring the page margins

Every page has *margins*. They provide the air around your document — that inch or so of breathing space that sets off the text from the rest of the page. As with other things in Word, these margins can be adjusted, fooled, cajoled, or otherwise obsessed over.

Word automatically sets page margins at 1 inch from every edge of the page. Most English teachers and book editors want margins of this size because these people love to scribble in margins. (They even write that way on blank paper.) In Word, you can adjust the margins to suit any fussy professional.

To change the margins, obey these steps:

1. **Click the Page Layout tab on the Ribbon.**

2. **Click the Margins button.**

Margins

It's found in the Page Setup group and shown in the margin.

Clicking the Margins button displays a menu full of common margin options.

3. **Pluck a proper margin from the list.**

The new margins affect all pages in your document — unless you split your document into sections, in which case the changes apply to only the current section. See Chapter 14 for information on sections.

The choices available on the Margins menu list settings for the top, left, bottom, and right margins. Yes, all four settings are changed at one time. When you want to set specific margins, choose the Custom Margins item from the bottom of the menu. Use the Margins tab in the Page Setup dialog box to set specific margins. Refer to the next section for more information.

✔ The margins set by using the Margins button menu format a page. To set margins for one or more paragraphs, refer to Chapter 11.

✔ The orange stars appearing on the Margin menu's icons represent popular or recent margin choices you've made.

✔ Keep in mind that most printers cannot print on the outside half inch of a piece of paper — top, bottom, left, or right. This space is an *absolute* margin; although you can tell Word to set a margin of 0 inches right and 0 inches left, text still doesn't print there. Instead, choose a minimum of 0.5 inches for the left and right margins.

Using the Page Setup dialog box

As with many features in Word, when you want more control over page formatting, you must flee from the fuzzy beneficence of the Ribbon interface and use an old-fashioned dialog box. In this case, it's the Page Setup dialog box, as shown in Figure 13-1.

To summon the Page Setup dialog box, click the Dialog Box Launcher in the lower-right corner of the Page Setup group on the Page Layout tab. Or you can use the keyboard shortcut: Alt+P, S, P.

The Page Setup dialog box sports three tabs: Margins for setting margins, Paper for selecting the page size, and Layout for dealing with other page formatting issues.

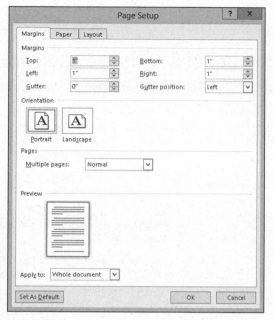

Figure 13-1:
The Margins
tab in the
Page Setup
dialog box.

Click the OK button to confirm your changes and close the Page Setup dialog box.

✔ To print on 3-hole paper, use the Margins tab in the Page Setup dialog box to set the gutter margin to about half an inch. That moves the entire margin "frame" one half inch from where the three holes are punched. You can set the Gutter Position to Left option, unless the holes are punched on the top of the page, in which case you set the Gutter Position to Top option.

✔ Changes made to a page's format — size, orientation, and margins — normally affect an entire document. By using the Apply To drop-down list in the Page Setup dialog box, however, you can determine which portion of a document will be affected by the margin change. You have three options:

- **Whole Document** changes the margins for your whole document, from bonnet to boot.

- **This Point Forward** makes the new margins take place from the insertion pointer's position onward.

- **Selected Text** applies the change only to the highlighted block of text. (This option appears in place of This Point Forward when text is elected.)

- **This Section** applies the margins to only the current section. See Chapter 14 for more information on sections.

Dangerous treading in the Multiple Pages area of the Page Setup dialog box

Nestled on the Margins tab of the Page Setup dialog box is the Pages area (refer to Figure 13-1). The Multiple Pages drop-down list tells Word how to use the paper on which your document is printed. Surprisingly, you have more than one way to print a document on a page. The following definitions help, as does the page preview image at the bottom of the Page Setup dialog box:

Normal means one page per sheet of paper. You can't get more normal than that.

Mirror Margins is used when the printer is smart enough to print on both sides of a sheet of paper. That way, every other page is flip-flopped so that their margins always line up. For example, the gutter may be on the left side of one page, but on the right for the page's back side.

2 Pages per Sheet splits the paper right down the center and forces Word to print two "pages" per sheet of paper. Note that this option works best when the pages are in landscape orientation.

Book Fold is Word's attempt to create a multiple-page booklet by printing the proper pages on both sides of a sheet of paper. The Sheets Per Booklet option that appears tells Word how long your booklet is.

Despite these options, Word is a poor bookbinding program. If you're into document publishing, consider getting a desktop publishing program, such as Adobe InDesign or Microsoft Publisher, which are far better equipped to deal with this topic.

Page Numbering

I'm still puzzled by people who manually number their pages when they use a computer and a word processor. Such a thing is silly beyond belief. That's because

Your word processor numbers your pages for you!

Memorize it. Live it. Be it.

Adding an automatic page number

Word can not only automatically number your pages, but it also lets you place the page number just about anywhere on the page and in a variety of fun and interesting formats.

Start your page numbering odyssey thus:

1. **Click the Insert tab.**

2. **In the Header & Footer area, click the Page Number command button.**

   A menu drops down, listing various page numbering options. The first three are locations: Top of Page, Bottom of Page, and Page Margins, or the sides of the page.

3. **Choose where to place the page numbers.**

   I want my page numbers on the bottom of the page, so I regularly choose the Bottom of Page option.

4. **Pluck a page numbering style from the scrolling list.**

   You can see oodles of samples, so don't cut yourself short by not scrolling through the menu. You can even choose those famous *page X of Y* formats.

Dutifully, Word numbers each page in your document, starting with 1 on the first page, up to however many pages long the thing grows. Plus, if you delete a page, Word renumbers everything for you. Insert a page? Hey! Word renumbers everything for you again, automatically. As long as you insert the page number by following the preceding set of steps, Word handles everything.

✔ The page numbers are placed into the document's header or footer. See Chapter 14 for information on headers and footers.

✔ To change the page number format, simply choose a new one from the Page Number menu.

✔ Page numbers can be removed just as easily: See the section "Removing page numbers," later in this chapter.

✔ See Chapter 23 for information on inserting a page number into your document's text, as opposed to in a header or footer.

Starting off with a different page number

You and I know that the first page of a document is page 1, but Word doesn't care. It lets you start numbering your document at whichever page number you want. If you want to start numbering your document at page 42, you can do so, if you follow these instructions:

1. **Click the Insert tab.**

2. **In the Header & Footer area, choose Page Number⇨Format Page Numbers.**

   The Page Number Format dialog box materializes, as shown in Figure 13-2.

Figure 13-2:
Gain more
control over
page
numbers.

3. **Select the Start At radio button, and type the beginning page number in the box.**

4. **Click OK to close the Page Number Format dialog box.**

Word starts numbering your document at the specified page number. So if you enter 47 in Step 3, the first page of the document is now page 47, the next page is 48, and so on.

For more page number control, such as suppressing the page number on the document's first page or having the page number jump in the middle of the document, you use sections. Different page numbering styles or sequences can be set for individual sections. See Chapter 14 for more information on sections.

Numbering with Roman numerals

When the urge hits you to regress a few centuries and use Roman numerals to tally a document's pages, Word is happy to oblige. Summon the Page Number Format dialog box (refer to Figure 13-2) by following Steps 1 and 2 in the preceding section. Simply choose the style you want from the Number Format drop-down list.

Removing page numbers

To strip out page numbers you inserted into your document, choose the Remove Page Numbers command from the Page Number menu (in the Header & Footer group on the Insert tab).

The Remove Page Numbers command rids your document of only those page numbers you inserted by using the Page Number menu. If you manually added a page number in a header or footer, you must manually delete it. See Chapter 14.

New Pages from Nowhere

As you type your document, Word adds new, blank pages for you to write on. These pages are appended to the end of the document, so even if you're typing in the midst of a chapter, the extra pages keep appearing so that no text is lost and nothing falls off the edge. That's all normal and good.

For those times when you need to stick a blank page in the middle of a document, or when you want to start your text at the top of a new page, Word provides two interesting commands. This section explains them.

Starting on a new page

To start typing on a new page in your document, you insert a manual page break, or *hard page break*. The simplest way to do this is to press the Ctrl+Enter key combination. Word then begins a new page On That Very Spot. All text before the insertion pointer is on the previous page, and all text afterward is on a new page.

You can also insert a hard page break by choosing the Page Break command from the Pages group on the Insert tab. If you don't see the Pages group, click the Pages button to choose the Page Break command.

Keep these points in mind when you're dealing with hard page breaks:

- ✔ Never, never, never start a new page by repeatedly pressing the Enter key until a new page pops up. That just leads to trouble later as you edit your document.

- ✔ Pressing Ctrl+Enter inserts a hard page-break *character* into your document. That character stays there, always creating a hard page break no matter how much you edit the text on previous pages.

- ✔ You can delete a hard page break by pressing either the Backspace or Delete key. If you do this accidentally, just press Ctrl+Z to undelete.

- ✔ You can see the hard page-break character if you use the Show/Hide command, found in the Paragraph group on the Home tab. (It's the ¶ button.) The hard page break appears as a dotted line with the text *Page Break* in the middle.

Inserting a whole, blank page

To shove a fresh, blank sheet of paper into the middle of a document, use the Blank Page command button, found in the Insert tab's Pages group. This command inserts *two* hard page breaks into a document, which creates a blank sheet of paper.

I don't recommend using this command unless you truly need a blank page in the midst of a document and you don't plan to write on that page. Putting graphics on the page is fine. Adding a table or any other single-page element to the blank page is also fine. But because the blank page is inserted by using two hard page breaks, writing on it leads to formatting woes down the line.

Page Froufrou

Page formatting happens above your text, below your text, to the sides of your text, and even *behind* your text. This section demonstrates the things you can format on a page that appear behind your words.

Coloring pages

When you can't think ahead to buy color paper for your printer, you can use Word's Page Color command button, found in the Design tab's Page Background group. Clicking this button displays a menu full of colors, some based on the document theme and some based on standard colors, or you can choose your own color by choosing the More Colors menu command. Use the Fill Effects menu command to choose *gradients,* or multiple colors.

As you move the mouse over the various colors on the Page Color menu, the document's page color is updated to reflect that new color (but only in Page Layout view). The text color may change as well, such as from black to white, to remain visible.

Your printer produces the color you choose, but you must direct the printer to print the page color by following these steps:

1. **Click the File tab.**

2. **Choose Options from the File screen.**

3. **Choose Display from the left side of the Word Options dialog box.**

4. **In the Printing Options area, put a check mark by the item labeled Print Background Colors and Images.**

5. **Click OK.**

   You can now print the background color — well, assuming that you have a color printer.

Because the color is printed, and isn't part of the paper, it doesn't cover the entire printed page. That's because your printer cannot mechanically access the outside edge of a page, so a white border (or whatever other color the paper is) appears around your colored page. At this point, ask yourself whether it's easier to use colored paper rather than all that expensive printer ink or toner.

- ✔ To remove page coloring, choose the No Color command from the Page Color menu.

- ✔ See Chapter 10 for information on coloring text. Chapter 18 discusses coloring the text background, which is a paragraph attribute and not a page format.

Adding a watermark

When finer papers are held up to the light, they show a *watermark* — an image embedded into the paper. The image is impressive but faint. Word lets you fake a watermark by inserting faint text or graphics behind every page in your document. Here's how:

1. **Click the Design tab.**

2. **In the Page Background group, click the Watermark button.**

   A menu plops down with a host of predefined watermarks that you can safely duck behind the text on your document's pages.

3. **Choose a watermark from the long, long list.**

   The watermark is applied to every page in your document.

You can customize the watermark by choosing the Custom Watermark command from the Watermark menu. Use the Printed Watermark dialog box to create your own watermark text, or you can import a picture, such as your company logo.

To rid your document's pages of the watermark, choose the Remove Watermark command from the Watermark command button menu.

If the watermark doesn't show up in the printed document, you may need to enable the Print Background Colors and Images setting. Refer to the steps in the preceding section.

Chapter 14

Document Formatting

I don't do much document formatting on my shopping lists or my kids' chore charts; it's not necessary. For the important stuff — the *real* documents — it's useful to employ some of Word's fancy document-formatting tricks. I'm talking about big-picture stuff that includes the handy-yet-weird concept of sections, headers and footers, cover sheets — all that jazz. The formatting information in this chapter might not be stuff you use all the time, but it's there for when you need to make documents look *extra* spiffy.

Slice Your Document into Sections

Word's page formatting commands usually affect every page in a document: The settings for margins, page orientation, paper size, and other types of formatting apply themselves not to a single page but rather to every dang doodle page, from 1 to *N*, where *N* is the mathematical concept best explained as "I don't know how huge this number could be."

Sometimes, however, you need a document that isn't formatted the same way, page after page. For example, you may want to change page number formats, or have the first page of a document be an unnumbered cover page, or you may need to display a table on page 6 in landscape orientation. All these tricks are possible with sections.

Understanding sections

A *section* is a part of a document that contains its own page formatting. It can be a single page or a range of pages, or a section can comprise the entire document.

All Word documents have one section. That's how page formatting works, and it's why all the page-formatting commands affect all pages in a document in the same way. When you need to change the page formatting within a document, you carve out a new section.

Figure 14-1 lists three examples of documents sliced up into sections.

Example 1

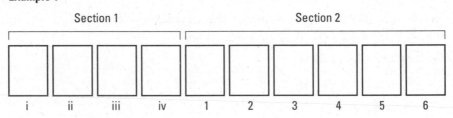

Example 2

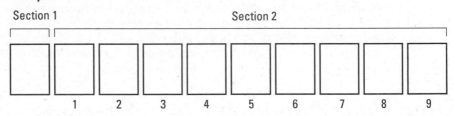

Example 3

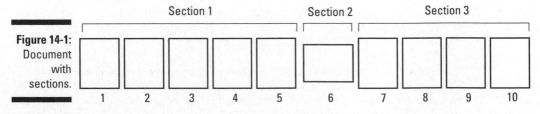

Figure 14-1:
Document
with
sections.

In Example 1, a single document contains two sections. The first section uses Roman numeral page numbers. The second section uses human numerals.

In Example 2, the document also contains two sections. The first section is a cover page that has no page numbering. The second section — all the remaining pages — uses page numbering. Also, see how the second page in the document is numbered as page 1? Again, that's because the page numbering applies only to section 2.

In Example 3, there are three sections in the document. The first and third sections sport the same formatting; the second section was created so that page 6 could be presented in landscape orientation.

When your document demands a change in page formatting, similar to the one shown in Figure 14-1, you use Word's section commands to make it happen.

> ✔ A *section* is basically a chunk of your document where page formatting can be different from, or unique to, the rest of your document.
>
> ✔ Text and paragraph formatting, as well as any styles you may create, don't give a hoot about sections. Sections affect only page formatting. See Chapter 13 for more information on page formatting.

Creating a section

Most often, a new section begins on a new page. It's called a *section break*, and it's similar in appearance to a page break. The difference is that the new section can sport its own formatting.

To create a new section in your document, heed these steps:

1. **Position the toothpick cursor where you want the new section to start.**

   Click the mouse where you need to begin a new section, similar to creating a new page break.

2. **Click the Page Layout tab on the Ribbon.**

3. **Click the Breaks button.**

   The Breaks button is found in the Page Setup group. Upon clicking that button, you see a menu with seven items. The last four items are various section breaks.

4. **Choose Next Page from the Breaks button menu.**

   A page break is inserted into your document; a new section has started.

After the section is created, you can then modify the page layout and format of each section in your document.

The new section looks like any old page break on the screen, but it's not. To confirm which section is which in your document, you can direct Word to display the Section indicator on the status bar: Right-click the Status bar and choose the Section item from the pop-up menu. The word *Section* appears on the far-left end of the status bar, followed by the current section number.

Using sections

To apply a specific page format to one section only, use the dialog box associated with the format, such as the Page Setup dialog box. In the dialog box, look for the Apply To drop-down list. To apply the format to the current section, choose This Section. That way, the format controls only the pages in the current section.

For example, to change the page numbering as shown in Examples 1 and 2 from Figure 14-1, follow these general steps:

1. **Set the page number for the first section.**

   Page numbering commands are found in Chapter 13. If the first section isn't to have page numbering, don't set a thing.

2. **Create a new section at the page where you want the numbering style to change.**

   You need to make a Next Page type of section break, as covered earlier in this chapter.

3. **In the new section, use the Page Number Format dialog box to set the new page numbering style: Choose the Start At option to start new numbering in the current section.**

4. **Click OK.**

The second section starts page numbering at the number and in the style you specified in Step 3.

To change page orientation in the middle of a document, shown in Example 3 in Figure 14-1, obey these general steps:

1. **Move the toothpick cursor to the page where you desire the new orientation.**

2. **Create a Next Page section break, as covered earlier in this chapter.**

3. **Choose the new orientation from the Orientation button on the Page Layout tab, as covered in Chapter 13.**

   The document at this point has two sections: The initial section uses one orientation, and then the last page has a different orientation. To set the rest of the document back to the original orientation, continue with Step 4:

4. **Create another Next Page section break.**

   The document now has three sections.

5. **On the new (last) page of the document, restore the original orientation.**

In the end, you have a document with three sections and two orientations, as shown in Example 3 in Figure 14-1.

Deleting a section break

A section break is just like a character in your document. To delete the break, you can use the Backspace or Delete keys. For example: Position the insertion pointer just before the section break and then press the Delete key.

When you have trouble finding the section breaks, switch to Draft view: Click the Views tab and choose Draft from the Views group. You can also summon the Section indicator on the status bar, as covered earlier in this chapter. In that case, position the toothpick cursor at the top of the page and then press the Backspace key.

Deleting a section removes any formatting, including headers and footers, that was unique to the section. If you accidentally delete a section break, you lose any special formatting that you applied to the section. In this case, press the Undo shortcut, Ctrl+Z, before you do anything else.

That First Page

One of the most common things to format in any document, and the bane of most folks, is that darn first page. It's a cover page. It's an introduction. It's different. The following sections describe how to deal with that pesky first page.

Adding a cover page

The sneakiest and quickest way to slap down a cover page in Word is to use Word's Cover Page command. Here's how it works:

1. **Click the Insert tab.**

2. **In the Pages group, click the Cover Page button.**

   If you don't see the Pages group or Cover Page button, click the Pages button and then click the Cover Page icon.

The Cover Page button displays a fat, fun menu full of various cover-page layouts.

3. **Choose a cover-page layout that titillates you.**

The cover page is immediately inserted as the first page in your document. The cover page is followed by a page break (not a section break), and it contains bracketed text, such as [Company Name].

4. **Click the bracketed text on the cover page.**

5. **Type the required replacement text.**

For example, click [Document title]. Then type the document's real title. The text you type replaces the bracketed text.

6. **Repeat Steps 4 and 5 until the cover page looks the way you like it.**

You can change a cover page at any time by choosing a new one from the Cover Page menu. The new cover page retains any replacement text you typed.

✔ To remove a cover page, follow Steps 1 and 2, but choose the item Remove Current Cover Page from the Cover Page menu. The cover page that Word inserted is removed.

✔ The Cover Page menu doesn't create a new section in your document. Even so, it's treated differently from certain page formatting commands applied to the rest of the document. That means if you add page numbers or a header or footer to your document, that formatting applies to only the second and later pages, not to the cover page.

✔ Leaving the bracketed text on the title page is tacky. Your boss doesn't want to see a report that has [Company Name] on it rather than your organization's name.

Making a cover page manually

Word's Cover Page command is quick, but I'm not really satisfied with any of its designs. I prefer instead to craft my own cover page, spiffing it up with formatting commands, graphics, artwork, and other goodies, as described throughout this book.

The best way to roll your own cover page is to follow Example 2 from Figure 14-1. Here are the general steps to take:

1. **Before writing the cover page, position the toothpick cursor at the tippy-top of the document.**

This step applies whether you've written the document or not. If you've already written the cover page, position the toothpick cursor at the end of the page. And if you've put in a hard page break after the cover page, delete it.

2. **Create a new, Next Page section break in your document.**

   The document now has two sections, and the first page is its own section.

3. **Create the cover page.**

   Add a title, additional text, graphics, and various document froufrou.

4. **On the second page, at the start of the new section, set the page numbering for the rest of the document.**

   Refer to the first set of steps in the earlier section, "Using sections," for the specifics of setting pages numbering for a section.

Because the cover page is its own section, the page numbering you apply to the second section doesn't affect the cover page. If you want the cover page numbered, dispense with sections and use a hard page break instead. Number the entire document, as described in Chapter 13.

Headers and Footers

Adding a header or footer to a document brings a smidgen of professionalism to your written creations and helps keep things organized. This section explains how to work with headers and footers without tying yourself into a knot.

Understanding headers and footers

There's a difference between a header and a heading, and between a footer and a footnote. Knowing that difference greatly helps you understand the whole header-footer concept.

A *header* is text that appears at the top of every page in a document.

A *footer* is text that appears at the bottom of every page in a document.

Both headers and footers exist as special, exclusive areas. Their content appears at the top and bottom of every page, respectively. Typical headers and footers contain page numbers, your name, the document name, the date, and other information that's handy to have on every page.

  ✔ A *heading* is a text style used to break up a long document, to introduce new concepts and help organize the text. See Chapter 15 for more information on headings.

  ✔ A *footnote* is a tiny bit of text that appears at the bottom of a page, usually a reference for some bit of text on that page. See Chapter 21.

✔ Word documents always have headers and footers, it's just that they're empty unless you put something there.

✔ Headers can also be called *eyebrows*. Weird, huh?

Using a preset header or footer

Word comes with a slate of uninspiring headers and footers. The good news is that they're easy to add to a document. Heed these steps:

1. **Click the Insert tab.**

2. **From the Header & Footer group, choose the Header button.**

   A list of preformatted headers is displayed.

3. **Choose the format you want from the list.**

   The header is added to your document, saved as part of the page format.

4. **Change any [Type here] text in the header.**

   Click the bracketed text to personalize your header. You can also add items to the header from the Header & Footer Tools Design tab that suddenly appears. See the next section for details.

5. **When you're done working on the header, click the Close Header and Footer button.**

Close Header and Footer

   The button is found on the far-right end of the Header & Footer Tools Design tab.

To add a footer, repeat these steps, but choose the Footer button in Step 2 and think of the word *footer* whenever you see the word *header* in the preceding steps.

✔ You can also exit from editing a header or footer by double-clicking the mouse in the main part of your document.

✔ After you exit from the header or footer, you can see its text at the top and bottom of your document. To edit the header or footer, double-click that ghostly text.

Editing a header or footer

Face it: Word's preset designs for the header are dull. Splashy, but dull. And chances are good that they don't contain all the information you want or need. That's no problem. You can edit the header by using what Word created as a starting point, or you can quickly whip up your own header.

Here's the secret to creating a new header or footer, or to editing an existing header or footer: Double-click in the space at the top or bottom of the page.

Here's a tip to make your creating-and-editing experience more enjoyable: Summon the ruler. Click the View tab, and ensure that a check mark appears by the Ruler item in the Show group.

After you're in header or footer editing mode, the Header & Footer Tools Design tab appears. On that tab, you find gathered a hoard of commands for working with headers. And footers, too. Anytime you read *headers* in this section, assume that I mean footers as well.

Type text

Any text you type in a header becomes part of the header. It doesn't have to be fancy text — just informative.

Word helps by giving you a center tab stop and a right tab stop in the header, as shown on the ruler in Figure 14-2. For example, you can type your name, press the Tab key twice, and then type a document title. Or type your name, the document title, and then the date, as shown in the figure's second example.

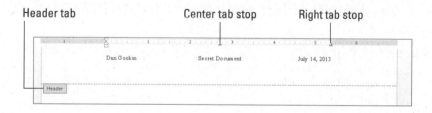

Figure 14-2: Text in a header.

Add a page number

Page numbers are added by inserting a *field* into the header or footer. Yeah, I wish this trick were easier, but that's how Word does things. Rather than repeat information here, you should review Chapter 23 on inserting fields into your document. The information there applies to headers and footers, as well as to the document's main text.

You don't have to go to page 1 to insert a page number in a header. Word is smart enough to place the proper number on the proper page, no matter where you're editing the header in your document.

Add the date and time

Unlike adding a page number, inserting a date or time field in the header is accomplished by using a command button found on the Header & Footer Tools Design tab: Click the Date & Time button found in the Insert group. The Date and Time dialog box appears. Choose a sample date or time format from the Date and Time dialog box, and then click the OK button to insert that item into the header.

Add graphics

The Insert area in the Header & Footer Tools Design tab sports a Picture button, which you can use to browse for graphical images that you can insert into the header. Of course, you can insert any graphical image by using Word's various graphics and drawing commands. Refer to Chapter 22 for tips and suggestions.

Working with multiple headers and footers

The header or footer you set is the same for every page in your document. Or is it? For example, this book uses different headers for its odd and even pages. Or maybe you have a document where you don't want the header on the first page. All of that is possible, as long as you peruse the following subsections.

Odd and even headers and footers

To spice up your document with a different header and footer on the odd (left) and even (right) pages, obey these steps:

1. **Create a header or footer, as described elsewhere in this chapter.**

   You don't really have to create a new header — just enter header or footer editing mode. As long as you see the Header & Footer Tools Design tab, you're in business.

2. **Click the Design tab.**

3. **Place a check mark by the Different Odd & Even Pages box.**

   This step tells Word that you want two sets of headers — one for odd pages and one for even pages. Notice how the tag identifying the header changes:

   Odd Page Header

The tag tells you which header you're editing; in this case, it's the Odd Page header.

4. **Create the header for the odd pages.**

5. **Click the Next button, found in the Navigation group on the Design tab.**

   Word displays the even page header, allowing you to create or edit its contents. The Header tag changes to reflect which header you're editing:

   ```
   Even Page Header
   ```

   By the way, you click the Next button to move from the odd header to the even header. You must click the Previous button to return to the odd header from the even header.

6. **Click the Go To Footer button to edit the footer's odd and even pages.**

   Edit the footer's contents and click the Next button to ensure that you work on both the odd and even footers (as you do in Steps 4 and 5 for the header).

7. **Click the Close Header and Footer button when you're done.**

Removing the Odd/Even Header option is as simple as deselecting the Different Odd & Even Pages option in the Options group (the opposite of Step 3). When you do that, the even-page header and footer are deleted, leaving only the odd-page header and footer.

No header or footer on the first page

Most people don't want the header or footer on the first page, which is usually the title page or a cover page. Suppressing the header for that page is easy: While editing a header, place a check mark by the Different First Page setting, found in the Options group on the Design tab. That's it.

When you set a different first-page header or footer, the tag on the first page changes to read First Page Header or First Page Footer. It's your visual clue that the first page of the document sports a different header from the one in the rest of the document.

You can still edit the first-page header or footer, if you like. It's merely different, not necessarily empty.

Headers/footers and sections

Just as Superman is limited in his powers by the crippling force of kryptonite, the mighty header is restricted in its scope and power by the document section. Normally, this limitation is minimal: Despite having different sections, the headers and footers you set for a document are the same across all sections. But when sections are implemented, you can change the headers and footers for each section, if you so desire.

Word flags each section's header and footer in the tag, as shown in Figure 14-3. Word also lets you know whether the header or footer is linked to the preceding section's header and footer, meaning that they're identical.

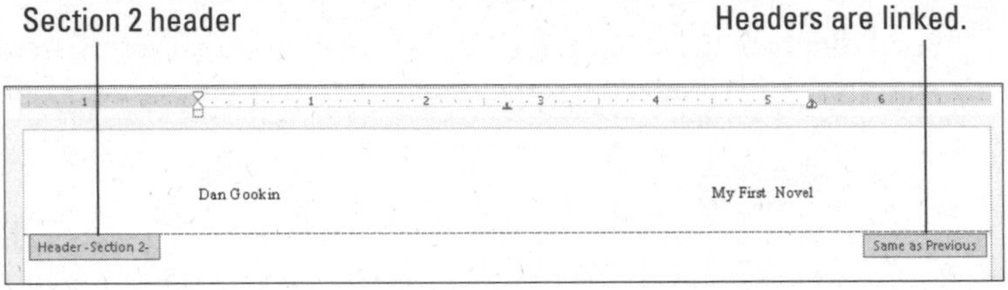

Section 2 header   Headers are linked.

Figure 14-3:
A header
in Section
2, linked to
Section 1.

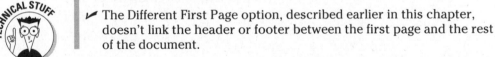

Dan Gookin   My First Novel

Header - Section 2-   Same as Previous

To unlink the header or footer, click the Link to Previous button, found in the Navigation group on the Design tab. If that button is highlighted, the header or footer isn't linked with the previous section.

- To hop between each section's header or footer, use the Next and Previous buttons on the Design tab.

- Changing a header in one section doesn't affect any other section in the document — unless they're linked. Check for the Same As Previous tab, as illustrated in Figure 14-3.

- The Different First Page option, described earlier in this chapter, doesn't link the header or footer between the first page and the rest of the document.

Removing a header or footer

The simplest way to remove a document header is to use the Header⇨Remove Header command, found in the Header & Footer group on the Insert tab. Likewise, to remove a footer, choose the Footer⇨Remove Footer command. Poof! The headers and footers are gone.

Another way to remove a header is to delete all text in a header: Press Ctrl+A to select all the text when editing the header, and then press the Delete key.

Chapter 15

Style Formatting

Formatting can certainly be a job. There's so much to format! In character and paragraph formatting alone, you'll find text sizes, colors, styles, margins, tabs, indents — lots of stuff and lots of time to spend doing it. So much time that lots of people don't bother much with formatting because they fear having to do it over and over and over. That fear is unfounded, however, because Word features something called styles, which make the process of formatting your text super cinchy.

The Big Style Overview

Styles are the virtual stew of formatting commands, all kept in one package. Apply a style, and you apply all the formatting of that style to your text. Even better, when you update or change a style, all text formatting with that style changes as well. In the end, you save time — and your documents look fabulous.

✔ A style is nothing more than a clutch of text and paragraph formats. You give the style a name and then you use it to format your text. Or you can format your text first and then create a style based on that text.

✔ Style names give you a clue to how to use the style, such as Heading 1 for the document's top-level heading, or Caption, used for figure and table captions.

✔ You've already been using styles and probably haven't realized it. All text in Word is formatted using the Normal style, which is Word's primary (or *default*) style. In Word 2013, the Normal style formats text in the Calibri font, 11 points tall, with left-aligned paragraphs, line spacing at 1.08, no indenting, zero margins, and 8 points of space after every paragraph.

✔ Styles are part of the document template. See Chapter 16 for more information.

Understanding style types

Word sports five different types of styles, each customized to format a different document element. You'll most likely only use (or even see) the first three:

✔ **Paragraph:** The paragraph style contains both paragraph- and text-formatting attributes: indents, tabs, font, text size, — you name it. It's the most common type of style.

✔ **Character:** The character style formats only characters, not paragraphs. All character formatting mentioned in Chapter 10 can be stuffed into a character style.

✔ **Linked:** The linked style is a combination style that can be applied to both paragraphs and individual characters. The difference depends on which text is selected when you apply the style.

✔ **Table:** The table style is applied to tables, to add lines and shading to the table cells' contents. Refer to Chapter 19 for more information on tables in Word.

✔ **List:** The list style is customized for presenting lists of information. The styles can include bullets, numbers, indentation, and other formats typical for the parts of a document that present lists of information. See Chapter 21 for info on lists.

These types come into play when you create your own styles, as well as when you're perusing styles to apply to your text. For example, if you want to create a new look for tables in a document, you make a Table style. Or when you want a style to affect only text and not paragraphs, you create a Character style.

Locating styles

In Word, styles dwell on the Home tab, in the aptly named Styles group, as shown in Figure 15-1. What you see is the Style Gallery, which can be expanded into a full menu of style choices.

The dialog box launcher, in the lower-right corner of the Styles group, is used to quickly display a task pane full of styles, also shown in Figure 15-1. To dismiss the Styles task pane, click the X (Close) button in its upper-right corner.

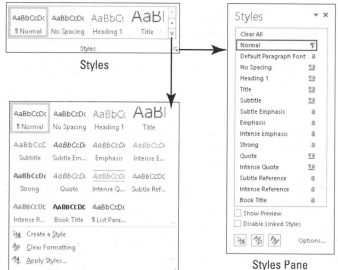

Styles Group

Styles

Styles Pane

Style Gallery

The Styles task pane lists only "recommended" styles. To see the whole slew of styles available in Word, follow these steps:

1. **Summon the Styles task pane.**

2. **Click the Options link in the lower-right corner of the Styles task pane.**

3. **In the Styles Pane Options dialog box, choose All Styles from the Select Styles to Show drop-down list.**

   Other options are Recommended, where Word decides which styles you need; In Use, where only those styles you're using show up; and In Current Document, which lists all styles available for the current document's template.

4. **Click OK.**

The Styles task pane is updated to list every dang-doodle style available in Word. You'll see quite a few of them.

✔ To preview the styles in the Styles task pane, put a check in the box by the Show Preview option, found at the bottom of the task pane. You can also see more information about a style by simply hovering the mouse pointer over the style's name in the Style task pane.

✔ The Styles task pane lists more styles than the Style Gallery, including styles you've created.

- ✔ Word's predefined styles are specified in the Style Gallery, though you can customize the list to replace Word's styles with your own. See the section "Customizing the Style Gallery," later in this chapter.

- ✔ A more abbreviated version of the Styles task pane is available: Press Ctrl+Shift+S to call forth the Apply Styles task pane.

- ✔ The keyboard shortcut for the Styles task pane is Ctrl+Shift+Alt+S. It helps to be quite dexterous with your left hand to conjure up this shortcut.

Applying a style

Working with a style is just like working with any other type of formatting. The major difference is that, instead of applying a single format, the style slaps down multiple formats on your text.

Most often, a style is applied by selecting text and then choosing a style from either the Style Gallery or the Styles task pane. The selected text is updated, reflecting the style's collective formatting.

You can also choose a new style and then just start typing; the new style affects the new text you type.

- ✔ To preview how a style affects text, use the Style Gallery; as you hover the mouse cursor over each item in the Gallery, text in your document is updated to reflect the style's appearance. (This trick doesn't work with older Word documents.)

- ✔ Styles can also be applied by using a keyboard shortcut, if one has been assigned. The shortcut for the Normal style is Ctrl+Shift+N. See the later section, "Assigning a shortcut key to your style."

- ✔ Also see the later section, "Removing style formatting."

Understanding heading styles

A special style in Word is the heading style. Word has several of them, starting with Heading 1, and then Heading 2, and progressing through however many Heading styles your document needs.

Heading styles are designed for organization: Heading 1 is for your document's main parts, Heading 2 is for breaking up those parts, and down the line through Heading 3, Heading 4, and so on. As an example, this section's heading, "Understanding heading styles," is Heading 2; the main section, "The Big Style Overview" is Heading 1.

Using heading styles is about more than simply document formatting. These styles not only help keep your document visually organized, but they also take advantage of other Word features.

For example, the heading styles appear whenever you use the vertical scroll bar to skim a document. You can collapse and expand headings by using the triangle button that appears just to the left of a heading (shown in the margin). Headings appear in the Navigation pane when you search for text. They can be used when creating a table of contents. And they're used in Word's Outline mode. These abundant examples are noted throughout this book.

- Try to make headings one line long.

- You can break up long headings between two lines: Press Shift+Enter to create a soft return in the middle of a long heading.

- When you're done typing a heading formatted with Heading 1 or Heading 2 or another heading level, press the Enter key. Automatically, the following paragraph is formatted using the Normal style. Normal is the "follow-me" style used for all Word heading styles. Refer to the sidebar "The follow-me style," later in this chapter, to find out how it works.

- Word's predefined Title style isn't a heading style.

- You can create your own heading styles. The secret is to set an outline level for the heading style in the Paragraph formatting dialog box. See the section "Make Your Own Styles," later in this chapter, for the details.

Checking the current style

You can discover which style is applied to your text by seeing which style is highlighted in the Style Gallery or in the Styles task pane. To be more specific, you can use the Style Inspector, as shown in Figure 15-2.

Attributes

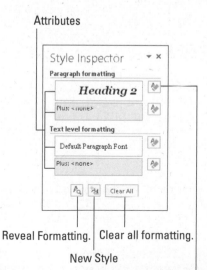

Figure 15-2:
Style
Inspector.

Reveal Formatting. Clear all formatting.

New Style

Clear specific attribute.

Activate the inspector by clicking the Style Inspector button, such as the one found at the bottom of the Styles task pane (refer to Figure 15-1).

To *really* see the details of how your text is formatted, you need to witness the gruesome Reveal Formatting task pane: Click the Reveal Formatting button in the Style Inspector (refer to Figure 15-2) or use the Shift+F1 keyboard shortcut.

The Reveal Formatting task pane shows the exact formatting applied to your document's text. Click any jot or tittle to expose the specifics. Choose a link in the task pane to summon the proper dialog box to alter or remove a formatting tidbit.

Removing style formatting

Word doesn't remove styles. Instead, the Normal style is simply reapplied to the text. Because many Word users don't understand or master the concept of styles, Word comes with the Clear Formatting command. Though this command would seem to remove styles, it doesn't; instead, it merely replaces a given style with whatever formatting is specified in the Normal style.

The Clear Formatting command is found loitering in the Font group on the Home tab. Use it to peel away stubborn style stains: Select the text you want to cleanse and click the Clear Formatting button. Whatever text you have selected is stripped of formatting by that command. Or any new text you type is created using the Normal style.

See Chapter 10 for additional details on the Clear Formatting command.

Make Your Own Styles

Considering all the restaurants out there in the world, why would you be so foolhardy as to cook your own food? The reason, I suppose, aside from home-cooked food being better and cheaper than restaurant food, is that you prefer to do things yourself. It's okay to be fussy, exacting. The same sentiment holds true for using styles in Word: Some people desire to create their own styles.

Word offers two ways to craft your own, unique styles: Format your text a certain way, and then base a new style on that text. Or build a style from scratch by using Word's version of a formatting style salad bar. This section covers the details.

Formatting and then making a style

The easiest way to make up a new style is to use all your formatting skills and power to format a single paragraph just the way you like. Then create the style based on that formatted paragraph. Here's how:

1. **Type and format a paragraph of text.**

   Choose the paragraph formatting and also any text formatting, such as size and font.

2. **Mark your paragraph as a block.**

   See Chapter 6 to find out how to mark a block of text.

3. **On the Home tab, in the Styles area, click the menu button to display the full Quick Styles Gallery.**

   Refer to Figure 15-1 to find the button, as well as to see the full Quick Styles Gallery.

4. **Choose the command Create a Style.**

   The Create New Style from Formatting dialog box appears.

5. **In the Name box, type a short and descriptive name for your style.**

   Short, descriptive names work best — for example, `proposal body` for the main text of a proposal, `character dialog` for the dialog part of a script, or `signature line` for the last part of a letter.

6. **Click the OK button to create the style.**

   The style is added to Word's repertoire of styles for your document.

The style is created and it has also been applied to the paragraph you typed (in Step 1). You can now use the style, applying it to other paragraphs in the document.

For more detail over the creation process, in Step 3 press the obnoxious keyboard shortcut Ctrl+Shift+Alt+S to summon a more detailed version of the Create New Style from Formatting dialog box. You can specify additional options in that dialog box, and even adjust formatting specifics.

 ✔ The styles you create are available only to the document in which they're created. They're saved with the document, along with your text.

 ✔ If you create scads of styles that you love and you want to use them for several documents, create a *template*. Chapter 16 covers this procedure, in the section about making a new template from scratch.

 ✔ You may have to tweak some settings in your style. See the section "Modifying a style," later in this chapter.

Creating a style from scratch

I've created a style from scratch fewer times than I've formatted first and then made a style. That's because it's easier to see what you're doing than to simply issue formatting commands and hope for the best. But if you're up to it, heed these steps to conjure a style from nothingness:

1. In the Styles task pane, click the New Style button.

If you don't see the Styles task pane, press Ctrl+Shift+Alt+S.

After clicking the New Style button, you see the Create New Style from Formatting dialog box, as shown in Figure 15-3.

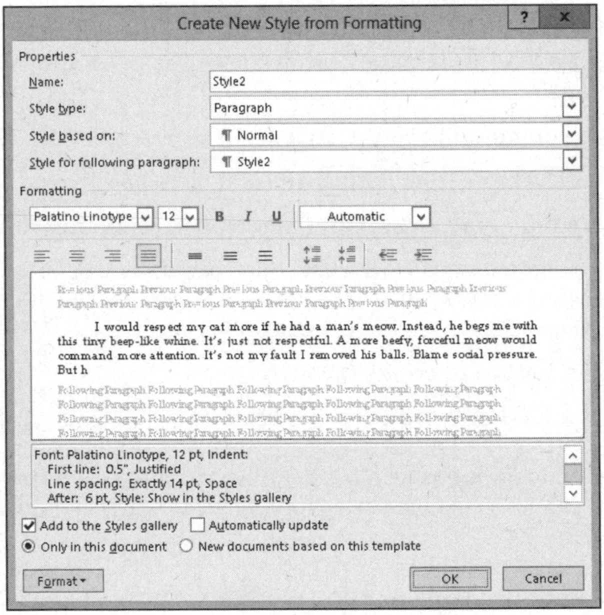

Figure 15-3: The Create New Style from Formatting dialog box.

2. Type a name for the new style.

3. Ensure that Paragraph is chosen for the style type.

If the format is a character style, choose Character. An example of a character style is blue, bold, Courier, 12-point — the one that I use in my documents for filenames.

4. Choose an existing style as a base from the Style Based On drop-down list.

This step can save time. If the style you're creating features a lot of the same formatting as an existing style, choose that style from the list. The settings from that style are not only copied over, but when you change one format for the original style, those formats also change for the new style.

5. **Use the controls in the dialog box to set the style's format.**

   Some controls are presented in the middle of the dialog box (refer to Figure 15-3). For others, use the Format button to choose something to format, and then to set options, use the dialog box that appears.

6. **Click the OK button when you're done.**

The new style is created.

Modifying a style

Styles change. Who knows? Maybe blow-dried hair and wide lapels will creep back into vogue someday.

Just as fashion styles change, you may need to change styles in your document. Nothing is wrong with that. In fact, by changing a style, you demonstrate the power of Word: Changing a style once causes all text formatted with that style to be updated. It beats the pants off making that change manually.

To modify a style, heed these steps:

1. **Summon the Styles task pane.**

   Keyboard shortcut: Press Ctrl+Shift+Alt+S.

2. **Point the mouse at the style you want to change.**

   A menu button appears on the right end of the style's entry.

3. **Click the menu button to display the style's menu.**

4. **Choose Modify.**

   The Modify Style dialog box appears, although it's the same Create New Style from Formatting dialog box (refer to Figure 15-3).

5. **Change the formatting for your style.**

   Use the Format button to alter specific styles: font, paragraph, tabs, and so on. You can even add new formatting options or assign a shortcut key (covered in the next section).

6. **Click OK when you're done.**

Close the task pane if you're done with it.

The follow-me style

When I write a new chapter in a book, I start with my own Chapter Title style. The next style I use is my Intro Paragraph style. Intro Paragraph is followed by TextBody, which is followed by TextBody, TextBody, TextBody, and so on. There's no point in my having to apply these styles because I can tell Word to change styles automatically.

In the Create New Style from Formatting dialog box (refer to Figure 15-3), locate the Style for Following Paragraph drop-down list. The style shown on this list tells Word which style to switch to when you press the Enter key to end a paragraph. Normally, it's the same style, which makes sense for most of your work. But in situations where you *know* that the style will switch, you can demand that Word do the switching for you.

For example, you can edit the Picture style so that the Picture Caption style is selected from the Style for Following Paragraph drop-down list. That way, pressing the Enter key after using the Picture style switches the style automatically to Picture Caption. Saves time.

Assigning a shortcut key to your style

Style shortcut keys make formatting even better because pressing Alt+Shift+T to apply the TextBody style is often faster than messing with the Style Gallery or the various task panes.

To give your style a shortcut key, follow these steps:

1. **Work through Steps 1 through 4 from the previous section.**

   Your goal is to display the Modify Style dialog box for your soon-to-be shortcut-key-blessed style.

2. **Click the Format button.**

   It dwells in the lower-left corner of the dialog box.

3. **Choose Shortcut Key from the menu.**

   The cryptic Customize Keyboard dialog box appears.

4. **Press your shortcut key combination.**

   Notice that the key combination you press appears as text in the Press New Shortcut Key box. (See the center-right side of the dialog box.) If you make a mistake, press the Backspace key to erase it and then choose another key combination.

Most of the good shortcut key combinations have already been put to work in Word. For example, Word uses Ctrl+B as the Bold character-formatting shortcut key. My advice is to use Ctrl+Alt and then a letter key for your style's shortcut. Most of the Ctrl+Alt key combinations are unassigned in Word.

5. **Confirm that the key combination you chose isn't already in use.**

   Refer to the text found below the Current Keys box. The text there explains which Word command uses the key combination you've pressed. When you see [unassigned], it means that your key combination is good to go.

6. **Click the Assign button.**

7. **Click the Close button.**

   The Customize Keyboard dialog box skulks away.

8. **Click the OK button.**

   You can also close the Style task pane, if you're done with it.

Congratulations! You now have a usable shortcut key for your style. Try it out: Position the insertion pointer in a block of text and press the key. Ta-da! The style is applied instantly.

Also see the earlier sidebar, "The follow-me style," for tips on automatically choosing one style after another.

Customizing the Style Gallery

The Style Gallery is handy, but only when you use those styles already stuck there. Word is understanding, however, so you're free to add any styles you like to the Style Gallery, or to remove them from it.

To add a style to the Style Gallery, follow these steps:

1. **Summon the Styles task pane.**

   Press the ungainly Ctrl+Shift+Alt+S key combination.

2. **Right-click the style you want to add.**

3. **Choose the command Add to Style Gallery.**

You can continue to add styles to the Style Gallery or close the Styles task pane.

To remove a style from the Style Gallery, right-click the style and choose the command Remove from Style Gallery from the shortcut menu that appears.

If the style you want to add doesn't show up, ensure that all styles are being shown in the Styles task pane's list. See the section "Locating styles," earlier in this chapter, and ensure that All Styles is displayed in the Styles task pane.

Deleting a style

You can delete any style you create. It's easy: Display the Styles task pane (press Ctrl+Shift+Alt+S), right-click the style's name in the list, and choose Delete from its menu. You're asked whether you're sure you want to delete the style. Click Yes.

You cannot delete the Normal or Heading or any other standard Word style.

Chapter 16

Template and Themes Formatting

*Y*ou have a choice. You can simply write and forget about formatting altogether. That's admirable, but why even have a word processor in that case? Or you can also spend even more amounts of time writing and formatting, getting your text to look just so. That's actually a waste of time, given that the computer is supposed to save you time. Or your third choice is to concentrate on your writing and take advantage of Word's templates and themes, which help automate the document-formatting chore.

Yep: I'd go for option three: Use Word's templates and themes to easily and rapidly format your prose. This chapter explains how.

Instant Documents with Templates

A template is a timesaver. It's a way to create documents that use the same styles and formatting without your having to re-create all that work and effort. Basically, the template saves time.

To use a template, you choose one when you start up a new document. You select a specific template instead of using the blank, new document option.

When the template opens, it contains all the styles and formatting you need. It may even contain text, headers, footers, or any other common information that may not change for similar documents.

Using templates isn't required in Word, just as you don't have to do any extra formatting or fancy stuff. But by using templates, you will save time. For example, I use one template for writing letters, another one for proposals, one for plays, and so on. This book has its own *For Dummies* template that contains all the text styles the publisher's production department demands I use to write the text.

- ✔ You can create documents by using your own templates or templates supplied with Word or available online.

- ✔ Every document in Word is based on a template. When you don't specify a template, such as when you start up a new, blank document, Word uses the Normal document template, `NORMAL.DOTM`.

- ✔ Word uses three filename extensions for its document templates: DOT was the template filename extension for older versions of Word. For Word 2013, DOTX and DOTM are used. DOTX refers to a template that doesn't employ macros; the DOTM indicates a template that uses macros. (This book doesn't cover macros; I wish it did, but there just isn't room.)

Starting a new document by using a template

Word comes with a host of templates already created, as well as any templates you whip up yourself. To see them, you must venture to the File screen's New menu, as shown in Figure 16-1. Follow these steps:

1. **Click the File tab.**

   The File screen appears.

2. **Choose New from the left side of the File screen.**

   The Featured part of the New screen appears. It lists Word's own templates, as well as some online templates. You can choose one of those templates; if you find one that suits you, skip to Step 4.

3. **To peruse your own templates, click the Personal heading, as illustrated in Figure 16-1.**

   The screen shows only those templates that you crafted yourself.

4. **Click on a template to start a new document using that template's formatting and any predefined text or graphics.**

   A new document window appears, ready for editing.

Word's templates are found here.

Your templates are found here.

Your templates

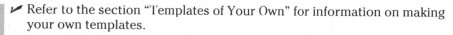

Figure 16-1:
Choosing a
template.

The new document contains the styles and formats and perhaps even some
text that's ready for you to use or edit. At this point, you work with the document just like you work with any other document in Word, though a lot of the
formatting and typing has been done for you.

- Refer to the section "Templates of Your Own" for information on making
  your own templates.

- Even though the template has saved you some time, you still need to
  save your work! Use the Save command and give your document a
  proper name as soon as possible!

- Editing the document doesn't change the template. To change or modify
  a template, see the section "Modifying a template," later in this chapter.

Attaching a template to a document

All hope isn't lost when you forget to choose a template, or when you decide
too late that your document needs a template, or even that you want to
change a template. In this case, you need to attach a new template to your
document. It sounds scary, but it's really quite easy. Follow these steps:

1. **Open the document that needs a new template attached.**

2. **Click the File tab.**

3. **On the File screen, choose the Options command.**

   The Word Options dialog box appears.

4. **Choose Add-Ins from the left side of the Word Options dialog box.**

5. **Choose Templates from the Manage drop-down list.**

   You find the Manage drop-down list near the bottom center of the dialog box.

6. **Click the Go button.**

   The Templates and Add-ins dialog box appears. You should see which template is attached to the document, such as `Normal`. Whichever template name appears there is whichever template is attached to the document.

7. **Click the Attach button.**

   Word displays the Attach Template dialog box, which looks and works like the Open dialog box.

8. **Select the template you want to attach.**

   The templates listed are stored on your computer; you don't see the full range of templates that you find on the New screen.

9. **Click the Open button.**

   The template is attached to your document.

10. **Ensure that the option Automatically Update Document Styles is selected.**

    Updating styles means that your document's current styles are changed to reflect those of the new template, which is probably what you want.

11. **Click OK.**

    The styles (plus custom toolbars and macros) stored in that template are now available to your document, and the document is now attached to the template.

Note that attaching a template doesn't merge any text or graphics stored in that template. Only the styles (plus custom toolbar and macros) are merged into your document.

You can also follow these steps to unattach a template. Do that by selecting Normal (`NORMAL.DOTM`) as the template to attach.

Templates of Your Own

If you enjoy the thrill and excitement of templates, you'll eventually have the desire to create your own. Eventually, you should have your own collection handy. These templates will greatly expedite your document production duties. Making these templates is the topic of this section.

Creating a template based on a document you already have

Rome wasn't built in a day, but building your own document template can take even less time. That's because you can easily create a template based on a document you've already slaved over. So when the formatting and styles and all that junk have already been created, making a template is a snap — and it doesn't require a large army or navy or any ambitious politicians.

To make a template based on a document you already created, follow these steps:

1. **Find or create the document, one that has styles or formats or text that you plan to use repeatedly.**

2. **Strip out any text that doesn't need to be in every document.**

   For example, my play-writing template has all my play-writing styles in it, but the text includes only placeholders — just to get me started.

   The template should contain only the styles you need for that document, plus any text that's common to all documents.

3. **Click the File tab.**

4. **On the File screen, choose the Save As command.**

   Don't worry about choosing the document's location. All Word templates are saved in a predefined folder, and Word automatically chooses that location for you.

5. **Click the Browse button.**

   The Save As dialog box appears. It's the same Save As dialog box that Word uses for saving everything. Refer to Chapter 8 if you need a refresher.

6. **Type a name for the template.**

   Type the name in the File Name box. Be descriptive.

   You don't need to name the template by using the word *template*.

7. **From the Save As Type drop-down list, choose Word Template.**

   Ah-ha! This is the secret. The document must be saved in a document template format. That's what makes a template superior over a typical, boring Word document.

8. **Click the Save button.**

   Your efforts are saved to disk as a document template, nestled in the proper place where Word keeps all its document templates.

9. **Close the template.**

   The reason for closing it is that any changes you make from now on are made to the template. If you want to use the template to start a new document, you choose that template from the New window, as described earlier in this chapter.

Refer to the later section, "Modifying a template," for information on updating or changing a template.

Making a new template from scratch

After you become well versed in creating Word styles, and after you fully understand the template concept, you can begin creating Word templates from scratch. It's easy, but only when you *truly* know what you want.

The basic trick is to build the styles you need and then add any text you may want. Then use the Save As dialog box to save the document as a template, as described in the preceding section.

The biggest drawback to this approach is that your template probably isn't complete. As you start creating new documents based on the template, you find that you need to modify existing styles as well as add new ones. That just means more template editing, which is covered in the next section.

Modifying a template

Changing or editing a document template is identical to changing or editing any document. You simply create a new document by using the existing template. Make your changes, and then use the Save As command to either overwrite the existing template or save the document as a new template, by following the steps from the earlier section, "Creating a template based on a document you already have."

Yes, you can edit a document template in other ways. You can open the template itself in Word, but the steps involved are rather convoluted because you have to have some computer-savvy skills just to find where Word hides the template files. No, you're much better to start with the template as though you're creating a new document and then simply save the document again as a template.

Changing a template has a widespread impact. When you update or modify a template, you're basically changing all documents that use the template. Be mindful of your changes!

The Theme of Things

Themes apply decorative styles to your document, such as fonts and colors, which gives your written efforts a professionally formatted feel with minimal fuss or talent. It's like having a graphics designer assist you but without having to suffer through her lamentable complaints about how her boyfriend pays no attention to her.

A theme consists of three elements:

Colors: A set of colors is chosen to format the text foreground and background, any graphics or design elements in the theme, plus hyperlinks.

Fonts: Two fonts are chosen as part of the theme — one for the heading styles and a second for the body text.

Graphical effects: These effects are applied to any graphics or design elements in your document. The effects can include 3-D, shading, gradation, drop shadows, and other design subtleties.

Each of these elements is organized into a theme, given a name, and placed on the Design tab's Themes menu for easy application in your document.

Refer to the next section for information on applying a theme.

✔ A professionally licensed, certified mentally stable graphics designer creates a theme's fonts, colors, and design effects so that they look good and work well together.

✔ A theme doesn't overrule styles chosen for a document. Instead, it accents those styles. The theme may add color information, choose different fonts, or present various graphical elements. Beyond that, it doesn't change any styles applied to the text.

REMEMBER

✔ The graphical effects of a theme are only applied to any graphics in your document; the theme doesn't insert graphics into your text. See Chapter 22 for information on graphics in Word.

✔ Choosing a theme affects your entire document all at once. To affect individual paragraphs or bits of text, apply a style or format manually. Refer to Chapter 15.

Applying a document theme

You choose a theme by using the Themes button found on the Design tab. Built-in themes are listed along with any custom themes you've created. Figure 16-2 illustrates the Themes menu.

Each of the built-in themes controls all three major theme elements, changing your document's contents accordingly. Hovering the mouse pointer over a theme changes your document visually, which is a way to preview the themes. Click on a theme to choose it.

TIP

✔ Because a document can use only one theme at a time, choosing a new theme replaces the current theme.

✔ To remove a theme from your document, choose the Office theme or the menu command Reset to Theme from Template (refer to Figure 16-2).

✔ If you would rather change only one part of a theme, such as a document's fonts, use the Colors, Fonts, or Effects command button on the Design tab.

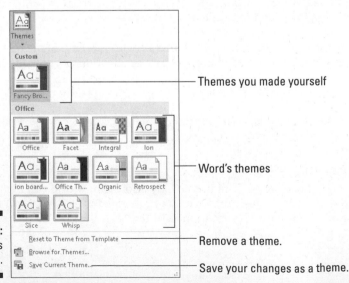

Figure 16-2:
The Themes
menu.

Themes you made yourself

Word's themes

Remove a theme.

Save your changes as a theme.

Modifying or creating a theme

You can't create your own themes from scratch, but you can modify existing themes to make your own, custom theme. You start by modifying existing theme colors and fonts:

To create a custom color theme, choose Colors⇨Customize Colors. Use the Create New Theme Colors dialog box to pick and choose which colors apply to text or various graphical elements in your document.

To create a custom font theme, choose Fonts⇨Customize Fonts. Use the Create New Theme Fonts dialog box to select fonts — one for the headings and another for the body text.

In each case, give the new theme a name and save it. You can then choose that theme from the Custom area of either the Colors or Fonts menu.

When you're using a set of theme colors, fonts, and graphics styles — even if you didn't create them yourself but, rather, used them merely to organize your document — you can collect the various elements as a theme: Choose Save Current Theme from the Theme menu, and use the dialog box to give your theme a proper descriptive name and save it. The theme you create then appears in the Custom area of the Themes menu (refer to Figure 16-2).

To remove a custom theme, right-click it on the Themes menu and choose the Delete command. Click the Yes button to remove the theme.

Chapter 17

Sundry Formatting

Say hello to the formatting leftovers, the items that are related to formatting but that may not fit into another chapter in this part of the book or that were, as is my feeling, added to the Word formatting mix in a weird or hodgepodge manner. In this chapter, you find a plethora of formatting tricks and tidbits. It's random stuff, various and sundry. Welcome to the Word formatting buffet dessert bar!

Weird and Fun Text Effects

 There's a fuzzy button in the Home tab's Font group. It looks like a big *A,* and it's one of those menu button items that dot the Ribbon like ticks on the back of an Alabama hound dog. Regardless, what it does is let you apply some interesting and nonstandard effects to your document's text.

To apply the text effects, simply choose one from the Text Effects menu. The effect you choose is applied to any new text you type or to any selected text in the document.

You can specifically apply an effect or change a color by choosing the specific item from the Text Effects menu, as shown in Figure 17-1. Or if you want to get fancy, you can use the Format Text Effects dialog box. To get there, follow these steps:

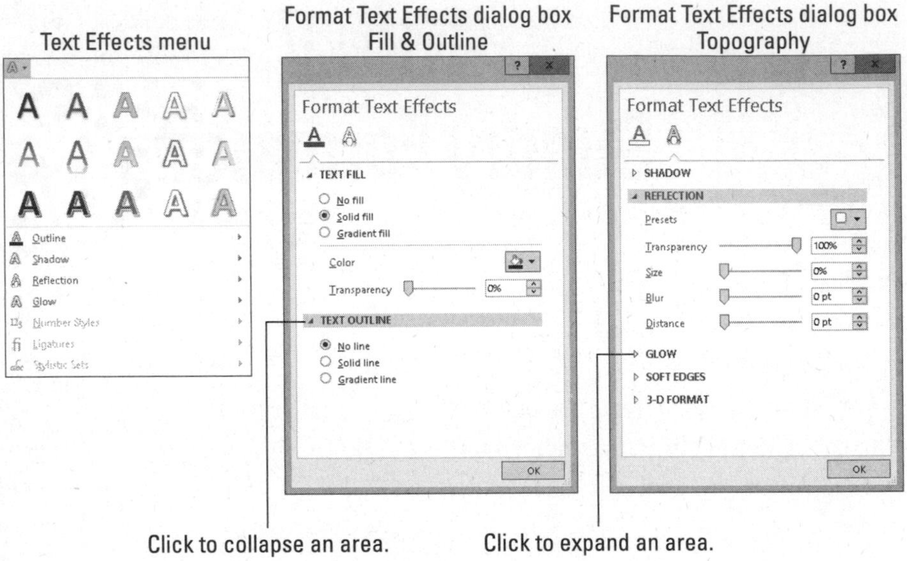

Text Effects menu

Format Text Effects dialog box
Fill & Outline

Format Text Effects dialog box
Topography

Figure 17-1:
Text effects
galore.

Click to collapse an area.   Click to expand an area.

1. **Summon the Font dialog box.**

   The keyboard shortcut is Ctrl+D. The longcut is to click the dialog box launcher, found in the lower-right corner of the Font group on the Home tab.

2. **Click the Text Effects button in the Font dialog box.**

   The Format Text Effects dialog box appears, as shown in Figure 17-1.

3. **Click the A button that has the underline to apply text fill and outline effects; other effects are added by clicking the hollow-looking A.**

   Refer to Figure 17-1 for the two types of effects that are applied in the Format Text Effects dialog box.

4. **Manipulate the controls in the dialog box to customize text effects.**

   Wonderful and detailed controls are available in the Format Text Effects dialog box, but sadly, no preview window.

5. **Click the OK button to dismiss the Format Text Effects dialog box.**

6. **Click the OK button to close the Font dialog box.**

The font effects you select affect any selected text in the document or any text you type from that point onward.

- ✔ The Text Attributes button doesn't look fuzzy when you're working on a Word document saved in an older, DOC file format.

- ✔ Font effects are best used for document headings and other decorative text.

✔ The text effects covered in this section are in addition to the standard font-formatting text attributes, such as bold, italic, and underline. See Chapter 10.

Steal This Format!

It's not a whisk broom, and you'd have to be old to think it's a shaving brush. No, it's a paintbrush. Not only that, but it's also a *special* paintbrush — one that steals text and paragraph formatting, by borrowing it from one place in your document and splashing it down in another. It's the Format Painter, and here's how it's used:

1. **Place the insertion pointer in the middle of the text that has the formatting you want to copy.**

   The insertion pointer must be in the midst of the word, not in the exact middle but neither to the left nor right of it. If it's not right, this trick doesn't work.

2. **On the Home tab, click the Format Painter command button in the Clipboard group.**

   The cursor changes to a paintbrush/I-beam pointer, as depicted in the margin. This special cursor is used to highlight and then reformat text in your document.

3. **Hunt for the text you want to change.**

4. **Highlight the text.**

   Drag the mouse over the text you want to change — to "paint" it.

Voilà! The text is changed.

✔ The Format Painter works with only character and paragraph formatting, not with page formatting.

✔ I like to think of the format painter this way: You dip the paintbrush into the "paint" of one format and then paint some text. So the first step is to click the mouse on the text that contains the formatting paint. Then choose the Format Painter tool, and paint the text you want to change.

✔ To change the formatting of multiple bits of text, double-click the Format Painter. That way, the Format Painter cursor stays active, ready to paint lots of text. Press the Esc key to cancel your Dutch Boy frenzy.

✔ If you tire of the mouse, you can use the Ctrl+Shift+C key combination to copy the character format from one location to another. Use the Ctrl+Shift+V key combination to paste the character format; highlight the text in your document, and press Ctrl+Shift+V to paste in the font formatting.

✔ You can sorta kinda remember to use Ctrl+Shift+C to copy character formatting and use Ctrl+Shift+V to paste, because Ctrl+C and Ctrl+V are the copy-and-paste shortcut keys. Sorta kinda.

✔ Don't confuse the Format Painter with the highlighting tool, found in the Font group. See Chapter 26.

Automatic Formatting

Part of Word's AutoCorrect function (covered in Chapter 7) is a feature named AutoFormat. Whereas AutoCorrect is used to fix primarily typos and common spelling boo-boos, AutoFormat is used to fix formatting fumbles. This section demonstrates AutoFormat's prowess.

Enjoying automagical text

AutoFormat controls some minor text formatting as you type. The settings are visible in the AutoFormat dialog box, as shown in Figure 17-2.

Figure 17-2:
AutoFormat
As You Type
settings.

To display that dialog box, heed these steps:

1. **Click the File tab.**

2. **On the File screen, choose Options.**

   The Word Options dialog box appears.

3. **Select Proofing from the left side of the window.**

4. **Click the button labeled AutoCorrect Options.**

5. **Click the AutoFormat As You Type tab in the AutoCorrect dialog box.**

   This part of the dialog box, shown in Figure 17-2, is where all the AutoFormat options dwell. Turning an option off or on is as easy as removing or adding a check mark.

The best way to demonstrate the AutoFormat-as-you-type concept is to have a Word document on the screen and then type the examples in the following sections. Note that these samples demonstrate only a few of the things AutoFormat can do.

When you find any of these tricks upsetting, see the later section, "Disabling the @#$%&! AutoFormat."

Smart quotes

The quote characters on the keyboard are *tick marks:* " and ' . AutoFormat converts them into the more stylish open and closed curly quotes. Type hither:

```
He said, "Yes, I'm being honest. I really do love
you, but the monster is coming and you broke your
ankle, and I figured that you'd understand."
```

Both the single and double quotes are properly used and converted.

Real fractions

You can format a fraction by typing the first value in superscript, the slash mark, and then the second value in subscript. Or you can let AutoFormat do it for you. Here's an example:

I spend twice the time doing ½ the work.

The characters *1/2* are converted into the single character ½. This trick works for some, but not all, common fractions. When it doesn't work, use the superscript/subscript trick described in Chapter 31, in the section about building your own fractions.

Hyperlinks

Word can underline *and* activate hyperlinks that are typed in your document, such as

```
I've been to http://www.hell.com and back.
```

The website `http://www.hell.com` is automatically underlined, colored, and turned into an active web page link for you. (You have to Ctrl+click to follow the link.)

Ordinals

You're guessing wrong if you think that *ordinals* are a baseball team or a group of religious leaders. They're numbers that end in the letters *st, nd,* or *rd,* as this line demonstrates:

```
There were two of us in the race; I came in 1st
and Barbara came in 3rd.
```

Word automatically superscripts ordinal numbers, making them look oh-so-spiffy.

Em dashes

An *em dash* is the official typesetting term for a long dash, longer than the hyphen (or its evil twin, the en dash). Most people type two hyphens to emulate the *em dash*. Word fixes that problem:

```
A red one is a slug bug--not a punch buggy.
```

As you type the–(dash-dash), AutoFormat replaces it with the official em dash character.

- ✔ The keyboard shortcut for typing an em dash is Ctrl+Alt+minus sign, where the minus sign is the minus key on the numeric keypad.

- ✔ The keyboard shortcut for typing an en dash is Ctrl+minus sign.

- ✔ The en dash is approximately the width of the letter *N.* Likewise, the em dash is the width of the letter *M.*

Formatting tricks for paragraphs

At the paragraph level, AutoFormat helps you quickly handle some otherwise irksome formatting issues. Some folks like this feature, some despise it. The following sections provide a few examples of what AutoFormat is capable of.

If you find any of these AutoFormat tricks annoying, refer to the later section, "Disabling the @#$%&! AutoFormat," for information on shutting the dern thing off!

Numbered lists

Anytime you start a paragraph with a number, Word assumes (through AutoFormat) that you need all your paragraphs numbered. Here's the proof:

```
Things to do today:
1. Get new treads for the tank.
```

Immediately after typing 1., you probably saw the infamous AutoFormat Lightning Bolt icon and noticed your text being reformatted. Darn, this thing is quick! That's AutoFormat guessing that you're about to type a list. Go ahead and finish typing the line; after you press Enter, you see the next line begin with the number 2.

Keep typing until the list ends or you get angry, whichever comes first. To end the list, press the Enter key again. That erases the final number and restores the paragraph formatting to Normal.

✔ This trick also works for letters (and Roman numerals). Just start something with a letter and a period, and Word picks up on the next line by suggesting the next letter in the alphabet and another period.

✔ Bulleted lists can also be created in this way: Start a line by typing an asterisk (*) and a space to see what happens.

✔ See Chapter 21 for more information on creating numbered or bulleted lists.

✔ I tell you earlier in this book not to press the Enter key twice to end a paragraph. That statement still holds true: When you press Enter twice to end an AutoFormat list, Word sticks only one Enter "character" into the text.

Borders (lines)

A line above or below a paragraph in Word is a *border.* Most folks call them lines, but they're borders in Word. Here's how to whip out a few borders by using AutoFormat:

```
---
```

Typing three hyphens and pressing the Enter key causes Word to instantly transmute the three little hyphens into a solid line that touches the left and right paragraph margins.

✔ To create a double line, type three equal signs and press Enter.

✔ To create a bold line, type three underlines and press Enter.

✔ Refer to Chapter 18 for more information on borders and boxes around your text.

Undoing an AutoFormat

You have two quick ways to undo AutoFormatting. The first, obviously, is to press Ctrl+Z on the keyboard, which is the Undo command. That's easy.

You can also use the Lightning Bolt icon to undo AutoFormatting. Clicking the icon displays a drop-down menu (see Figure 17-3) that you use to control the AutoFormat options as you type. Three options are usually available: Undo what has been done, disable what has been done so that it never happens again, and last, open the Control AutoFormat Options dialog box, which is covered in the next section. Choose wisely.

Figure 17-3:
AutoFormat
options.

Undo Border Line

Stop Automatically Creating Border Lines

Control AutoFormat Options...

Disabling the @#$%&! AutoFormat

Formatting is subjective. Sometimes you want AutoFormat to help you out, and sometimes AutoFormat makes you angry enough to want to hurl the computer out an open window. Either way, the AutoCorrect dialog box, shown earlier in Figure 17-2, controls AutoFormat.

To disable settings in the AutoCorrect dialog box, follow the Steps (1 through 4) in the earlier section, "Enjoying automagical text." Remove the check marks by the options that vex you on the AutoFormat As You Type tab in that dialog box. But you're not done!

You also need to click the AutoFormat tab in the AutoCorrect dialog box. There are even more options to undo on that tab.

Click the OK button when you're done, and close the Word Options window.

You can also disable options as you type by using the AutoFormat options menu, shown in Figure 17-3, and described in the preceding section.

Center a Page, Top to Bottom

Nothing makes a document title nice and crisp like having it sit squat in the center of a page. The title is centered left to right, which you can do by selecting Center alignment for the title's paragraph. But how about centering the title top to bottom?

If you're thinking about whacking the Enter key 17 times in a row to center a title top to bottom, stop! Let Word do the math to make the title perfectly centered. Here's how:

1. **Move the insertion pointer to the start of your document.**

   The Ctrl+Home key combination moves you there instantly.

2. **Type and format your document's title.**

   It can be on a single line or on several lines.

   To center the title, select it and press Ctrl+E, the Center keyboard short-cut. Apply any additional font or paragraph formatting as necessary.

   Avoid the temptation to press the Enter key to add space above or below the title. Such space isn't needed, and would wreck Word's auto-matic centering powers.

3. **Insert a section break after the title's last line: On the Page Layout tab, choose Breaks⇨Next Page from the Page Setup area.**

   The section break ensures that only the first page of your document is centered from top to bottom. Review Chapter 14 for more information on document sections.

4. **Ensure that the insertion pointer is again on the document's first page.**

   You need to be on the page you want to format.

5. **Summon the Page Setup dialog box: Click the Page Layout tab, and choose the dialog box launcher from the lower-right corner of the Page Setup area.**

   The Page Setup dialog box appears.

6. **Click the Layout tab.**

7. **Select Center from the Vertical Alignment drop-down list.**

   You can find this item in the bottom half of the dialog box.

8. **Confirm that the Apply To drop-down list shows This Section.**

9. **Click OK.**

The first page of the document will be centered from top to bottom.

Part IV
Spruce Up a Dull Document

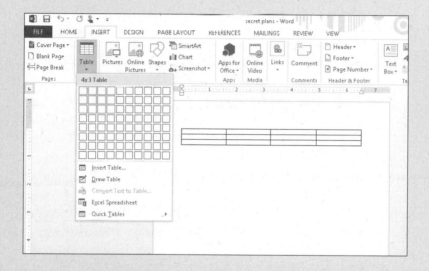

See how you can assign a shortcut key to a symbol at www.dummies.com/extras/word2013.

In this part . . .

- ✔ Learn how to use borders, draw lines, and add color to your background.

- ✔ Get to know tables and how to use them within your Word 2013 documents.

- ✔ Find out how you can split your text into multiple columns.

- ✔ Discover how to make several types of lists, including bulleted lists, numbered lists, and indexes.

- ✔ Learn how you can insert images and captions into your Word 2013 document.

- ✔ See how you can assign a shortcut key to a symbol at www. dummies.com/extras/word2013.

Chapter 18

Lines and Shading

· ·

· ·

*T*he days of whacking the hyphen, equal sign, or underline key to decorate your text are long over. It's sad, too, because I knew quite a few people who were adept at using the computer keyboard's more interesting symbol keys to draw boxes and lines and even graphics within their text. I can understand the need, but what I don't understand is why people don't simply use the borders, lines, and shading commands in Word, which are so cleverly discussed in this very chapter.

The Basics of Lines and Shading

Two command buttons found in the Home tab's Paragraph group handle lines and colors in Word. That's the easy part. The difficult part is remembering that a line is known as a *border* in Word. Furthermore, background colors are known as *shading*. Keep these two concepts in your head, and you're well on your way to drawing all sorts of lines in, on, around, above, and over your text, as well as to coloring the background of that text.

REMEMBER

    ✔ A line is a *border* in Word.

    ✔ An exception to the line-is-a-border concept is the Horizontal Line, a special border that's applied between paragraphs. See the later section, "Drawing a fat, thick line."

✔ Word's Shading (background color) command affects the text background. Text color is applied by using the Font Color command, which is covered in Chapter 10.

✔ Not all lines in Word are borders. A vertical red line in the left margin can be a sign that something was changed on that line. Refer to Chapter 26 for more information on revision marking.

Working the Borders command button

Word places its basic text decoration doodlings on the Borders command button menu, as shown in the margin. It's found in the Home tab's Paragraph group. Clicking that button immediately applies the indicated border to your text, or removes the borders, as is the case with the No Border button.

The Border command button can also be used to display a menu full of border choices, as shown in Figure 18-1. Choosing a border from the menu not only applies that border to your text but also changes the Border command button to reflect the new border style.

Figure 18-1: The Border menu.

For details on setting specific borders in your text, see the later section, "Lines, Borders, and Boxes."

✔ You can use only one border style at a time from the Border menu. Choosing another style replaces the first style.

✔ If you want a combination of borders, you must use the Borders and Shading dialog box, as described in the later section, "Summoning the Borders and Shading dialog box." This dialog box also allows you to change the line style, color, and thickness of the border.

Using the Shading command button

Background color is applied to your text by using the Shading button. As with the Borders command button, the background color shown on the button is applied to selected text or to new text you type. You can choose a new color from the menu that's displayed when you click the Shading command button's down-arrow thing. Normally, I'd put a figure of that menu here, but this book isn't in color, so it would look gross.

> ✔ The basic palette of colors is chosen by the current document theme. See Chapter 16 for more information on themes and theme colors.

> ✔ You can also set background grayscale colors and patterns by using the Shading tab in the Borders and Shading dialog box, covered in the next section.

Summoning the Borders and Shading dialog box

For true control over borders, you summon the Borders and Shading dialog box, as shown in Figure 18-2. Choosing the Borders and Shading command from the bottom of the Border menu (refer to Figure 18-1) does the job.

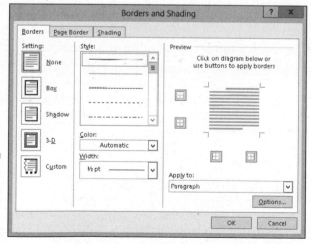

Figure 18-2: The Borders and Shading dialog box.

Unlike on the Border menu, several options are available in the Borders and Shading dialog box for setting borders. Most notably, you can set the border line style, thickness, and color.

You can also use the Borders and Shading dialog box to create a page border and apply background color (shading). Later sections in this chapter discuss the details.

Click the OK button to apply your border settings and close the dialog box, or press Cancel, to give up and quit.

Lines, Borders, and Boxes

Here a line. There a line. Everywhere a line-line. This section describes various ways to apply lines, borders, and boxes to your text. This section refers to the Border menu and the Borders and Shading dialog box, as described earlier in this chapter.

The process of applying a line, border, or box to your text changes the paragraph formatting. The format sticks with the paragraph, even when you press Enter to start a new paragraph. To remove the line, border, or box, see the later section, "Removing borders."

Putting a line above a heading

A common use of lines in Word is to apply a line to a heading in your document. It's a form of text decoration; plus, it helps to break up the document. Here's how it's done:

1. **Place the insertion pointer in a heading or paragraph.**

2. **From the Borders command button, choose the Top Border command.**

If you want to change the border thickness, color, or style (dashed or dotted), you summon the Borders and Shading dialog box. Use the Color and Width menus to apply color and thickness.

Boxing text or paragraphs

To stick a box around any spate of words or paragraphs, summon the Borders and Shading dialog box (refer to Figure 18-2), and choose a box style from the Setting column: Box, Shadow, or 3-D. Click OK.

To ensure that the border is applied to text (words) and not to the entire paragraph, select the text first and then choose Text from the Apply To drop-down list in the Borders and Shading dialog box.

Another way to place a box around a passage of text is to use a text box. Unlike text formatting, a text box is a graphical element you can insert into your document. See Chapter 23.

Boxing a title

Someday when you're tasked with creating an organizational newsletter, you can surprise all your friends and others who were smart enough to avoid that task by coming up with a fancy title, similar to the newsletter heading shown in Figure 18-3. It looks complex and such, but it's nothing more than the crafty application of borders; plus, some deft text, paragraph, and tab stop skills.

Figure 18-3: Top and bottom borders.

Vol. XXVI, Issue 13   November 2013

Zamboni Professional

Frank's Favorite Patterns   *You* are the show!
Your Second Business: Shaved Ice   Hockey Players: Don't get me started!

The key to creating such a heading is to type all the text first and then use the Borders and Shading dialog box to add different border styles above and below the paragraphs.

- ✔ Use the Preview window in the Borders and Shading dialog box to set the line style. Click the mouse in the Preview window to add or remove lines above or below or to either side of the text.

- ✔ The title shown in Figure 18-3 takes advantage of the center and left tab stops, as described in Chapter 12.

Making rules

A common trick in page design is to apply a line above or below text. The line is a *rule,* and it helps to break up the text, highlight a specific paragraph, or create a *block quote, callout,* or *pull quote.* Here's how:

1. **Click the mouse to place the insertion pointer into a given paragraph of text.**

   Yes, it works best if you've already written that paragraph. Remember my admonition: Write first, format later.

   2. **Summon the Borders and Shading dialog box.**

   3. **Choose a line style, width, and color, if needed.**

   4. **Click the Top button.**

      The Top button is found on the right side of the Borders and Shading dialog box, in the Preview area. (Refer to Figure 18-2.)

   5. **Click the Bottom button.**

   6. **Click OK.**

You may also want to adjust the paragraph margins inward so that your text further stands out on the page. Refer to Chapter 11 for more information.

If you press Enter to end the paragraph, you carry the border formatting with the insertion pointer to the following paragraph. See the section "Removing borders," later in this chapter, to find out how to prevent that situation.

Drawing a fat, thick line

Sometimes, you need one of those fat, thick lines to break up your text. I dunno *why,* but the *how* is to choose the Horizontal Line command from the Border menu (refer to Figure 18-1). Word inserts a thin, inky stroke, running from the left to right margins.

   ✔ Unlike a border, the horizontal line isn't attached to a paragraph, so it doesn't repeat for every new paragraph you type.

   ✔ To adjust the horizontal line, click to select it with the mouse. Six "handles" appear (top and bottom and the four corners) around the selected image. You can drag these handles with the mouse to set the line's width or thickness.

   ✔ Double-clicking the horizontal line displays the Format Horizontal Line dialog box, where further adjustments can be made and color added.

   ✔ To remove the horizontal line, click once to select it and then press either the Delete or Backspace key.

Putting a border around a page of text

Compared with putting a border around a paragraph, you would think that putting a border around a page of text would be easy. Wrong! It's not that you can't figure out such a thing on your own — it's that it takes a certain level of finesse to get it done correctly. I've studied the puzzle of page borders and have devised this solution:

1. **Put the insertion pointer on the page you want to border.**

   For example, you might put it on the first page in your document.

2. **Summon the Borders and Shading dialog box.**

3. **Click the Page Border tab.**

   Whoa! The Page Border tab looks almost exactly like the Borders tab (refer to Figure 18-2).

4. **Choose the border you want: Use a preset box or pick a line style, color, and width.**

   You can select a funky art pattern from the Art drop-down list.

5. **Choose which pages you want bordered from the Apply To drop-down list.**

   You can select Whole Document to put borders on every page. To select the first page, choose the This Section–First Page Only item. Other options let you choose other pages and groups, as shown in the drop-down list.

   And now, the secret:

6. **Click the Options button.**

   The Border and Shading Options dialog box appears.

7. **From the Measure From drop-down list, choose the Text option.**

   The Edge of Page option just doesn't work with most printers. Text does.

8. **Click OK.**

9. **Click OK to close the Borders and Shading dialog box.**

To add more "air" between your text and the border, use the Border Shading Options dialog box (from Step 6) and *increase* the values in the Margin area.

Refer to Chapter 14 for more information on creating a section break in your document. By using sections, you can greatly control which pages in a document have borders and which do not.

To remove the page border, choose None under Settings in Step 4 and then click OK.

Removing borders

When you don't listen to my advice and you format a paragraph before you type its contents, notice that the borders stick with the paragraph like discarded gum under your shoe. To peel annoying borders from a paragraph, you choose the No Border style.

From the Border menu, choose No Border.

In the Borders and Shading dialog box, double-click the None button and then click OK.

You can also use the Borders and Shading dialog box to selectively remove borders from text. Use the Preview window and click a specific border to remove it; refer to Figure 18-2.

Background Colors and Shading

 Word lets you splash a dash of color behind any text, as well as inside any borders you create. It's all done by simply using the Shading command button, found in the Paragraph group, or, for more complexity, by using the Shading tab in the Borders and Shading dialog box.

The key to applying a background color is to first mark the text, such as a document title, as a block. (See Chapter 6 for block-marking instructions.) Then choose a color from the Shading command button's menu. Or if the colors don't suit you, choose the More Colors command from the menu and conjure up your own, custom color.

To apply a gray background, you summon the Shading tab in the Borders and Shading dialog box. Choose the gray scale percentage from the Style menu in the Patterns area. You can also choose a pattern from that menu, though I recommend against patterns because they aren't well suited for shading text.

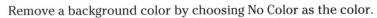

✔ You can best apply background color to a page by using the Page Color command, described in Chapter 13.

 ✔ To create white text on a black background, select the text and apply white as the text foreground color (refer to Chapter 10). Then from the Shading command button, choose black as the background color.

Remove a background color by choosing No Color as the color.

Chapter 19

Able Tables

*W*ord processing is a linear task. Characters flow into words, which flow into sentences, which form paragraphs. You start reading here and end up there. It's basic stuff. That is, until the information you're trying to organize is best presented in a grid. That's when you need to summon a table in your document.

Sure, you can cobble together a grid of text by using tabs and fancy paragraph formatting, but it's best to let Word do the work. This happens by employing the Table command, which I believe you'll find far easier than assembling that build-it-yourself furniture that comes from Scandinavia.

There's a Table in Your Document

In Word, tables have an advantage over organizing information with rows and columns, courtesy of the Tab key. That's because a table is considered its own document element, one that Word manipulates as a unit.

In a table, you can easily add, remove, or reorganize the rows and columns. You can format a table all at once, using predefined formatting options. While you could do all that with tabs, the process would undoubtedly drive you insane. You probably don't want to go insane, so I highly recommend using Word's Table command any time you need to present information in a grid of rows and columns.

Before you venture into Table Creation Land, I recommend that you peruse these points:

- Anytime you need information in a grid, or in columns and rows, you're better off creating a table in Word than fussing with tabs and tab stops.

- Rows in a table appear from left to right across the screen.

- Columns in a table go up and down.

- Each "cubbyhole" in a table is a *cell*.

- Cells can have their own margins, text, and paragraph formats. You can even stick graphics into cells.

- Unlike when you work with tabs, Word tables can be resized and rearranged to fit your data. Try doing that with tabs!

Working with tables in Word

A table is something you insert into your document, so Word's Table commands are found on the Ribbon's Insert tab, in the aptly named Tables group. Only one button is in that group. Click that button to see the Table menu, as shown in Figure 19-1.

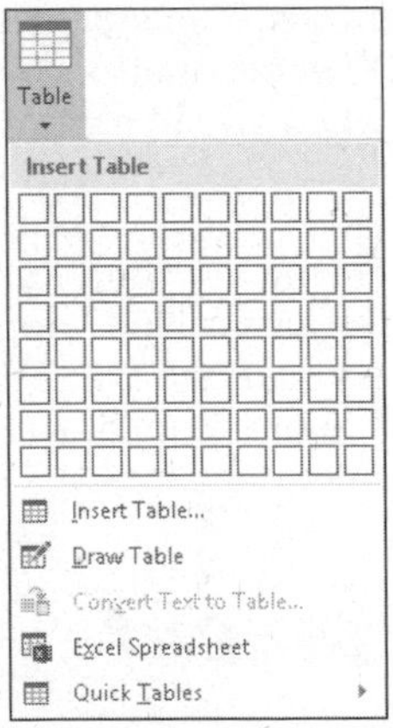

Figure 19-1: The Table menu.

The following sections describe how to use the menu, though here's a quick overview:

1. **Insert the table into your document.**

   Word offers various table-creating commands, all of which plop down a nice, blank empty table for you to fill.

2. **Add the table's text.**

   Unlike at other times where it works best to first write your prose and then format it, I highly recommend that you create the table first and then fill it with text.

3. **Format the table.**

   The job of formatting takes place by using two special tabs that appear on the Ribbon: Design and Layout. They both appear beneath the Table Tools label. Using these tabs is covered in the section "Table Modification," later in this chapter.

The formatting job also includes adding or removing rows or columns in the table. Again, it takes place after the table is initially created and after you add text. The rest of this chapter explains the details.

- ✔ Don't fret if you've already started a table by using tabs and tab stops. Word deftly converts plain text into a table; refer to the section "Converting text into a table," later in this chapter.

- ✔ Word lets you easily add or remove rows or columns to or from a table. Don't worry about getting the table dimensions wrong when you first create it. See the later section, "Adjusting the table."

- ✔ The table is initially created at the same width as your document's paragraph margins. As you add more columns, each column gets smaller.

- ✔ The two special tabs that appear on the Ribbon, Design and Layout, show up anytime the insertion pointer dwells in a table's midst.

- ✔ I recommend starting the table on a blank line by itself. Furthermore, type a second blank line *after* the line you put the table on. That makes it easier to continue typing text after the table is created.

Making a table

Just to confuse you, Word offers multiple ways to create a table. It's one of those let's-deluge-the-user-with-options things that Microsoft does so well. Depending on how well you get along with Word, you can choose one of the various ways.

The best way to create a table

The most consistent way to make a table in Word is to use the grid on the Table button's menu, as shown in Figure 19-1. Follow these steps:

1. **Move the insertion pointer to the location where you want the table in your document.**

   Tables dwell in your document like paragraphs, existing on a line by themselves.

2. **Click the Insert tab.**

3. **Click the Table button.**

4. **Drag the mouse through the grid to create in your document a table that has the number of rows and columns you need for the table.**

   For example, Figure 19-2 shows a 4-column-by-3-row table being created by dragging the mouse. As you drag the mouse pointer on the menu, the table's grid appears in your document.

5. **Release the mouse button to begin working on the table.**

4x3 Table selected

Table button

Table preview in document

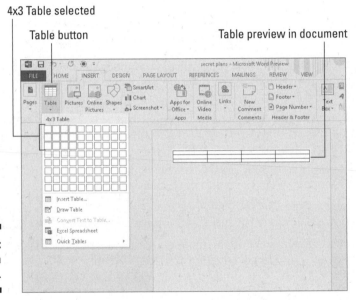

Figure 19-2:
Creating a
4-by-3 table.

See the later section, "Text in Tables," for filling in your table.

The right-brain approach to creating a table

When dialog boxes make more sense than using menus and graphical goobers, choose the Insert Table command from the Table menu (refer to Figure 19-1). Use the Insert Table dialog box to manually enter the number of rows and columns you need. Click the OK button to plop down your table.

The completely left-brain approach to creating a table

Free your mind from the constraints of conventionalism, clutch a crystal, and use the mouse to draw a table inside your document: From the Table menu on the Insert tab, choose Draw Table. The insertion pointer changes to a pencil, as shown in the margin. Drag the mouse to "draw" the table's outline in your document, as shown in Figure 19-3.

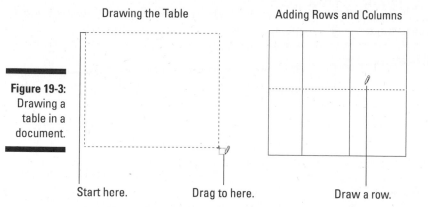

Drawing the Table   Adding Rows and Columns

Figure 19-3:
Drawing a
table in a
document.

Start here.   Drag to here.   Draw a row.

Start in the upper-left corner of where you envision your table and drag to the lower-right corner, which tells Word where to insert the table. You see an outline of the table as you drag down and to the right (refer to Figure 19-3).

Continue to create the table by drawing rows and columns, as illustrated in the figure. As long as the mouse pointer looks like a pencil, you can use it to draw the rows and columns in your table.

Press the Esc key to end table-creation mode.

The "I can't do anything — please help" approach to creating a table

Word comes with an assortment of predefined, formatted tables. Plopping one down in your document is as easy as using the Quick Tables submenu, chosen from the Table menu on the Insert tab (refer to Figure 19-1). Keep scrolling that menu; you'll discover more tables available than just the calendars.

After inserting a Quick Table, all you need to do is add or edit the existing text. You can even use the Table Tools Design tab to instantly reformat the table. Or just succumb to the desire to manually format your table, as described elsewhere in this chapter.

Text in Tables

Text pours into a table on a cell-by-cell basis. You can type a word, sentence, or even a paragraph. All that text stays in the cell, though the cell changes size to accommodate larger quantities of text.

You can format a table's cell just like any paragraph in Word, even adding margins and tabs. All the standard text and paragraph formats apply to cells in a table just as they do to regular text, but your first duty is to get text into a table's cell.

- ✔ Truly, if you have large quantities of text in a single cell, you probably don't need a table to present your information.
- ✔ Even though you can format first-line indents for text in a cell, I don't recommend it. Such formatting can be a pain to manipulate.
- ✔ Show the Ruler when you work with formatting a table — it's a boon: Click the View tab and place a check mark by the Ruler item in the Show group.

Navigating a table

Text appears in whichever cell the toothpick cursor is blinking. Though you can simply click the mouse in a cell to type text, you can use keyboard shortcuts to move around the table: Press the Tab key to move from cell to cell. To move back, press Shift+Tab.

When you press the Tab key at the last cell in a row, the toothpick cursor moves down to the first cell in the next line. Pressing the Tab key in the table's last, lower-right cell automatically adds another row to the table.

- ✔ To produce a tab character within a cell, press Ctrl+Tab.
- ✔ When you press the Enter key in a cell, you create a new paragraph in a cell, which probably isn't what you want.
- ✔ The Shift+Enter key combination (a soft return) can be used break up long lines of text in a cell.

Selecting in a table

Selecting text in a table can get funky. That's because you can select the text itself, or you can select a cell, row, or column. Here are my suggestions:

- ✔ Triple-click the mouse in a cell to select all text in that cell.
- ✔ Select a single cell by positioning the mouse in the cell's lower-left corner. The mouse pointer changes to a northeastward-pointing arrow, as shown in the margin. Click to select the cell, which includes the cell's text but primarily the cell itself.

✔ Move the mouse into the left margin and click to select a row of cells.

✔ Move the mouse above a column, and click to select that column. When the mouse is in the "sweet spot," the pointer changes to a downward-pointing arrow (shown in the margin).

✔ Selecting stuff in a table can also be accomplished from the Table group on the Table Tools Layout tab. Use the Select menu to select the entire table, a row, a column, or a single cell.

✔ Clicking the table's "handle" selects the entire table. The handle is visible whenever the mouse points at the table or when the insertion pointer is placed inside the table.

See the later section, "Adjusting the table," for suggestions on what to do after selecting individual parts of a table.

Doing math in a table

Yes, Word can do math in its tables, just as you can do math in an Excel spreadsheet. The main difference is that Word's math commands aren't as sophisticated as the ones you find in Excel. Some would consider that a blessing.

Of all the math formulas available, the one I use the most is SUM. What it does is to add values in a row or column. Follow these steps:

1. **Create a table that contains values you want to add.**

   The values can be in a row or column. The last cell in that row or column must be empty. It's into this cell that you paste the SUM formula.

2. **Click the mouse in the cell where you want to place the formula.**

3. **Click the Table Tools Layout tab.**

4. **Click the Formula button in the Data group.**

   The Formula dialog box appears.

5. **Choose SUM from the Paste Function menu.**

6. **Click the OK button.**

   The values in the row or column are totaled and the result displayed in the table.

When you change the values in the table, you need to refresh or update the formula. To do so, right-click on the total in the table. From the pop-up menu, choose the command Update Field. If you don't see the Update Field command, you clicked on the wrong text.

Also see Chapter 23 for more information on fields in Word documents.

Converting text into a table

If you started working on your document before you discovered the Table command, you probably have fake tables created by using tabbed text. If so, you can easily convert that text into a bona fide table by following these simple steps:

1. Select the text you want to convert into a table.

It helps if the text is arranged into columns, with each column separated by a tab character. If not, things get screwy but still workable.

2. From the Insert tab, choose Table⇨Convert Text to Table.

The Convert Text to Table dialog box appears.

3. Ensure that Tabs is selected in the Convert Text to Table dialog box.

Confirm that your text-to-table transition is set up properly by consulting the Number of Columns item in the Convert Text to Table dialog box. If the number of columns seems correct, the conversion most likely is a good one. When the number of columns is off, you have a rogue tab somewhere in your text.

4. Click OK.

A table is born.

You probably need to make adjustments, reset column widths, and so on and so forth. These tasks may be a pain, but they're better than retyping all that text.

Turning a table into plain text

To boost your text from the confines of a table's cruel and cold cells, obey these steps:

1. Click the mouse inside the table you want to convert.

Don't select anything — just click the mouse.

2. Click the Table Tools Layout tab.

3. From the Table group, choose Select⇨Select Table.

4. From the Data group, choose Convert to Text.

The Convert to Text dialog box appears.

5. Click OK.

Bye-bye, table. Hello, ugly text.

As with converting text to a table, some cleanup is involved. Mostly, it's resetting the tabs (or removing them) — nothing complex or bothersome.

When a table's cells contain longer expanses of text, consider choosing Paragraph Marks from the Convert to Text dialog box (before Step 5). The text then looks less ugly after the conversion.

Table Modification

Rarely have I created the perfect table. Oh, maybe I've had instant success with a 1-column table or something simple. Most of the time, however, you'll find that your table requires some adjustments, some formatting, or tines and tweaks to get things just right. That's all possible, using the Table Tools tabs after the table has been created.

✔ The Table Tools tabs show up only when a table is being edited or selected.

✔ The best time to format and mess with a table is after you finish putting text into the table.

Manipulating a table with the mouse

For quick-and-dirty table manipulation, you can use the mouse. Here are some tips:

✔ Positioning the mouse on a vertical line in the table's grid changes the mouse pointer to the thing shown in the margin. You can adjust the line left or right and resize the surrounding cells.

✔ You can also adjust cell width by using the Ruler, by pointing the mouse at the Move Table Column button that appears above each table cell gridline.

✔ Pointing the mouse at a horizontal line changes the mouse pointer to the one shown in the margin. At that time, you can use the mouse to adjust the line up or down and change the row height of surrounding cells.

✔ Insert a new row by pointing the mouse outside the table's left edge and clicking on the + (plus) button, as shown in the margin. The row is inserted below the location where you click the button.

✔ Just as you can insert a new row, you can insert a new column by pointing the mouse at the table's top edge. Click the + (plus) button, shown in the margin, to add a row.

Adjusting the table

It's the Table Tools Layout tab that harbors many of the command buttons and items that let you manipulate and adjust a table. Start your table design journey by placing the insertion pointer somewhere within the table itself. Then you can peruse this section for some popular things to do with the table by using the Table Tools Layout tab.

Insert columns or rows

You can expand a table by adding rows or columns, and the rows or columns can be added inside the table or appended to any of the table's four sides. Four commands in the Rows & Columns group make this task possible: Insert Above, Insert Below, Insert Left, and Insert Right. The row or column that's added is relative to where the insertion pointer is within the table.

Delete cells, columns, or rows

The key to deleting all or part of a table is to first position the insertion pointer in the part of the table you want to remove. Then choose the table element to remove from the Delete button's menu; the Delete button is found in the Rows & Columns group.

When you choose the Delete Cells command, you see a dialog box asking what to do with the other cells in the row or column: Move them up or to the left. Yes, deleting a cell may make your table asymmetrical.

Adjust row and column size

Gizmos in the Cell Size group let you fine-tune the table's row height or column width. Adjustments that are made affect the row or column containing the insertion pointer.

The Distribute Rows and Distribute Columns command buttons, found in the Cell Size group, help clean up uneven column or row spacing in a table. With the insertion pointer anywhere in the table, click either or both buttons to even things out.

Align text

Text within a cell can be aligned just like a paragraph: left, center, or right. Additionally, the text can be aligned vertically: top, middle, or bottom. Combine these options and you have an explanation for the nine orientation buttons in the Alignment group.

Reorient text

The Text Direction button in the Alignment group changes the way text reads in a cell or group of selected cells. Normally, text is oriented from left to right. By clicking the Text Direction button once, you change the text direction to top-to-bottom. Click the button again, and the direction is changed to bottom-to-top. Clicking a third time restores the text to its normal direction.

Sadly, you cannot create upside-down text with the Text Direction button.

Merge cells

You can combine two or more cells in a table by simply erasing the line that separates them. To do so, click the Eraser command button found in the Draw group on the Layout tab. The mouse pointer changes to a bar of soap, but it's supposed to be an eraser (shown in the margin). Use that tool to erase lines in the table: Click a line and it's gone.

Click the Eraser button again when you're done merging.

- ✔ To merge a clutch of cells, select them with the mouse, then click the Merge Cells button in the Merge group found on the Layout tab.

- ✔ Merging cells combines the cells' contents, gluing together all the cells' text.

- ✔ You cannot remove the outside lines of the table. Those lines hold the table together, and removing them would (theoretically) delete the table.

Split cells

To turn one cell into two, you simply draw a line, horizontally or vertically, through the cell. Do so by clicking the Draw Table command button in the Draw group. The mouse pointer changes to the pencil pointer, which you can use to draw new lines in the table.

Click the Draw Table button again to turn off this feature.

You can also split cells by selecting a single cell, and then choose the Split Cells command from the merge group. Use the Split Cells dialog box to determine how to best mince up the cell.

Designing a table

The Table Tools Design tab is used to help you quickly (or slowly) format your table. The tab shows up whenever the insertion pointer lies somewhere in a table's realm. This section covers some common table design tricks and tips you can pull by using the Table Tools Design tab.

Quickly apply styles

The Table Styles group can quickly apply formatting to any table. Choose a style or click the menu button to see a smattering of styles. It's easy work.

Set table line styles

The lines you see in a table's grid are the same borders you can apply to text with the Border command button, as discussed in Chapter 18. The Borders group features lots of commands and options for creating borders in your table. For example, you can choose a line style and thickness and then use the Border Painter button to apply that style to any line you click on inside the table.

Remove a table's lines

Occasionally, you may want a table without any lines. For example, I typically use a 1-column, 2-row table to insert a picture and its caption into my text. To remove the table's grid in that situation and others, select the table and choose No Border from the Borders menu.

Having no lines (borders) in a table makes working with the table more difficult. The solution is to show the table *gridlines,* which aren't printed. To do that, select the table and choose the View Gridlines command from the Borders menu.

Deleting a table

To utterly remove the table from your document, click the mouse inside the table and then choose Delete⇨Table from the Rows & Columns group on the Layout tab. The table is blown to smithereens.

✔ Yes, deleting the table deletes its contents as well.

✔ If you'd rather merely convert the table's contents into plain text, refer to the section "Turning a table into plain text," earlier in this chapter.

Chapter 20

Columns of Text

. . . .

. . . .

*H*ere's a pop quiz: If someone asks about columns and you immediately think of something written in a magazine or newspaper, you're probably a writer. If you think Doric, Ionic, and Corinthian, you're probably a nerd. What you probably don't think of are text columns in Word. That's because placing columns across a page of text is a task that you probably don't believe a word processor can do. Man, are you wrong!

All about Columns

Here's a secret: All text you write in Word is already formatted in columns. Yep, although it's only one column of text per page, it still counts as a column.

Most folks don't think of their text in columns — that is, until you start talking about two or three columns of text per page. Such a thing is entirely possible in Word. The secret is the Columns command button, found on the Page Layout tab in the Page Setup group.

Clicking the Columns button displays a menu of handy column-formatting options, as shown on the left in Figure 20-1. Splitting text into columns is as easy as choosing a column format from that list.

To be more specific with the number of columns or their layout, choose the More Columns command. You can then use the Columns dialog box, as shown on the right in Figure 20-1.

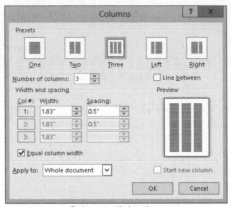

Figure 20-1:
The
Columns
menu and
dialog box.

Columns menu   Columns dialog box

Use the Columns dialog box to create and design multiple columns for your document — specifically, those not available on the Columns menu: Set the number of columns you want by using the Number of Columns box. Use the Preview window to help determine how your page is formatted. Click the OK button to apply the column format to your document.

✔ Rather than use the cursor-movement keys to move the insertion pointer between columns, use the mouse. Pointing and clicking in a column is easier than watching the insertion pointer fly all over the page.

✔ Choosing a column format from the Columns button menu affects the entire document, splitting it (or reducing it) into the number of columns specified — that is, unless you split the document into sections. In that case, the column type you chose affects only the current section. See Chapter 14 for more information on sections in Word.

✔ Use the Preview window in the Columns dialog box to get an idea of what the heck you're doing.

✔ To have only a portion of your document use columns, refer to the section "Mixing column formats in a document," a little later in this chapter.

✔ When you're working with columns and notice that Word starts acting slow and fussy, *save your work!*

✔ Although using columns for a short document seems to work well in Word, putting text into columns in a document of ten pages or more is better done in a desktop publishing program (DTP). See the nearby sidebar, "For advanced formatting, nothing beats DTP."

✔ Maximum number of columns per page? That depends on the size of the page. Word's minimum column width is half an inch, so a typical sheet of paper can have up to 12 columns on it — not that such a layout would be appealing or anything.

For advanced formatting, nothing beats DTP

I'll be honest up front: When you desire columns for whatever you're writing, what you need is *desktop publishing,* or *DTP,* software. Desktop publishing isn't about writing; it's about assembling text that you've already written with graphics and other design elements and then laying them out as a professional would. DTP is built for such a task. It can handle it.

Word's ability to march text into columns isn't its best feature. Columns work for smaller documents — say, one-sheet newsletters, trifold brochures, or fliers. Beyond that, I highly recommend using DTP software for your demanding documents. Both Adobe InDesign and Microsoft Publisher are good places to start, if you're interested in DTP software.

Making two-column text

Two columns are sufficient to impress anyone. More columns make your text skinnier and more difficult to read. Here's how you create a two-column document on a standard sheet of paper, in the vertical orientation:

1. **Start up a new document.**

   Or if you have an existing document, move the toothpick cursor to the document's tippy-top: Press Ctrl+Home.

2. **From the Columns menu, choose Two.**

   You're done.

The entire document flows in two columns, or if you're starting out, you'll notice that text is organized in columns.

✔ To restore the document to one column, repeat the steps in this section, but in Step 2, choose One.

✔ You can make specific column adjustments in the Width and Spacing area of the Columns dialog box (refer to Figure 20-1).

✔ If you want an attractive line to appear between the columns of text, visit the Columns dialog box and put a check mark in the Line Between box. You may not, however, find the line between columns attractive.

✔ The space between columns is the *gutter.* Word sets the width of the gutter at 0.5" — half an inch. This amount of white space is pleasing to the eye without being too much of a good thing.

Building a trifold brochure

The three-column text format works nicely on paper in Landscape mode. This method is how most trifold brochures are created. Obey these steps:

1. **Start a new document, or work with an existing document — if you're so bold.**

2. **On the Page Layout tab, choose Landscape from the Orientation button.**

    The button is found in the Page Setup group.

3. **From the Columns button, choose Three.**

    Your trifold brochure is effectively formatted. Three columns are evenly spaced across the page.

4. **Optionally, visit the Columns dialog box to adjust the columns' width and spacing.**

    This step works best when you have text in your document.

Refer to Chapter 13 for information on Landscape mode.

Mixing column formats in a document

Your whole document doesn't have to sport just one column format. You can split things up so that part of the document is in one column and another part is in two columns and then maybe another part goes back to only one column. The secret is to use the Columns dialog box (refer to Figure 20-1).

When you're choosing a new column format, be sure to select the Apply To drop-down list. When you choose Whole Document, the format applies to the entire document. If you choose This Point Forward, the new columns start at the insertion pointer's location.

Choosing This Point Forward inserts a continuous section break into your document. So the real solution to mixing column formats is to read about sections in Chapter 14 and then divide your document into sections and apply the column formats accordingly.

Column Termination

You can stop the multicolumn format in one of several ways. For a newspaper column, the newspaper can go under. For a Doric, Ionic, and Corinthian column, your civilization can collapse. For a column of text, however, Word offers a number of tricks, none of which involves bankruptcy or revolution.

Giving up and going back to one column

The easiest way to undo a multicolumn document is to return it to a single column. It's cinchy: From the Columns button on the Page Layout tab, choose the item One. It restores your document to single-column mode, which is how Word naturally creates documents.

When that doesn't work, summon the Columns dialog box (refer to Figure 20-1) and choose One from the list of presets. Ensure that Whole Document is chosen from the Apply To menu and then click the OK button. The columns are gone.

> ✔ In Word, you don't "remove" column formatting as much as you choose the standard column format, One.
>
> ✔ Removing columns from a document doesn't remove sections or section breaks. See Chapter 14 for more information on deleting section breaks.

Ending multiple columns in the middle of a document

Say that you're using multiple columns in a document when suddenly, and for good reason, you decide to switch back to single-column format. Here's how:

1. **Place the insertion pointer wherever you want your columns to stop.**

2. **Summon the Columns dialog box.**

   Directions are offered earlier in this chapter.

3. **In the Columns dialog box, choose One from the Presets area.**

4. **From the Apply To drop-down list, select This Point Forward.**

5. **Click OK.**

   The columns stop, and regular, one-column text is restored.

When you work these steps, you place a continuous section break into your document. The multicolumn format is applied to the previous section, and the single ("One") column format is applied after the section break.

A continuous section break doesn't contain a page break; the new column format can pick up in the middle of a page. Refer to Chapter 14 to bone up on section breaks.

Placing a column break

When you want to continue using columns but want the text you're writing to start at the top of the next column, you need a *column break*. Figure 20-2 illustrates what I'm talking about.

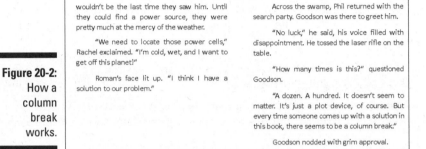

Figure 20-2:
How a
column
break
works.

wouldn't be the last time they saw him. Until they could find a power source, they were pretty much at the mercy of the weather.

"We need to locate those power cells," Rachel exclaimed. "I'm cold, wet, and I want to get off this planet!"

Roman's face lit up. "I think I have a solution to our problem."

Across the swamp, Phil returned with the search party. Goodson was there to greet him.

"No luck," he said, his voice filled with disappointment. He tossed the laser rifle on the table.

"How many times is this?" questioned Goodson.

"A dozen. A hundred. It doesn't seem to matter. It's just a plot device, of course. But every time someone comes up with a solution in this book, there seems to be a column break."

Goodson nodded with grim approval.

To create such a thing, heed these steps:

1. **Place the insertion pointer where you want your text to start at the top of the next column.**

   For example, you might place it at the beginning of the word *across* in Figure 20-2.

2. **On the Page Layout tab, in the Page Setup group, choose Breaks⇨Column.**

   The text hops to the top of the next column.

Column breaks don't end columns; they merely split a column, ending text at a certain point on a page and starting the rest of the text at the top of the next column.

Use the Show/Hide command in the Home group (the Paragraph Mark button) to know where exactly to place the column break. You might want to insert the column break *after* a paragraph mark (¶) to have the columns line up at the top of the page.

Chapter 21

Lots of Lists

A variety of information can lurk in your documents — stuff that I refer to as *lists*. Here's my list of these lists: lists of items noted with bullets (asterisks or dots) and lists of items that are numbered. You can also consider a table of contents as a list, a list of document headings. A list of keywords in your document is an index. And don't forget academic lists, such as footnotes and endnotes. All these lists are listed here, in this chapter of lists.

Lists with Bullets and Numbers

Whenever you have more than two items to describe in your document, consider creating a list. To draw attention to such a list, to call it out from the rest of your text, you can try hanging indents, make the first few words **bold**, or take advantage of the Word bullets and line numbering features, covered in this section.

Making a bulleted list

In typesetting, a *bullet* is merely a graphical element, such as a ball or a dot, used to highlight items in a list. The word *bullet* comes from the French word *boulette,* which has more to do with food than with round pieces of lead quickly exiting a firearm, like this:

- Bang!
- Bang!
- Bang!

To apply bullets to your text, highlight the paragraphs you want to shoot and choose the Bullets command button, found in the Home tab's Paragraph group. Instantly, your text is not only formatted with bullets but also indented and made all neat and tidy.

TIP

✔ You can choose a different bullet style by clicking the menu button next to the Bullets command. Choose your new bullet graphic from the list that appears, or use the Define New Bullet command to dream up your own bullet style.

✔ Because the bullet is a paragraph format, it *sticks* to the paragraphs you type. To halt the bullets, click the Bullet command button again and they're removed from the paragraph format.

✔ Bullets can also be applied by using Word's AutoFormat ability. See Chapter 17.

Numbering a list

When a list contains items that are in a certain order or that need to be referenced elsewhere, you can apply numbers or letters or another type of sequential marking. To make it happen, select the paragraphs as a block and choose the Numbering command button from the Paragraph group on the Home tab.

When you click the button, each paragraph is numbered. You can use the Numbering command button's menu to choose another sequential format, such as letters or Roman numerals, or choose a specific numbering style. Or when none of the predefined formats in the menu pleases you, choose Define New Number Format to create your own numbered list.

✔ List Numbering is a paragraph format. It sticks with every successive paragraph you type until you turn off numbering.

✔ To remove numbers, simply click the Numbering button again. This action removes numbering from the paragraph format.

✔ You can also choose the None command from the Numbering button's menu to remove numbering from one or more paragraphs.

TECHNICAL STUFF

✔ You can break and resume paragraph numbering, but it's tricky: Try to apply the numbering as you type paragraphs. Simply press the Backspace key to disable automatic paragraph numbering. To resume numbering, click the Numbering command button again, and the paragraph numbering should continue from where it left off.

Creating a multilevel numbered list

 The Multilevel List button, found in the Paragraph group on the Home tab, is used to number a multileveled list, consisting of sublevels and indents, as shown in Figure 21-1. It's a tricky type of list to create, so pay attention!

> **North Diamond Mosquito Abatement Board By-Laws**
> 1. Purpose.
>   a. We exist to abate mosquitos.
> 2. Board composition.
>   a. The board shall consist of seven (7) members.
>   i. Two members shall be at large.
>   ii. Five members shall be elected by district.
>   b. Members shall be elected every year.
>   c. The term of each member shall be 3 years.
>   d. No mosquitoes are allowed to be members.
> 3. Duties

Figure 21-1:
A multilevel
list.

You can create a multilevel list from scratch, or you can apply the format to a selected block of text. The secret is to use the Tab and Shift+Tab keys at the start of the paragraph to shuffle the paragraphs higher and lower in the multilevel list hierarchy. It works like this:

- ✔ Press the Tab key at the start of a paragraph to indent that paragraph to a deeper level in the multilevel list format.

- ✔ Press the Shift+Tab key combination at the start of a paragraph to unindent a paragraph to a higher level in the multilevel list format.

- ✔ Press the Enter key twice to end the list.

- ✔ Also see Chapter 25 for information about Word's Outline mode.

Numbering lines on a page

Word lets you slap down numbers for every line on a page, which is a feature that's popular with those in the legal profession as well as with folks who write radio scripts. It was also a feature that many former WordPerfect users demanded in Word. Here's how it goes:

1. **Click the Page Layout tab.**

2. **In the Page Setup group, click the Line Numbers command button to display its menu.**

3. **Choose a numbering format from the menu.**

The continuous option numbers all the lines in your document, from first to last. The Restart Each Page option simply numbers a page from line 1 through the last line.

To remove the line numbers, choose None from the Line Numbers command button.

Lists of Document Contents

Word sports a References tab that contains groups of commands you can use to build custom lists in your documents. This section covers the two most common list-making tricks: the table of contents and the index.

Creating a table of contents

One helpful example of how computers can save you time — and I'm not kidding — is to let Word create a table of contents (TOC) from your document. No, there's no need to manually type a TOC. As long as you use the built-in heading styles, Word can slap down a custom TOC in your document as easily as following these steps:

1. **Create a separate page for the TOC.**

   Word places the TOC at the insertion pointer's location, though I prefer to have the thing on its own page. Refer to Chapter 13 for information on creating new pages; a new, blank page near the start of your document is ideal for a TOC.

2. **Click the mouse to place the insertion pointer on the new, blank page.**

   The TOC is inserted at that point.

3. **Click the References tab.**

4. **In the Table of Contents group, click the Table of Contents button.**

   The Table of Contents menu appears.

5. **Choose an item from the menu based on what you want the table of contents to look like.**

   And there's your TOC, page numbers and all.

You may have to scroll up to see the table of contents. You may also want to add a title above the TOC — something clever, such as *Table of Contents*.

✔ When the steps in this section don't produce the effect you intended, it usually means that your document headings aren't formatted with the Heading styles.

✔ Cool people in publishing refer to a table of contents as a *TOC,* usually pronounced "tee-o-see" (or "tock").

✔ Things change. To update the TOC, click once to select it. Then Click the Update Table button on the References tab. Use the Update Table of Contents dialog box to choose what to update. Click OK.

✔ Word bases the TOC on text formatted with the Heading styles in your document. As long as you use Heading 1 for main heads, Heading 2 for subheads, and Heading 3 (and so on) for lower-level heads and titles, the TOC is spot-on. Or you can use your own heading styles, if you format them with a specific outline level. See Chapter 15 for more information.

✔ The table of contents exists as a *field* in your document. See Chapter 23 for more information about fields.

Building an index

An *index* is a reference list like a table of contents, but with more detail and at the opposite end of the document. Also, the index is organized by topic or keyword, as opposed to the organizational description a table of contents offers.

Creating an index in Word is a two-step process. The first step is to identify the words or phrases in a document that need to be indexed. The second part involves using those references to automatically build the index for you. The following sections explain the details.

All indexing actions and commands take place under the realm of the References tab, in the Index group.

Select text for the index

To flag a bit of text for inclusion in the index, follow these steps:

1. **Select the text you want to reference in the index.**

   The text can be a word or phrase or any old bit of text. Mark that text as a block.

2. **In the Index group on the References tab, click the Mark Entry button.**

   The Mark Index Entry dialog box appears. The text you selected in your document appears in the Main Entry box.

3. **Type a subentry in the Mark Index Entry dialog box (optional).**

The subentry further clarifies the main entry. The subentry is especially useful when the main entry is a broad topic.

4. **Click *either* the Mark button or the Mark All button.**

Use the Mark button when you want to mark only instances that you think will most benefit the reader. Use the Mark All button to seek out and flag all instances of the text in your document, to create an index entry for every single one.

When you mark an index entry, Word activates the Show/Hide command, where characters such as spaces, paragraph marks, and tabs appear in your document. Don't let it freak you out. Step 7 tells you how to turn that thing off.

Because Show/Hide is on, you see Index code in the document after you mark an index item. It looks something like this: {·XE·"pustule"·}

5. **Continue scrolling your document and looking for stuff to put into the index.**

The Mark Index Entry dialog box stays open, allowing you to continue to create your index: Simply select text in the document and then click the Mark Index Entry dialog box. The selected text appears in the Main Entry box. Click the Mark or Mark All button to continue building the index.

6. **Click the Close button when you're done.**

The Mark Index Entry dialog box disappears.

7. **Press Ctrl+Shift+8 to cancel the Show/Hide command.**

Use the 8 key on the keyboard, not on the numeric keypad.

Create the index

After marking bits and pieces of text for inclusion in the index, the next step is to create the index. Do this:

1. **Position the insertion pointer where you want the index to appear.**

If you want the index to start on a new page, create a new page in Word (see Chapter 13). I also recommend putting the index at the *end* of your document, which is what the reader expects.

2. **Choose the Insert Index button from the Index group on the References tab.**

The Index dialog box appears. Here are my recommendations:

- The Print Preview window is misleading. It shows how your index will look but doesn't use your actual index contents.

- Use the Formats drop-down list to select a style for your index. Just about any choice from this list is better than the From Template example.

- The Columns setting tells Word how many columns wide to make the index. Note that two columns is the standard, though I usually choose one column, which looks better on the page, especially for shorter documents.

- I prefer to use the Right Align Page Numbers option.

3. **Click the OK button to insert the index into your document.**

Review your index. Do it now. Press Ctrl+Z to undo if you dislike the layout; start over with the steps in this section. Otherwise, you're done.

Obviously, the index needs to be updated when you go back and change your document. To update a document's index, click the mouse on the index. Then choose the Update Index command button from the Index group. Instantly, Word updates the index to reference any new page numbers and include new marked index entries.

- ✔ Feel free to add a heading for the index because Word doesn't do it for you.

- ✔ Word places the index into its own document section by using continuous section breaks. Refer to Chapter 14 for more information on sections.

Footnotes and Endnotes

The difference between a footnote and an endnote is that one appears on the same page as the reference and the other appears at the end of the document. Content-wise, a footnote contains bonus information, a clarification, or an aside, and an endnote is a reference or citation. That's just a guess.

In both cases, the footnote or endnote is flagged by a superscripted number or letter in the text[1]. And both are created in the same manner, like this:

[1]See? It works!

1. **Click the mouse so that the insertion pointer is immediately to the right of the text that you want the footnote or endnote to reference.**

2. **Click the References tab.**

3. **From the Footnotes group, choose either the Insert Footnote or Insert Endnote command button.**

    A number is superscripted to the text, and you're instantly whisked to the bottom of the page (footnote) or the end of the document (endnote), where you type the footnote or endnote.

4. Type the footnote or endnote.

There's no need to type the note's number; it's done for you automatically.

Here are some nonfootnote endnote notes:

- ✓ The keyboard shortcut for inserting a footnote is Alt+Ctrl+F.

- ✓ The keyboard shortcut for inserting an endnote is Atl+Ctrl+D.

- ✓ The footnote and endnote numbers are updated automatically so that all footnotes and endnotes are sequential in your document.

- ✓ Use the Next Footnote button's menu to browse between footnote and endnote references in your document; the Next Footnote button is found in the Footnotes group on the References tab on the Ribbon.

- ✓ You can see a footnote or endnote's contents by pointing the mouse at the superscripted number in the document's text.

- ✓ Use the Show Notes button (Footnotes group, References tab) to help you examine footnotes or endnotes themselves. That same button can also be used to hop back to the footnote/endnote reference in your text.

- ✓ To delete a footnote or endnote, highlight its reference number in your document and press the Delete key. Word magically renumbers any remaining footnotes or endnotes.

- ✓ To convert a footnote to an endnote, right-click on the footnote itself. Choose the command Convert to Endnote. Likewise, you can convert endnotes to footnotes by right-clicking on the endnote text and choosing the command Convert to Footnote.

- ✓ For additional control over the footnotes and endnotes, click the dialog box launcher button in the Footnotes group. Use the Footnote and Endnote dialog box to customize the reference text location, format, starting number, and other options.

Chapter 22

Here Come the Graphics

*1*f you want your document to have pictures, you may believe that you can write a thousand words and they will suffice. But believe me, doing such a thing would be more effort than it's worth. That's because Word easily lets you slap down images and pictures and even draw and edit graphics right there amidst the plain old boring text in your document. This chapter explains how it works.

✔ Word lets you use graphics from any other graphics program you have in Windows. Use those other programs to create and refine an image, save the image using that program, and then put it into Word as described in this chapter.

✔ The more images you add in Word, the more sluggish it becomes. My advice: Write first. Add graphics last. Save often.

Graphical Goobers in Your Text

When you feel the urge, when your text is just plain lonely, or when you want to push Word's abilities to the wall, you can stick a graphical goober into your document. This section highlights what you can do with graphics in Word.

✔ The different types of goobers are found on the Insert tab, in the Illustrations group.

✔ You can also copy any image from another program in Windows and paste the image into Word by using the Paste button found in the Clipboard group on the Home tab — or just press Ctrl+V.

✔ The easiest type of image to paste is one that's found on the Internet. Right-click the image on a web page, all while dutifully remaining aware of various copyright laws around the world, and choose the Copy Image (or similar) command from the pop-up menu. Then you can paste the image into your document: Press Ctrl+V.

✔ Images are placed *inline* with your text, which means that they appear wherever the insertion pointer is blinking. You can, however, lay out the image in a variety of ways inside your document. Refer to the directions in the section "Images in and around Your Text," later in this chapter.

Plopping down a picture

The most common type of graphical goober you stick into a document is a picture. Assuming that the image exists and you know where to find it on your computer, you can follow these steps to plop the image into your document:

1. **Click the mouse wherever you want to place the image in your document, or at an approximate spot.**

   You can always move the image later; the job for now is to get the image into the document.

2. **From the Insert tab's Illustrations group, click the Pictures button.**

3. **Use the Insert Picture dialog box controls to browse for the image you want.**

4. **Click to select the image.**

5. **Click the Insert button.**

   The image is slapped down into your document.

Figure 22-1 illustrates how the image looks, highlighting some of the features you can use to adjust the image.

Rotation handle   Layout Options button

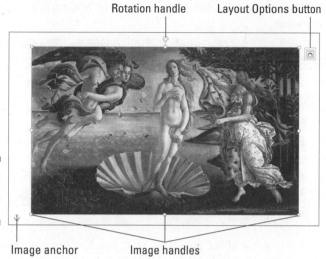

Figure 22-1:
An image in
a document.

Image anchor   Image handles

The controls highlighted in Figure 22-1 are necessary because working with graphics in Word involves more steps than simply inserting pictures into a document. See the section "Image Editing," later in this chapter.

✔ After you insert a picture, or anytime an image is selected, the Picture Tools Format tab appears on the Ribbon. Later sections in this chapter explain how to use the tools found on that tab.

✔ Word recognizes and understands nearly all popular graphics file formats. The one format it doesn't understand is probably the one you need the most.

✔ A cool thing to stick at the end of a letter is your signature. Use a desktop scanner to digitize your John Hancock. Save your signature as an image file on your computer, and then follow the preceding steps to insert the signature in the proper place in your document.

Inserting clip art

Clip art is a collection of images, both line art and pictures, that you're free to use in your documents. Inserting a clip art image works much like inserting a graphics image (see the preceding section), except that the clip art is organized. You can search for an image by name or category. Here's how it goes:

1. **On the Insert tab, in the Illustrations group, click the Online Pictures button.**

   The Insert Pictures window appears.

2. **In the text box by the option Office.com Clip Art, type a description of what you want.**

   For example, a picture of a politician may go well with your report on misbehaving in public. Type **politician** in the box.

3. **Press the Enter key.**

   Peruse the results that are displayed. You may have to scroll a bit to see all of them.

4. **Click the image you want, or refine your search by repeating Steps 2 and 3.**

5. **Click the Insert button.**

   The image is downloaded from the Internet and thrust into your document, looking similar to Figure 22-1.

Word sticks the clip art graphic into your text, just like it's a big character, right where the insertion pointer is blinking. At this point, you probably want to move the image, resize it, or do other things. Later sections in this chapter explain the details.

   ✔ Apparently, the clips are free to use; I don't see anything saying otherwise. But, then again. . . .

   ✔ The problem with clip art is that it's inanely common. That means the image you choose will doubtless be used by someone else, which gives clip art an air of unoriginality.

Slapping down a shape

Word comes with a library of common shapes ready to insert into your document. Graphics professionals call the shapes *line art*. You can call forth line art into your document by following these steps:

1. **Choose a predefined shape from the Shapes button menu, found in the Illustrations group on the Insert tab.**

   After you choose a shape, the mouse pointer changes to a plus sign (+).

2. **Drag the mouse in the document to wherever you want the shape to appear.**

   Drag down, from the upper-left corner of the shape to the lower right. The shape appears at the location where you draw it, at a size determined by how you drag the mouse. Some shapes may require you to click the mouse two or three times to draw a line or create a curve.

The shape you insert floats over your text, hiding your document. To fix it, you use one of Word's text wrapping tools. See the section "Wrapping text around an image," later in this chapter. Also see the later section, "Grouping images," for combining simple shapes into more-complex graphics.

Control the shape's colors and look by using the Format tab's Shape Styles group. Here are some things you can do:

- To set the shape's color style, click the Theme Fill button. The theme's colors are set when you choose a document theme, as described in Chapter 16.

- Choose the Shape Fill button to determine which color to use for the shape's interior.

- The Shape Outline button sets the color for the line that defines the shape.

- Set the shape's line thickness by choosing the Weight submenu from the Shape Outline button's menu.

- To stick a picture into the shape, effectively making it a picture frame, click the Shape Fill button and choose Picture from the menu. Use the Select Picture dialog box to hunt down an image to place into the shape.

Adding some WordArt

Perhaps the most overused graphic that's stuck into any Word document is WordArt. It's quite popular. If you haven't used it yourself, you've probably seen it in a thousand documents, fliers, and international treaties. Here's how it works:

1. **On the Insert tab, in the Text group, click the WordArt button to display the WordArt menu.**

2. **Choose a style from the gallery for your WordArt.**

   A WordArt graphic placeholder appears in your document.

3. **Type the (short and sweet) text that you want WordArt-ified.**

Your bit of text appears as an image in your document. Yes, even though it's text, it's also a graphical element and can be edited and changed as described elsewhere in this chapter.

Including a caption

Some graphics are used as text decorations, other graphics are extensions of your text. To best reference such an image, you should add a caption. The caption's text can identify the image with boring text ("Figure 1"), or it can explain what's in the image ("John touches the plant that he swore to us was not poison sumac").

To add a caption to an image, heed these steps:

1. **Click to select the graphic.**

2. **From the References tab's Captions group, click the Insert Caption button.**

   The Captions dialog box appears.

3. **In the Caption text box, type the figure caption text.**

   Windows supplies the figure number in the form of the text, Figure 1. You cannot remove that reference, but you can place a check mark in the Exclude Label From Caption box to shrink it down to just a number.

4. **Choose a position for the caption from the Position drop-down list.**

   The caption position is relative to the figure.

5. **Click the OK button.**

   The caption is applied to the figure.

The caption itself is a special type of text box, which resembles a graphical image but contains text. It's not grouped with the image, so if you move or resize the image, you have to move or resize the caption box as well. To avoid that, you can group the two items. See the later section, "Grouping images."

✔ See Chapter 23 for more information on text boxes.

✔ You can change the caption at any time simply by clicking the mouse in the caption text box and typing a new caption.

✔ Captions are removed like any other graphic in your document; see the next section.

✔ An advantage to applying captions this way is that you can create a list of captions or figures for your document, summarizing them all along with their page references. To do so, use the Insert Table of Figures button, found in the References tab's Captions group.

Deleting an image or some artwork

Getting rid of artwork in a document isn't the same as removing text. Graphics are special. The proper way to delete them is to click the image once to select it. Then press the Delete key. Poof — it's gone.

Images in and around Your Text

You can place graphics into your document in three different ways:

- ✔ **Inline:** The graphic works like a large, single character sitting in the middle of your text. The graphic stays with the text, so you can press Enter to place it on a line by itself or press Tab to indent the image, for example.

- ✔ **Wrapped:** Text flows around the graphic, avoiding the image like all the girls at a high school dance avoid the guys from the chess club.

- ✔ **Floating:** The image appears behind the text as though it's part of the paper, or the image slaps down on top of the text like some bureaucratic tax stamp.

 Each of these ways to place an image features various options, which help you create the look you want. The options are found by clicking the image to select it and then clicking the Layout Options button, as shown in the margin (refer to Figure 22-1). This section describes some of the popular choices.

Wrapping text around an image

The most common way to place an image in your text is to wrap the text around the image. Heed these steps to create an image in your document with text wrapping:

1. **Place the image into your document.**

    Refer to earlier sections in this chapter. At this point, the specific image placement doesn't matter.

2. **Click the image so that its handles and various options appear, shown earlier, in Figure 22-1.**

3. **Click the Layout Options button.**

    Word features four options in the text wrapping area that deal specifically with keeping text away from the image: Square, Tight, Through, and Top and Bottom. Refer to Table 22-1 for specifics.

4. **Choose a text wrapping option.**

Examine your image and the text to see whether it wraps the way you like. If it doesn't, repeat these steps and choose another setting in Step 3.

 To remove text wrapping, choose the In Line with Text option from Step 3.

Table 22-1		Image Layout Options
Icon	*Setting*	*What It Does*
	Square	The image sits on the same plane as the text, but the text flows around the image in a square pattern, regardless of the image's shape.
	Tight	Text flows around the image and hugs its shape.
	Through	Text flows around the image as best it can, similar to the Tight option.
	Top and Bottom	Text stops at the top of the image and continues below the image.
	Behind Text	The image floats behind the text, looking almost like the image is part of the paper.
	In Front of Text	The image floats on top of your text, like a photograph dropped on the paper.

Floating an image

When you want an image to be placed in your document independently of the text, you float the image, either behind the text or in front of the text. It's cinchy: Follow the steps from the preceding section, but choose either the Behind Text or In Front of Text option.

After choosing either Behind Text or In Front of Text, you see the image released from the confines of the text. The image floats freely, either behind or in front of your text. You can drag the image anywhere to position it.

Moving an image hither and thither

You can lug around graphics in a document as easily as you move text. Consider the graphic as a block, or a single large character, and simply drag it by using the mouse: As you point the mouse at the image, it changes to a four-way arrow, as shown in the margin. At that point, you can drag the image nigh and yon.

How the graphic sits with your text (covered in the preceding section) determines where and how you can move it. When an image floats behind your text, you may need to "open up" a spot so that you can grab the image. To do so, press the Enter key a few times by the image or on the same line. After moving the image, delete the extra blank paragraphs created by pressing the Enter key.

Try not to point the mouse at one of the image's handles and drag (refer to Figure 22-1.) When you do, you end up resizing the image rather than moving it.

Attaching an image to some text

Some images need to move with the text, and other images need to stay at a specific spot on the page to make things look right. You can choose which way you want your images placed and switch between those ways at any time.

To unattach an image from text, select the image and click the Layout Options button. Choose the setting Fix Position on Page. The image becomes stuck on the page at that position, with the text moving up or down around it as you edit.

To attach an image to text, choose the command Move with Text from the Layout Options button menu. The image moves up and down the page as you write and edit.

✔ To keep an image associated with a specific chunk of text, use the Anchor icon, as shown in the margin. Drag the icon by the paragraph that references the image. That way, if the paragraph moves to another page, the image moves with it.

✔ Choose the Behind Text or In Front of Text layout setting when you attempt to keep an image on a specific page, unattached to any text.

Image Editing

I hope you follow my earlier advice in this chapter and prepare your images before you slap them down in Word. That's because Word lets you work with graphics, even though it's not a graphics program. Still, Word offers some touch-up features for dealing with a document's illustrations. This section offers some suggestions.

- ✔ Use Word's Undo command, Ctrl+Z, to undo any image editing boo-boos.
- ✔ When you're using a document theme, theme effects are automatically applied to any graphic that's inserted into your document. Refer to Chapter 16 for more information on themes.

Resizing an image

To change an image's size on the page, heed these steps:

1. **Click to select the image.**

   The image grows handles, shown earlier, in Figure 22-1.

2. **Use the mouse to drag one of the image's four corner handles inward or outward to make the image smaller or larger.**

   If you press and hold the Shift key as you drag the mouse, the image is proportionally resized.

You can use the buttons in the Format tab's Size area to nudge the image size vertically or horizontally or to type specific values for the image's size.

Cropping an image

In graphics lingo, *cropping* works like taking a pair of scissors to the image: You make the image smaller, but by doing so, you eliminate some content, just as an angry, sullen teen would use shears to remove his cheating scumbag former girlfriend from a prom picture. Figure 22-2 shows an example.

To crop, click the image once to select it, and then click the Crop button in the Format tab's Size group. You're now in Cropping mode, which works much like resizing an image: Drag a cropping handle inward, which slices off a side or two from the image.

Figure 22-2:
Cropping an
image.

I use the outside (left, right, top, or bottom) handles to crop. The corner handles never crop quite the way I want them to.

To finish cropping, click the Crop command button again.

Rotating an image

You have two handy ways to rotate an image, neither of which involves turning the computer's monitor or craning your neck to the point of chiropractic necessity.

To freely rotate an image, use the mouse to grab the rotation handle at the top of the image. (Refer to Figure 22-1.) Drag the mouse to twist the image to any angle.

 For more precise rotation, use the Rotate menu found in the Format tab's Arrange group. From the menu, you can choose to rotate the image 90 degrees to the left or right or to flip the image horizontally or vertically.

Changing an image's appearance

Pictures can be manipulated by using the tools found in the Adjust group on the Picture Tools Format tab. Only a few tools are available, but the good news is that each tool's button shows a menu full of options previewing how the image will be affected. To make the change, simply choose an option from the appropriate button's menu. Here are some suggestions:

✔ Brightness and contrast settings are made from the Corrections button menu.

✔ To wash out a picture you placed behind your text, choose the Washout color from the Recolor area of the Color button's menu.

✔ To convert a color image to monochrome ("black and white"), choose the first item, Saturation 0%, from the Color Saturation list on the Color button's menu.

✔ A slew of interesting, artistic brush strokes and other effects are found on the aptly named Artistic Effects button menu.

Image Organization

When things grow complicated with your document's graphics, you enter the realm of image organization. Multiple images often require positioning, aligning, arranging, and grouping into a unit. It's not a complex thing, but rather a timesaver that you can employ. This section covers the details.

✔ All commands referenced in this section are found on the Format toolbar, in the Arrange group. Obviously, the graphical image(s) must be selected for that toolbar to appear.

✔ To select multiple images, press and hold the Shift key as you click each image.

Lining up your graphics

One way to help organize and lay out multiple images on a page is to show the grid: Choose the View Gridlines command from the Align button's menu. Instantly, the page turns into graph paper, to assist you in positioning your graphics and text, similar to what you see in Figure 22-3.

When you find the grid annoying, you can disable gridlines: Choose the View Gridlines command from the Align button's menu again. But you can also employ the Alignment Guides feature. It's also found on the Align button's menu.

With the Alignment Guides option on, a lime green line appears as you drag an image close to the page margins, or when the image is aligned with the top or bottom edge of another graphic on the page. Use that green line to more precisely position the image.

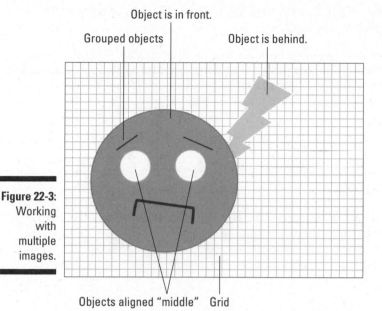

Object is in front.

Grouped objects

Object is behind.

Figure 22-3:
Working
with
multiple
images.

Objects aligned "middle"   Grid

Arranging multiple images

New images are plunked down on a page one atop the other. You don't notice this arrangement unless two images overlap (refer to Figure 22-3). When you're displeased with the overlapping, you can change the order of an image by selecting it and using the Bring to Front and Send to Back buttons in the Format tab's Arrange group.

 To help you keep multiple images lined up, use the Align button's menu. After selecting multiple images, choose an alignment option. For example, in Figure 22-3, using the Align Middle command sets the eyeballs on the face image. Further, the Align Selected Objects option was chosen from the menu to ensure that the objects align with each other and not with the edge of the page or the paragraph's margins.

✔ To align objects to the page's edge, choose the option Align to Page from the Align menu. With this setting on, images can be aligned with the page's edge by using the Align menu.

 ✔ To line up a caption box below an image, ensure that the setting Align Selected Objects is chosen from the Align menu. Start by selecting both the image and its caption and then choose the Align Center option. You might also want to group the image and its caption, as discussed in the next section.

✔ The Distribute Horizontally and Distribute Vertically commands on the Align menu can help you evenly space out a row or column of images.

Grouping images

When you cobble together a complex image using smaller pieces, or when you arrange shapes or pictures — or an image and its caption — keep those items together. That way, you can move them as a single unit, copy and paste, or apply image effects. The trick is to group the separate items into a single object.

 To group images in your document, select the images and then choose the Group command from the Group Objects menu. The images are then treated as a unit, such as the face shown in Figure 23-3, which is a collection of individual Word shapes.

To ungroup, click on the grouped images and then choose the Ungroup command from the Group Objects menu.

Chapter 23

Fun with the Insert Tab

- -

- -

*I*f inserting weird and wonderful things into a document weren't a vital part of using Word, the program wouldn't sport the Insert tab on the Ribbon. Further, the Insert tab is the second tab over, next to the preeminent Home tab. The Insert tab isn't over at the far-right end, down there with the oddball Review and View tabs. Verily, inserting stuff into your document is a worthwhile endeavor.

Characters Fun and Funky

The computer's keyboard lets you type all 26 letters of the alphabet — plus, numbers 1 through 9 and 0, a smattering of symbols, and punctuation thingies. That's a lot to type, and some authors spend their entire lives weaving those characters into a tapestry of text heretofore unseen in literary history. As if that weren't enough, you can sprinkle even more characters into your document, spicing it up like garlic in a salad. Foreign language letters, symbols — all sorts of fun stuff is covered in this section.

Nonbreaking spaces and hyphens

Two unique characters in a document are the space and the hyphen. These characters are special because Word uses either of them to wrap a line of text: The space splits a line between two words, and the hyphen (using hyphenation) splits a line between a word's syllables.

Sometimes, however, you don't want a line to be split by a space or a hyphen. For example, splitting a phone number is bad — you want the phone number to stay intact. And you may desire to have two words that are separated by a space to be stuck together like glue. For those times, you need *unbreakable* characters.

- ✔ To prevent the hyphen character from breaking a line, press Ctrl+Shift+- (hyphen).
- ✔ To prevent the space character from breaking a line, press Ctrl+Shift+spacebar.

In either case, a nonbreaking character is inserted into the text. Word doesn't break a line of text when you use one of these special characters.

The only way to discern whether your document has a nonbreaking space or hyphen is to use the Show/Hide command on the Home tab. (It's the ¶ symbol button.) The code for a nonbreaking hyphen is a box with a tiny question mark in it. The code for a nonbreaking space is the degree symbol.

Typing characters such as Ü, Ç, and Ñ

You can be boring and type *deja vu* or be all fancy and type *déjà vu* or *café* or *résumé*. Your readers will think that you know your stuff, but what you really know is how to use Word's diacritical prefix keys.

Diacritical symbols appear over certain letters in foreign languages and in foreign words borrowed (stolen, really) into English. To create a diacritical in Word, you press a special Control-key combination. The key combination you press somewhat represents the diacritical you need, such as Ctrl+' to produce the ' diacritical. The Ctrl-key combination is followed by the character that needs the new "hat," as shown in Table 23-1.

Table 23-1	Those Pesky Foreign Language Characters
Prefix Key	**Characters Produced**
Ctrl+'	á é í ó ú
Ctrl+`	à è ì ò ù
Ctrl+,	ç
Ctrl+@	å
Ctrl+:	ä ë ï ö ü
Ctrl+^	â ê î ô û
Ctrl+~	ã õ ñ
Ctrl+/	ø

For example, to insert an é into your document, press Ctrl+' and then type the letter *E*. Uppercase *E* gives you É, and lowercase *e* gives you é. It makes sense because the ' (apostrophe) is essentially the character you're adding to the vowel.

Be sure to note the difference between the apostrophe (or *tick*) and back tick, or *accent grave.* The apostrophe (') is next to your keyboard's Enter key. The back tick (`) is below the Esc key.

For the Ctrl+@, Ctrl+:, Ctrl+^, and Ctrl+~ key combinations, you also need to press the Shift key, which is required anyway to produce the @, :, ^, or ~ symbols that are on your keyboard. Therefore, Ctrl+~ is really Ctrl+Shift+`. Keep that in mind.

Word's AutoCorrect feature has been trained to know some special characters. For example, when you're typing *café,* Word automatically sticks that whoopty-doop over the *e.*

Inserting special characters and symbols

The Symbol menu is nestled in the Symbols group on the Insert tab. Clicking the Symbol command button lists some popular or recently used symbols. Choosing a symbol from the menu inserts the special symbol directly into your text.

Choosing More Symbols from the Symbol menu displays the Symbol dialog box, as shown in Figure 23-1. Choose a decorative font, such as Wingdings, from the Font menu to see strange and unusual characters. To see the gamut of what's possible with normal text, choose (normal text) from the Font drop-down list. Use the Subset drop-down list to see even more symbols and such.

To stick a character into your document from the Symbol dialog box, select the symbol and click the Insert button.

You need to click the Cancel button when you're done using the Symbol dialog box.

- ✔ Click the Insert button once for each symbol you want to insert. When you're putting three Σ (sigma) symbols into your document, you must locate that symbol on the grid and then click the Insert button three times.

- ✔ Some symbols have shortcut keys. They appear at the bottom of the Symbol dialog box (refer to Figure 23-1). For example, the shortcut for the degree symbol (°) is Ctrl+@, spacebar — press Ctrl+@ (actually, Ctrl+Shift+2) and then type a space. Doing so gives you the degree symbol.

✔ You can insert symbols by typing the symbol's character code and then pressing the Alt+X key combination. For example, the character code for Σ (sigma) is 2211: Type **2211** in your document and then press Alt+X. The number 2211 is magically transformed into the Σ character.

Highlighted symbol

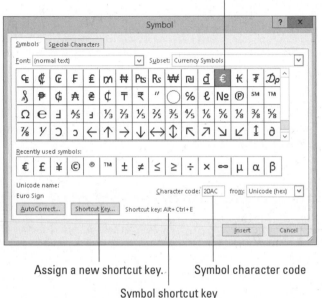

Figure 23-1: The Symbol dialog box.

Assign a new shortcut key.

Symbol shortcut key

Symbol character code

Spice Up Your Document with a Text Box

A *text box* is a graphical element that contains — hold your breath, wait for it, wait — *text*. The text can be used as a decorative element (as a *pull quote*) to highlight a passage of text on the page, or it can be simply an information box or an aside, such as those that litter the pages of *USA Today*. The primary purpose of the text box is to prevent your document from becoming what graphic designers refer to as the dreaded Great Wall of Text.

Text boxes are easily shoved into a document by following these steps:

1. **Click the Insert tab.**

2. **In the Text group, choose Text Box.**

3. **Choose a preformatted text box from the list.**

   The text box is splashed onto the current page in your document.

4. **Rewrite the text in the box.**

   La-di-da.

The Drawing Tools Format tab appears whenever a text box is ready for editing on the screen. The tab hosts a hoard of text box formatting and style commands. Most of them are similar, if not identical to, the formatting commands used on images and graphics in Word. Indeed, text boxes are basically graphical elements, just like images and pictures. Refer to Chapter 22 for details, hints, and tips.

✐ If you prefer to create your own text boxes, choose the Draw Text Box command from the Text Box menu (refer to Step 2). Drag the mouse to create a text box at a specific location and size. The text box appears empty, ready for you to type something.

✐ Text in a text box can be formatted the same as any text outside the box.

✐ It's common to copy and paste text from the document into the box, which is how pull quotes work.

✐ Turn text sideways inside the text box by using the Text Direction button. Look in the Text group on the Text Box Tools Format tab.

✐ To delete a text box, click it with the mouse and press the Delete button on the keyboard.

✐ You can create a text box of any shape by inserting that shape into your document, right-clicking the shape, and then choosing the Add Text command from the pop-up menu. See Chapter 22 for more information on shapes.

Fields of Dreams

The phrase "carved in stone" refers to text that doesn't change. What you write in Word isn't carved in stone — well, unless you have a cool printer I've not heard of. Still, the text you scribble remains the same until you change it or until the computer screws up.

To liven things up a bit, Word has a way to let you add *dynamic* (changing) elements to your document. Unlike the text you normally compose, dynamic text changes to reflect a number of factors. These dynamic elements are added to a document by using *fields*. This section discusses these ever-changing tidbits of text.

Understanding fields

To take advantage of fields, you use the Field dialog box, as shown in Figure 23-2. To summon this dialog box, click the Insert tab, and then choose Explore Quick Parts⇨Field. The Explore Quick Parts button is found in the Text group.

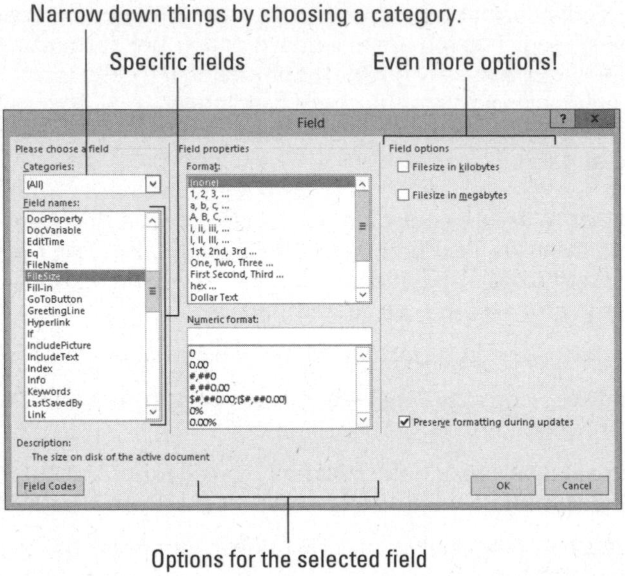

Narrow down things by choosing a category.

Specific fields

Even more options!

Figure 23-2:
The Field
dialog box.

Options for the selected field

The left side of the Field dialog box contains scrolling lists of categories in the Field Names list. These categories represent various dynamic scraps of text you can insert into your document. When you choose a category, the right side of the dialog box changes to show more detailed options.

After you click the OK button, the field is inserted into your document. It looks like regular text, but it's not: The field reflects some changing aspect of the document or other conditions, like the date and time.

✔ Many other commands in Word insert fields into a document, such as the Page Number commands, discussed in Chapter 13, or the table of contents and index, covered in Chapter 21. The Field dialog box, however, lists them all.

✔ Your best clue that you have a field and not text comes when you try to delete a field. See the later section, "Deleting fields."

Updating a field

Just because a field contains dynamic text doesn't mean that the field is always accurate. Occasionally, fields need updating. It happens in two ways: First, you can update a field by closing your document and opening it again; second, and more conveniently, you can manually update a field.

To ensure that a field displays up-to-date information, right-click it and choose the Update Field command. The field's text is refreshed.

The mystery of content controls

Word's fields aren't the only gizmos you can stick into a document that contains dynamic text. Another gizmo is the content control. It's not really a field, though it can be inserted as though it's a field and then updated. The primary difference is how a content control looks, which is something like this:

Content controls are usually inserted by Word commands, such as those that automatically create headers or footers or insert page numbers. You can also choose the Quick Parts⇨Document Property command (found in the Insert tab's Text group) to insert a property control. The Equation menu, found in the Insert tab's Symbols group, also inserts content controls.

You can edit a content control's contents, if you like, and some controls are designed that way. But editing the text in other controls changes the thing to plain text, so be careful.

Time-sensitive content controls can be updated by pressing the F9 key.

Some Date content controls have a pick-the-date button, displaying a tiny calendar from which you can set the property's date.

If you're unsure which text in your document is a field, click the mouse on that text. Fields are highlighted in Word with a dark gray background.

Changing a field

You cannot edit text in a field, which kind of ruins the point of the field. Instead, you can adjust the field's contents: Right-click the field and choose Edit Field from the pop-up menu. The Field dialog box is redisplayed, allowing you to make whatever modifications you deem necessary.

Just as those mutants at the end of *Beneath the Planet of the Apes* removed their human masks, you can remove a field's mask by right-clicking it and choosing the Toggle Field Codes command. For example, the FileSize field looks like this:

```
{ FILESIZE \* MERGEFORMAT }
```

To restore the field to human-readable form, right-click it again and choose the Toggle Field Codes command. All praise be to the bomb.

Deleting fields

Removing a field works almost like deleting text. The main difference is that you have to press the Delete or Backspace key twice. For example, when you press Backspace to erase a field, the entire field becomes highlighted. It's your clue that you're about to erase a field, not regular text. Press Backspace again to erase the field (and its text).

Putting various fields in a document

Of all the zillions of fields you can insert and use in Word, you might use only a smattering. This section covers some of my favorites. It assumes that the Field dialog box (refer to Figure 23-2) is open and ready for business as you start working the steps.

Page numbers

My favorite fields are page number fields. To ensure that the document accurately reflects the current page number, insert a current page number field:

1. **In the Field dialog box, select Numbering from the Categories drop-down list.**

2. **Select Page from the Field Names list.**

3. **In the Field Properties section of the Field dialog box, select a format for the page number.**

4. **Click OK.**

The current page number dynamically appears in your document. Of course, the page number can also land in a header or footer or anywhere else.

Total number of pages

To insert the total number of pages in your document, heed these directions:

1. **Select Document Information from the Categories drop-down list.**

2. **Select NumPages from the Field Names list.**

3. **Select a format.**

4. **Click OK.**

Word count

Getting paid by the word? Stick an automatic word count at the end of your document:

1. **From the Categories list, select Document Information.**

2. **Select NumWords from the Field Names list.**

3. **Click OK.**

Document filename

Many organizations place the document's filename into a document header or footer. Rather than guess, why not use a field that contains the document's exact name? Do this:

1. **From the Categories list, select Document Information.**

2. **Select FileName from the Field Names list.**

3. **In the field properties, choose the format (text case).**

4. **Optionally (though recommended), put a check mark by the option Add Path to Filename.**

5. **Click OK.**

The FileName field is updated even when you change the filename; the field always reflects the file's name. It's an advantage of using fields over typing static text.

If filenames are to be part of a document's header or footer, consider adding the FileName field to the template that creates the document. See Chapters 14 and 16.

The Date and Time

Here's a tip: With few exceptions, time travelers are the only ones who bother asking for the current year. Otherwise, you probably have people who want to know the current date and time, or maybe you simply want to insert the date or time, or both, into your document. Word has many tricks for making it happen.

Adding the current date or time

Aside from looking at a calendar and typing a date, you can use the Date and Time button (shown in the margin), found in the Text group on the Insert tab. Click the button to display a dialog box from which you can choose how to insert the current date or time into your document.

✔ Click the Update Automatically option in the dialog box so that the date-and-time text is always current.

✔ The keyboard shortcut for the current date is Alt+Shift+D. This command inserts a content control into your document to display the current date.

✔ The keyboard shortcut for inserting the current time is Alt+Shift+T. Unlike the current date, this shortcut inserts a field, not a content control, into your document.

✔ See the sidebar "The mystery of content controls," earlier in this chapter, for information on content controls.

Using the PrintDate field

One of the date fields I use most often is PrintDate. This field reflects the current date (and time, if you like) that a document is printed. Here's how it's done:

1. **Summon the Field dialog box.**

   Directions are found earlier in this chapter.

2. **Select Date and Time from the Categories drop-down list.**

3. **Select PrintDate from the Field Names list.**

4. **Choose a date-and-time format from the Field Properties area.**

5. **Click OK.**

The field looks gross until you print the document, which makes sense.

I like to put the PrintDate field into the header of important documents, which lets people know the date the thing was printed. PrintDate works well for that purpose; the other fields in the Date and Time category are updated only when you manually refresh them.

Part V
The Rest of Word

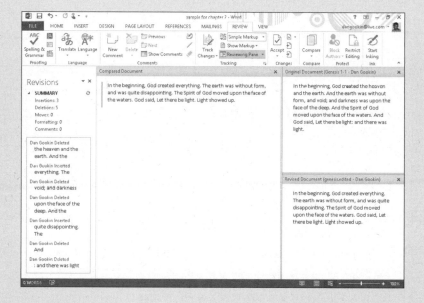

Discover how to add new tabs and commands to the Ribbon at www. dummies.com/extras/word2013.

In this part . . .

- ✔ Find out how to work with multiple Word 2013 documents at one time.

- ✔ Learn all you need to know about working with outlines and the thesaurus in Word 2013

- ✔ Get familiar with how to insert comments in your documents and how to use Word 2013's track changes feature.

- ✔ Find out how to use mail merge in Word 2013.

- ✔ Learn about how to use and print labels.

- ✔ Discover how to add new tabs and commands to the Ribbon at www.dummies.com/extras/word2013.

Chapter 24

Multiple Documents, Windows, and File Formats

*W*ord is flexible. If Word were a person, I'm sure it could bend over and touch its toes, lick the end of its nose, and possibly even stick its own elbow into its ear — all at once. You never get to see that (thankfully), but you can see how Word is flexible when it comes to playing with documents: Word can open and display multiple documents, work with a single document in multiple windows, and even toy with multiple document formats.

Multiple Document Mania

You need not limit your word processor usage to toiling with a single document in a single window. Oh, no! You can open multiple documents, you can work on the lot, you can even split a document in a window or open a single document in two or more windows. It's not impossible. It's not insane. It's covered in this section.

Opening several documents at once

It's not a question of whether Word can work on more than one document at a time. No, it's a question of how you open those documents. Let me count the ways:

- ✔ **Just keep using the Open command to open documents.** (See Chapter 8.) No official limit exists on the number of documents Word can have open, though I would avoid having too many open (more than ten or so), because they slow down your computer.

- ✔ **In the Open dialog box, select multiple documents to open.** Press and hold the Ctrl key as you click to select documents. Click the Open button, and all the documents open, each in its own window.

- ✔ **From any folder window, select multiple Word document icons.** Lasso them with the mouse, or Ctrl+click to select multiple documents. Press the Enter key to open the lot.

See the next section for information on how to handle multiple document windows.

Switching between multiple documents

Each document dwells in its own Word program window. One way to switch between them is to use the Switch Windows menu on the View tab. The menu lists as many as nine open documents in Word: To switch to another document, choose it from the menu.

When more than nine documents are open at a time, the last item on the Switch Windows menu is the More Windows command. Choosing this item displays the Activate dialog box, which lists *all* open document windows. Select a document from the window and click OK to switch to it.

Watch out for any document in the list named Document1, Document2, or similar. Such a name means that you haven't yet saved your stuff. *Do so now!* Refer to Chapter 8.

Viewing more than one document at a time

To see two or more documents displayed on the screen at the same time, select the View tab and click the Arrange All button. Immediately, Word organizes all its windows, by placing them on the screen like the pieces of a jigsaw puzzle.

✔ Using the Arrange All command is fine for a few documents, but for too many, you end up with a useless mess.

✔ Word doesn't arrange minimized windows.

✔ Yes, the Ribbon disappears when the document window gets too small.

✔ Although you can see more than one document at a time, you can *work* on only one at a time. The document with the highlighted title bar is the one "on top."

✔ Clicking a window's Maximize button restores the document to its normal, full-screen view.

Comparing two documents side by side

A quick and handy way to review two documents is to arrange them side by side in two windows and lock their scrolling so that you can peruse both at one time. Here's how to accomplish this trick:

1. **Open both documents.**

2. **On the View tab, in the Window group, click the View Side by Side button.**

   Word instantly arranges both documents in vertical windows, with the current document on the left and the other on the right.

3. **Scroll either document.**

   Scrolling one document also scrolls the other. In this mode, you can compare two different or similar documents.

   You can disable synchronous scrolling by clicking the Synchronous Scrolling button, found in the Window group.

4. **When you're done, choose View Side by Side again.**

Refer to Chapter 26, which tells how to detect changes made to a document.

Viewing the same document in multiple windows

A handy document-viewing trick — especially long documents — is to open a single document in two windows. This trick makes writing and editing easier than hopping back and forth within the same document window and potentially losing your place.

To open a second window on a single document, click the View tab. In the Window group, click the New Window button. A second window opens, showing the current document. You can confirm that the same document is in two windows by checking the window's title bar: The first window's filename is followed by :1, and the second window's filename is followed by :2.

When you no longer need the second window, simply close it. You can close either window :1 or :2; it doesn't matter. Closing the second window merely removes that view. The document is still open and available for editing in the other window.

- Even though two windows are open, you're still working on only one document. The changes you make in one window are updated in the second.

- This feature is useful for cutting and pasting text or graphics between sections of a long document.

- You can even open a third window by choosing the New Window command again.

Using the old split-screen trick

Splitting the screen allows you to view two parts of your document in the same window. No need to bother with extra windows here: The top part of the window shows one part of the document; the bottom part, another. Each half of the screen scrolls individually, so you can peruse different parts of the same document without switching windows.

To split a window, click the Split button. It's found on the View tab, in the Window area. The current document is then split into two views. Each part can be scrolled individually so that you can peruse or edit different parts of the document in the same window.

To undo the split, double-click it with the mouse. Poof! It's gone.

- When the ruler is visible, a second ruler appears just below the split.
- You can move the split up or down by dragging it with the mouse.

Many, Many Document Types

Word doesn't restrict you to working with only its own documents. You can work with just about any type of available word processing or text document. This feature allows you to read and edit non-Word documents as well as share your stuff with others.

Understanding document formats

When you save a document, Word not only places the document's text into a file but also stores other information: formatting, graphics, page layout — everything. To keep it all organized, Word uses a specific *file format* for your document. It's the Word file format that makes a Word document unique and different from other types of files you may store on the computer's hard drive.

The Word document format is popular, but it's not the only word processing document format available. Other word processors (believe it or not) use their own formats. Plus, some common file formats exist, designed to simplify the sharing of documents between incompatible computers. Yes, Word accepts these formats and allows you to save your documents in those formats, if you want.

The key to opening or saving a document in one file format or another is to use the file type drop-down list in the Open or Save As dialog box, respectively. This list specifies which file format Word uses, for either opening a file or saving a file under a format other than the standard Word document format.

- The file type list in the Open dialog box has no name. Instead, it appears as a button menu, found just to the right of the File Name text box. Choosing a file type from that list directs the Open dialog box to not only display those specific file types but also open them properly for editing in Word.

- In the Save As dialog box, the drop-down list is named Save As Type. It lists file formats you can use to save your document in addition to Word's own Word Document file type. Even so:

- The best way to save a file in another format is to use the Export command, discussed in Chapter 9.

- Basic document opening and saving information is found in Chapter 8.

- Later sections explain how to use the file type menus.

- The standard Word document format is named DOCX, after the filename extension Word applies to documents you save. The older Word document format was the DOC format, used by Word versions 2003 and earlier.

Opening a non-Word document

Word can magically open and display a host of weird, non-Word documents. Here's how it works:

1. **Press the Ctrl+O key combination to summon the Open screen.**

2. **Choose Computer.**

   Or you can choose SkyDrive to hunt down files shared on the Internet.

3. **Click the Browse button to bring forth the Open dialog box.**

4. **Choose a file format from the menu button.**

   The menu button has no label, though it might say *All Word Documents*, as shown in Figure 24-1.

Figure 24-1:
Change file types in the Open dialog box.

File type menu

By choosing a specific file format, you direct Word to narrow the number of files displayed in the Open dialog box. Only files matching the specific file format are shown.

If you don't know the format, choose All Files from the drop-down list. Word then makes its best guess.

5. **Choose the file from the list.**

   Or work the controls in the dialog box to find another storage media or folder that contains the file. Chapter 8 explains in detail how it works.

6. **Click the Open button.**

   The alien file appears onscreen, ready for editing, just like any other Word document.

Well, the document may not be perfect. It may not even open. But be prepared to fix things or do some tidying up. Word tries its best.

✔ For some document types, Word may display a special file-conversion dialog box that lets you preview the document. Generally speaking, clicking the OK button in this step is your best bet.

✔ The Recover Text from Any File option is useful for peering into unknown file formats, especially from antique and obscure word processing file formats.

✔ Word *remembers* the file type! When you use the Open dialog box again, the same file type is already chosen from the Files of Type drop-down list. That means your regular Word document may be opened as a "plain text" document, which looks truly ugly. Remember to check the Files of Type drop-down list if such a thing happens to you.

✔ Accordingly, when you want to open a Word document after opening an HTML document, or especially by using the Recover Text from Any File option, you *must* choose Word Documents from the list. Otherwise, Word may open documents in a manner that seems strange to you.

✔ Don't blame yourself when Word cannot open a document. Many, many file formats are unknown to Word. When someone is sending you this type of document, ask them to resend it using a common file format, such as HTML or RTF.

Updating an older Word document

Microsoft Word has been around for a long, long time. In 2007, Word changed the file format used for its documents, moving from the older DOC file format to the present DOCX format. Because a lot of people still use older versions of Word, not to mention the abundance of older DOC files out there, it becomes necessary to work with and convert those older documents.

Working with an older Word (DOC) document is cinchy: Simply open the document. You see the text [Compatibility Mode] appear after the filename at the top of the window. This text is a big clue that you're using an older Word document. Another clue is that a lot of Word's features, such as the ability to preview format changes and document themes, don't work when you're editing an older document.

To update an older document, use the Export command. After opening an older Word document, follow these steps to convert it:

1. **Click the File tab.**

2. **On the File screen, choose Export.**

3. **Click the Change File Type option.**

4. **Choose Document from the list of Document File Types.**

   It's the first item on the list.

5. **Click the Save As button.**

   This button is found at the bottom of the screen. (You may have to scroll down to see it.)

6. **Click the Save button in the Save As dialog box to update the document.**

   Or you can work the controls in the Save As dialog box to rename the document or save it in a different location.

7. **Click the OK button after not reading the warning.**

   The file is updated.

Though the document has been updated and saved in the newer Word DOCX format, the older document still exists. You have to obliterate it by using Windows file management commands if you truly want to be done with it.

 ✔ To save a document using the older Word (DOC) file format, refer to Chapter 9.

 ✔ Word 2013, Word 2010, and Word 2007 all use the same document format; their files are compatible.

Chapter 25

Word for Writers

The word processor is the best tool for writers since the ghostwriter. Seriously, I don't need to explain to anyone the horrors of using a typewriter. The mere dawn of the word processor, back in the primitive, steam-powered era of computing, was a welcome relief. Heck, I remember being overjoyed at being able to backspace and erase text, ecstatic at the concept of word wrap, and floored by the miracle of on-the-fly spell checking.

Writing words in a word processor doesn't make you a writer any more than working with numbers in a spreadsheet makes you a mathematical genius. Even so, beyond its basic word processing abilities, Word comes with an armada of tools for making a writer's job easier. Whether you're writing your first guest piece for the church newsletter or crafting your 74th horror-thriller, you'll enjoy Word's features for writers.

Organize Your Thoughts

All writers I know use an outline to organize their thoughts. In the old days, you put the outline on a stack of 3-by-5 cards. Today, you put it on a computer, which is far easier to use and will never get mixed in with grandma's recipes.

Word's Outline feature allows you to group ideas or plot elements in a hierarchical fashion. You can then shuffle topics around, make subtopics, and toss around notions and concepts to help get your thoughts organized. Even if you're not a writer, you can use Word's Outline mode to create lists, work on projects, or look busy when the boss comes around.

Entering Outline view

An outline in Word is just like any other document. The only difference is in how Word displays the text. To enter Outline view, click the Outline button found on the View tab, in the Views group. Word's window changes, growing an Outlining tab and changing to Outline view, as shown in Figure 25-1.

Move topic.

Set topic level.

Open/Close topic.   Set which levels appear.

Outlining tab   Exit Outline View.

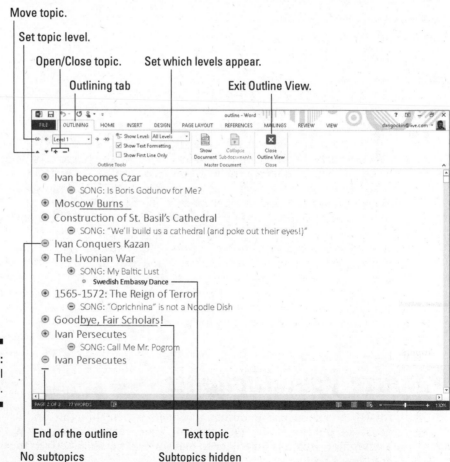

Figure 25-1:
A typical
outline.

End of the outline   Text topic

No subtopics   Subtopics hidden

Outlining details are covered in the next few sections. In the meantime, I offer some general tidbits:

- ✔ To leave Outline view, you can choose another document view, such as Print Layout, or simply click the big, honkin' Close Outline View button on the Ribbon's Outlining tab.

- ✔ That thick, short, horizontal line marks the end of your outline. The line also appears in Draft view, where it also marks the end of a document. The bar doesn't go away, so don't try to delete it.

- ✔ All basic Word commands work in Outline view. You can use the cursor keys, delete text, check spelling, save, insert oddball characters, print, and so on. Don't worry about formatting the text.

- ✔ Word uses the Heading 1 through Heading 9 styles for your outline. Main topics are formatted in Heading 1, subtopics in Heading 2, and so on.

- ✔ The Body, or Normal, style is used in an outline for making notes and such. See the section "Adding a text topic," later in this chapter.

Typing topics in the outline

Outlines are composed of topics and subtopics. *Topics* are your main ideas, with *subtopics* describing the details. You should start your outline by adding the main topics. To do so, just type them out.

In Figure 25-2, you see several topics typed out, each on a line by itself. Each topic, as well as any subtopics, sports a gray circle. The circle acts as a handle for the topic; you can use the circle to expand or collapse the topic as well as move it around. Later sections in this chapter explain the details.

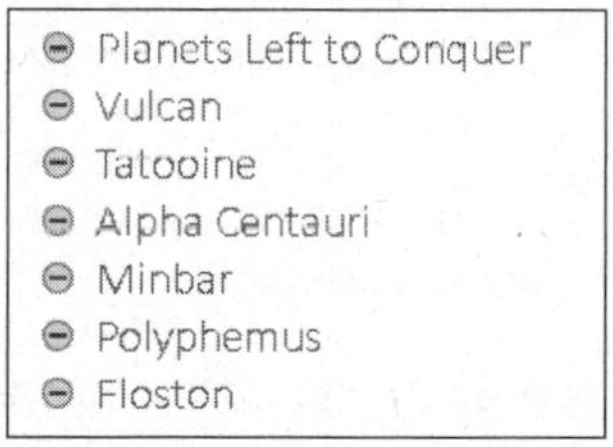

Figure 25-2:
Level 1
topics.

- ⊖ Planets Left to Conquer
- ⊖ Vulcan
- ⊖ Tatooine
- ⊖ Alpha Centauri
- ⊖ Minbar
- ⊖ Polyphemus
- ⊖ Floston

- ✔ Press Enter at the end of each topic. This creates another topic at the same *level* as the first topic.

- ✔ See the next section for information on creating a subtopic.

- ✔ Main topics should be short and descriptive, as in a book's table of contents.

- ✔ Word automatically selects the Heading 1 style for main-level topics.

- ✔ Use the Enter key to split a topic. For example, to split the topic Pots and Pans, first delete the word *and,* and then with the insertion pointer placed between the two words, press the Enter key.

- ✔ To join two topics, put the insertion pointer at the end of the first topic and press the Delete key. (This method works just like joining two paragraphs in a regular document.)

- ✔ It doesn't matter whether you get the order right at first. The beauty of creating your outline with a word processor is that you can rearrange topics as your ideas solidify. My advice is just to start writing things down now and concentrate on organization later.

Demoting a topic (creating subtopics)

Outlines have several levels. Beneath topics are subtopics, and those subtopics can have their own subtopics. For example, your main topic may be Things I Regret, and the subtopics would be what those things actually are.

To create a subtopic, simply type at the main topic level, but don't press Enter when you're done. Instead, click the Demote command button, found in the Outlining tab's Outline Tools group and shown in the margin.

The keyboard shortcut to demote a topic is Alt+Shift+→.

Demoting a topic has these effects in Outline mode:

- ✔ The topic is shifted one notch to the right in the outline.

- ✔ The paragraph style changes to the next-highest-numbered heading style, such as from Heading 1 to Heading 2.

- ✔ The Level item in the Outline Tools group changes to reflect the new topic level.

- ✔ The parent topic's circle grows a plus-sign (+) symbol. It's the sign that subtopics exist or that the topic can be expanded.

You can continue creating subtopics by typing them and then pressing the Enter key at the end of each subtopic. Word keeps giving you subtopics, one for each press of the Enter key.

- ✔ You don't really *create* subtopics in Word as much as you *demote* main topics.

- ✔ You can also use the Level drop-down list, found on the Outlining tab, to instantly promote or demote the topic to any specific level in the outline.

✔ Unlike when you're creating main topics, you can get a little wordy with your subtopics. After all, the idea here is to expand on the main topic.

✔ According to Those Who Know Such Things, there must be at least two subtopics for them to qualify as subtopics. When you have only one subtopic, either you have a second main topic or you've created a text topic. See the later section, "Adding a text topic," for information.

Promoting a topic

To convert a subtopic into a higher-level topic, you promote it. For example, as you work on a subtopic, it grows powerful enough to be its own, main-level topic. If so, promote it:

✔ To promote a subtopic, place the insertion pointer in the topic's text and click the Outlining tab's Promote command button. You can also press Alt+Shift+← on the keyboard.

✔ You can also drag the topic's circle with the mouse; move one notch left to promote.

✔ Promoting a topic changes its heading style.

✔ To instantly make any topic a main-level topic, click the Promote to Heading 1 button.

Adding a text topic

When you feel the need to break out and actually write a paragraph in your outline, you can do so. Although it's perfectly legit to write the paragraph on the topic level, what you should do is stick in a text topic by using the Demote to Body Text button. Here's how:

1. **Press the Enter key to start a new topic.**

2. **Click the Demote to Body Text button.**

    Or you can press Ctrl+Shift+N, the keyboard shortcut for the Normal style.

What these steps do is change the text style to Body Text. Changing the text style to Body Text in your outline allows you to write a bit of text for your speech, some instructions in a list, or a chunk of dialogue from your novel.

The joy of collapsible headers

One benefit of using Word's header styles is that you can work with any document as an outline without entering Outline view. Word displays tiny triangle buttons by a heading-style paragraph. You can click that button to expand or collapse the heading and all its contents — including any subheadings.

The main difference between viewing a document as an outline and using the heading-style triangle buttons is that only the Outlining tab gives you the commands to collapse all headings or show only a certain heading level. That's fine, because any document can be viewed in Outline view.

Rearranging topics

The beauty of creating an outline on a computer is that you can not only promote and demote topics but also shuffle them around and reorganize them as your thought process becomes more organized. To move a topic, click the mouse so that the insertion pointer is blinking inside that topic. Then choose one of these techniques to rearrange it:

   ✔ Click the Move Up button (or press Alt+Shift+↑) to move a topic up a line.

   ✔ Click the Move Down button (or press Alt+Shift+↓) to move a topic down a line.

The mouse can also lug topics around. The secret is to drag the topic by its circle. When the mouse is positioned just right, the mouse pointer changes to a four-way arrow (see the margin). I recommend using this trick only when you're moving topics around a short distance; dragging with the mouse beyond the current screen can prove unwieldy.

Subtopics are moved with a topic only when the topic is collapsed. When the topic is expanded (open), then only that line is moved.

Expanding and contracting topics

Unless you tell Word otherwise, it displays all topics in your outline, from top to bottom — everything. That's fine for the details, but as your outline grows, you may want to see only part of the picture — perhaps a grand overview of only the main topics or only Level 2 topics. That's done by expanding and contracting portions of the outline.

A topic with subtopics has a plus sign in its circle. To collapse the topic and temporarily hide its subtopics, click the Collapse button or press Alt+Shift+_ (underline). You can also double-click the plus sign with the mouse to collapse a topic.

To expand a collapsed topic, click the Expand button or press Alt+Shift++ (plus sign). Again, you can also click the plus sign with the mouse to expand a collapsed topic.

Rather than expand and collapse topics all over, you can view your outline at any level by choosing that level from the Show Level drop-down list. For example, choose Level 2 from the list so that only Level 1 and Level 2 topics are displayed; Levels 3 and higher are hidden.

- ✔ When a topic is collapsed and it has subtopics, you see a fuzzy line extend over the last part of the topic text (refer to Figure 25-1).
- ✔ To see the entire outline, choose Show All Levels from the Show Level drop-down list on the Outlining tab.
- ✔ If you have wordy topic levels, you can direct Word to display only the first topic line by clicking to put a check mark by the Show First Line Only option, found on the Outlining tab in the Outline Tools group.

Printing an outline

Printing an outline works just like printing any other document in Word. But because it's an outline, there's one difference: Only the topics that are visible in the outline are printed.

For example, if you want to print only the first two levels of your outline, choose Level 2 from the Show Level drop-down list. To print the entire outline, choose All Levels from the Show Level drop-down list. Whatever option is chosen determines how many levels are printed.

- ✔ The outline isn't printed with indents, though it's printed using the heading styles of each topic level.
- ✔ See Chapter 9 for more information on printing documents in Word.

The outline shortcut-key summary box

I like using shortcut keys whenever possible. You may be the same way, in which case you'll enjoy using the following keyboard shortcuts when you're dealing with an outline:

Key Combo	What It Does
Alt+Shift+→	Demotes a topic
Alt+Shift+←	Promotes a topic
Alt+Shift+↑	Shifts a topic up one line
Alt+Shift+↓	Shifts a topic down one line
Ctrl+Shift+N	Inserts or demotes a topic to body text
Alt+Shift+1	Displays only top topics
Alt+Shift+2	Displays first- and second-level topics
Alt+Shift+#	Displays all topics up to a number you specify
Alt+Shift+A	Displays all topics
Alt+Shift++ (plus sign)	Displays all subtopics in the current topic
Alt+Shift+_ (underline)	Hides all subtopics in the current topic

Novels and Other Large Documents

The first novel I wrote (and never published, of course) was several hundred pages long. It was saved as a single document. That length works because Word documents can be *any* length, but putting everything into one document that way is impractical. Moving around the document takes forever, and rearranging text is cumbersome.

A better solution for long documents is to keep each chapter, or large chunk, as its own file. You can then take advantage of Word's Master Document feature to put everything together when it comes time to print or publish.

✔ The *master document* stitches together all individual documents, or subdocuments, even continuing page numbers, headers, footers, and other ongoing elements. The end result is a large document that you can print or publish.

✔ What qualifies as a large document? Anything over 100 pages qualifies, as far as I'm concerned.

✔ When writing a novel, create each chapter as its own document. Keep all those chapter documents in their own folder. Further, use document filenames to help with organization. For example, I name chapters by using numbers: The first chapter is 01, the second is 02, and so on.

✔ This book is composed of 42 individual Word documents — one for each chapter, each part introduction, the front matter, the index, and so on.

Creating a master document

Word's Master Document feature allows you to collect and coordinate individual documents — called *subdocuments* — and cobble them all into one, large document. When you have a master document, you can assign continuous page numbers to your work, apply headers and footers throughout the entire project, and take advantage of Word's Table of Contents, Index, and other list-generating features.

To create a big, whopping document from many smaller documents — to create a *master* document — obey these steps:

1. **Start a new, blank document in Word.**

   Press Ctrl+N to quickly summon a new, blank document.

2. **Save the document.**

   Yeah, I know — you haven't yet written anything. Don't worry: By saving now, you get ahead of the game and avoid some weird error messages.

3. **Switch to Outline view.**

   Click the Outline button on the View tab, as described earlier in this chapter.

4. **On the Outlining tab in the Master Document group, click the Show Document button.**

   More choices appear in the Master Document group. One of those choices is the Insert button, used to build the master document.

5. **Click the Insert button.**

6. **Use the Insert Subdocument dialog box to hunt down the first document to insert into the master document.**

   The documents must be inserted in order. I hope you used a clever document-naming scheme, as recommended in the preceding section.

7. **Click the Open button to stick the document into the master document.**

   The document appears in the window, but it's ugly because Outline view is active. Don't worry: It won't be ugly when it prints! Word has set itself up for you to insert the next document:

If you're asked a question about conflicting styles, click the Yes to All button. It keeps all subdocument styles consistent with the master document.

8. **Repeat Steps 5 through 7 to build the master document.**

9. **Save the master document when you're done.**

At this point, the master document is created. You can edit the headers and footers, create a table of contents, and work on other items that affect the entire document.

✓ Ensure that you're completely done with the individual documents — the chapters in your novel or parts of a large report — before you move forward with the master document. Otherwise, creating the master document involves too much effort.

✓ When you're ready, you can publish the master document just as you publish any individual document. See Chapter 9 for information on publishing a document.

✓ Editing a document included in the master document automatically updates the master document. So, if you need to tidy up Chapter 3 in your novel, work on only that individual document. You don't need to worry about reinserting it into the master document.

✓ Use the Collapse Subdocuments button to instantly hide all subdocument text. This action makes it easier to build a table of contents or work on the master document's headers and footers.

✓ See Chapter 21 for more information on creating a table of contents and an index for your document.

Splitting a document

Splitting a document isn't a part of creating a master document, but it might be, if you mistakenly start out with a humongous document. To split any document into smaller documents, you basically have to cut and paste; no specific Word command splits a document.

Here's how to split a document:

1. **Select half the document — the portion you want to split into a new document.**

   Or if you're splitting a document into several pieces, select the first chunk that you want to plop into a new document.

   Split a document at a natural break within the document, such as at a new main header (Heading 1 style).

2. **Cut the selected block.**

I press Ctrl+X to cut the block.

3. Summon a new, blank document.

Ctrl+N does the trick.

4. Paste in the portion of the first document you cut in Step 2.

Press Ctrl+V to paste. If the text doesn't paste in with the proper formatting, click the Paste Options button and then choose Keep Source Formatting (shown in the margin).

5. Save both documents.

You now have two documents where you started with one.

Dan's Writing Tips

Nothing beats advice from someone who has been there and done that. As a professional writer, I'm excited to pass along my tips, tricks, and suggestions to any budding scrivener. That's why I wrote this section.

Finding the best word

When two words share the same meaning, they're said to be *synonyms* — for example, *big* and *large*. Synonyms are helpful in that they allow you to find better, more descriptive words and, especially, to avoid using the same tired old words over and over. Obviously, knowing synonyms is a handy skill for any writer.

To find the synonym of any word, right-click the word in your document. From the pop-up menu, choose the Synonyms submenu to see a list of words that have a similar meaning. Choosing a word from the menu replaces the word you right-clicked in your document.

✔ To see more alternatives than are displayed on the Synonyms submenu, choose the Thesaurus item. The Thesaurus pane opens up, listing lots of alternative words.

✔ The keyboard shortcut for opening the Thesaurus pane is Shift+F7.

✔ To insert a word from the Thesaurus pane, right-click the word and choose the Insert command.

✔ *Antonyms,* or words that mean the opposite of the selected word, might also appear on the Synonyms submenu.

✔ Not all words have synonyms. If so, the Synonyms submenu displays (No Suggestions). Oh, well.

Writing for writers

Here's a smattering of tips for any writer using Word:

- You'll notice that, thanks to AutoFormat, Word fixes ellipses for you. When you type three periods in a row, Word inserts the ellipsis character: . . . Don't correct it! Word is being proper. When you don't use the ellipsis character, be sure to separate the three periods with spaces.

- You can format paragraphs by separating them with a space or by indenting the first line of each paragraph. Use one or the other, not both.

- Keep the proper heading formats: Heading 1, Heading 2, and so on. Or create your own heading styles that properly use the Outline Level format. That way, you can easily create a table of contents as well as use other Word features that display headings in your documents.

- Use Outline mode to collect your thoughts. Keep filling in the outline and organizing your thoughts. When you find yourself writing text-level topics, you're ready to write.

- Use the soft return (Shift+Enter) to split text into single lines. I use the soft return to break up titles and write return addresses, and I use it at other times when text must appear one line at a time.

- Word is configured to select text one word at a time. This option isn't always best for writers, where it sometimes pays to select text by character, not by word. To fix that setting, from the File tab menu, choose Options. In the Options dialog box, click the Advanced item and then remove the check mark by the item When Selecting, Automatically Select Entire Word. Click OK.

- Refer to Chapter 21 for information on footnotes and endnotes, often required for serious documents.

Making every word count

You pay the butcher by the pound. The dairyman is paid by the gallon. Salesmen are paid by a percentage of their sales. Writers? They're paid by the word.

If you're lucky enough to be paid for your writing, you know that "word count" is king. Magazine editors demand articles based on word length. "I need 350 hilarious words on tech-support phone calls," an editor once told me. And novel writers typically boast about how many words are in their latest efforts. "My next book is 350,000 words," they say in stuffy, nasal voices. How do they know how many words they wrote?

The best way to see how many words dwell in your document is to view the status bar. The word count appears after the *Words* label, and the count is updated as you type.

ABC 123 When the status bar word count isn't enough for you or isn't visible, you can click the Review tab and then, from the Proofing group, click the Word Count button, as shown in the margin. The detailed Word Count dialog box appears, listing all sorts of word-counting trivia.

Click the Close button to banish the Word Count dialog box.

Also see Chapter 23 for information on inserting a Word Count field into your document.

Avoiding writer's block

I don't get writer's block. I don't even know what it is, though I can imagine. That's because I know the secret to getting rid of writer's block. As with all deep truths and wisdom, foolish people will scoff at this advice. They'll mock it. But the wise writer will understand the meaning and press on, to write more and more stuff.

The secret to getting rid of writer's block? *Lower your standards.* If you can't get the words on the page, you're shooting higher than you need to.

Don't think it's for a lack of talent that you have writer's block; it's merely that you haven't yet found how to exploit your talent at the level at which it works best. Therefore, lower your standards. You'll find that not only will you be more prolific but your stuff will read better as well.

It's all in your head, right?

Chapter 26

Let's Work This Out

*W*riting isn't considered a team sport, but it can be. Eventually, writers encounter collaboration, welcome or not. Often it comes in the form of an editor, but occasionally others chime in. To assist in that task, Word gives you some work-it-out-together tools. They help you share ideas, point out issues that need attention, and even see who has done exactly what to your precious text.

Comments on Your Text

How can you get comments into your text? I can think of two ways.

The silly way: You type a comment (something you don't intend to include in the final document) in ALL CAPS. Or you color the text red or blue. You add parentheses or square brackets around the text. These are all desperate acts.

The best way: You use Word's comment feature, as described in this section.

Adding a comment

To shove a comment into your document, follow these steps:

1. **Select the chunk of text on which you want to comment.**

   Be specific. Although you may be tempted to select the entire document, only the first few words of a longer chunk are necessary.

2. **On the Review tab, click the New Comment button in the Comments group.**

   Several things happen. First, a Comments box appears by the selected text, similar to the one shown in Figure 26-1. You also see a cartoon bubble (shown in the margin), which is a visual indication that a comment exists somewhere in the text.

Close comment.

Click to add a comment on the comment.

Original comment

Figure 26-1:
Comments
on a text
passage.

Comment on the comment.

3. **Type your comment.**

   Jot down your thoughts.

4. **Press the Esc key when you're done typing the comment.**

   You can also close the comment: Click its Close (X) button (refer to Figure 26-1). Or just click the mouse outside the Comments box.

The comments and the markup area stay visible until you hide them; hiding comments is covered in the next section.

✔ You cannot undo a comment. Comments can only be deleted, as covered later in this chapter.

✔ Even if you change your mind and don't write a comment, the comment stays. Its text is empty, but it's still a comment.

✔ Other readers and editors and various meddlers can comment on your comments, shown later, in Figure 26-2. Click the button shown in that figure to add a comment to the comment. Names appear by each comment so that you know whom to blame.

✔ You can edit the comments the same as you edit any text in Word.

Displaying comments

Normally Word uses the cartoon bubble, shown in the margin, as your clue that a comment exists in the text. When you point the mouse at text, it becomes highlighted, showing where the comment is. But when you're really curious about what was commented on and who said what, you can reveal all the comments at once. Follow these steps:

1. **Click the Review tab.**

2. **Click the Display for Review button menu.**

   The button is found in the Tracking group, and its icon is shown in the margin. The button's name depends on which Display for Review mode is chosen.

3. **Choose the All Markup command.**

The document changes its view again. Comments are highlighted in the text with a color specific to whoever made the comment. A dashed list extends beyond the right edge of the onscreen page, and you see comment text.

To restore the cartoon-bubble view, choose the Simple Markup command from the Display for Review button menu.

✔ Choose the No Markup command from the Display for Review button menu to hide all comments in your document.

✔ The Inking command switches the display to All Markup view. See the later section, "Marking with digital ink," for information on the Inking command.

✔ Word also has the Show Comments button, though clicking this button doesn't control whether comments are displayed as cartoon bubbles or full comments.

✔ Clicking the Next and Preview buttons to review your comments also switches the display to All Markup view. See the next section, which also covers using the Reviewing pane.

Reviewing comments

Peruse comments by using two commands in the Comments group:

Next   Choose the Next Comment button to jump to the next comment in the document.

Previous   Choose the Previous Comment button to jump to the previous comment in the document.

To see all comments in a document at one time, summon the Reviewing Pane button: Click the Reviewing Pane button, found in the Review tab's Tracking group, to show or hide the Reviewing pane. The button's menu sets whether the pane appears vertically or horizontally.

Close the Reviewing pane by clicking the Reviewing Pane button again, or click the X in the top-right corner.

- ✔ The Reviewing pane displays all comments in your document in a single list, as shown on the left (vertical) or bottom (horizontal) edge of the window.

- ✔ Click a comment in the Reviewing pane to instantly go to that location in your document.

Printing comments (or not)

I'll bet you were surprised! You went to print your document and, lo, there on the page was all your wonderful, formatted text — and all the silly comments. That's probably not what you wanted.

To control whether a document's comments appear when printed, follow these steps:

1. **Visit the Print screen.**

   The keyboard shortcut is Ctrl+P.

2. **Click the Print All Pages button to display what I call the "print what" menu.**

   At the bottom of the menu, you see a set of options, the first of which is Print Markup. This setting controls whether comments, as well as other text markup covered in this chapter, print with the rest of the document.

3. **Choose the Print Markup command.**

   When this command has a check mark by it, the comments print. When no check mark appears, you're directing Word not to print comments (and other types of text markup).

Use the Print Preview window to confirm whether comments will print.

4. Make any other settings in the Print window as needed.

5. Click the big Print button to print the document.

The change made by completing these steps isn't permanent. You must follow these steps every time you print the document or else the comments print as well.

See Chapter 9 for more information on printing documents in Word.

Deleting comments

To delete a comment, point at its highlighted text and click the right mouse button. Choose Delete Comment from the pop-up menu. That's the cinchy way.

You can also use the Delete button in the Comments group on the Review tab to remove the current comment. The Delete button is available only when the insertion pointer is blinking inside commented text.

To delete all comments from a document at one time, use the Delete button's menu: Choose Delete⇨Delete All Comments in Document.

Scribble, Scribble

Your eighth grade English teacher, Mrs. Hawkins, didn't use Word. No, she preferred a much more old-fashioned way of commenting on your text: the dreaded red pen. I once had a publisher instruct each of my books' editors to use a different colored pen when editing pages from my book. (And each was required to make at least four marks on every page.)

Those days of drawing comments on paper may be gone, but they're not entirely forgotten. Today, you can use digital ink to mark up a document. You can highlight text and you can digitally scribble on the page — just like Mrs. Hawkins and with equal vigor.

Whipping out the yellow highlighter

Word comes with a digital highlighter pen that lets you mark up and color-ize the text in your document without damaging your computer monitor. To highlight your text, abide by these steps:

1. **Click the Home tab.**

2. **Click the Text Highlight button in the Font group.**

   The mouse pointer changes to a — well, I don't know what it is, but the point is that Word is now in Highlighting mode.

3. **Drag the mouse over the text you want to highlight.**

   The text becomes highlighted — just like using a highlighter on regular paper, but far neater.

4. **Click the Text Highlight button again to return the mouse to normal operation.**

   Or press the Esc key to exit Highlighting mode.

The highlight doesn't necessarily need to be yellow. Clicking the menu button to the right of the Text Highlight button displays a palette of highlighter colors to choose from.

To remove highlighting from your text, you can highlight it again in the same color, which erases it. Or you can choose None as the highlight color and then drag the mouse over any color of highlighted text to remove the highlight.

- ✔ Highlighting isn't the background color. It is its own text format.

- ✔ You can also highlight a block of text by first marking the block and then clicking the Highlight button that appears on the Mini toolbar.

- ✔ The highlighted text prints, so be careful with it. If you don't have a color printer, highlighted text prints in black or gray on hard copy.

Marking with digital ink

When the urge to draw on a document hits you, or you have a touchscreen monitor or a Tablet PC with a digital stylus, you can whip out Word's ink tools: On the Review tab, click the Start Inking button. The document's view changes to All Markup (with comments to the right of the page), and the Ink Tools Pens tab appears.

Choose a pen from the Pens gallery and start drawing on the screen. The object you draw becomes a graphical thingie in your document, which is saved and even prints. You can draw with the mouse, or with your finger on a touchscreen monitor.

To switch back to text-editing mode, click the Stop Inking button on the Ink Tools Pens tab.

- ✔ To remove an ink — uh, *stain* — on the page, click the Eraser button and then click on the ink mark.

✔ Word treats the ink objects you draw just like they're images. You can wrap text around them, move them, rotate them, and so on. See Chapter 22 for details.

✔ If the Start Inking button is disabled (if you can't click it), click the mouse in your document's text.

✔ You may not have the ability to use the Start Inking button if your PC lacks a multitouch monitor or is running under Windows 7.

Look What They've Done to My Text, Ma

I'm elated when someone comments on my text. The feedback is good. But then, oftentimes, those so-called literary critics — nay, mortal enemies of the pen — descend upon the text with their viperous scissors and cruel word choices. Sometimes, those who change (they say "edit") text are vicious; their modifications are odiously obvious. At other times, the modifications are satanically subtle. Either way, it helps to employ Word's revision-tracking tools to know what truly is yours and what isn't.

Comparing two versions of a document

You have the original copy of your document — the stuff you wrote. You also have the copy that Barbara, the vixen from the legal department, has worked on for a week or so. Both documents have different names, of course. Your job is to compare them to see exactly what's been changed from the original. Here's what to do:

1. **Don't open the original document just yet.**

   If you already opened the original document in anticipation of what I was about to write here, go ahead and close the thing. Don't ever again let me catch you trying to guess my steps!

2. **Click the Review tab.**

3. **From the Compare group, choose Compare⇨Compare.**

   The Compare Documents dialog box shows up.

4. **Choose the original document from the Original Document drop-down list.**

5. **Choose the edited document from the Revised Document drop-down list.**

   In either case (in Step 4 or 5), when you cannot find the original or revised document, click the Wee Folder icon (shown in the margin) to browse for the documents you want to open.

6. **Click OK.**

Word compares the two documents and notes all changes. Then it displays a list of changes. You see the compared document with changes marked, plus the original and revised documents, laid out as shown in Figure 26-2.

If your screen doesn't look like Figure 26-2, click the Compare button again, and from its menu, choose Show Source Documents⇨Show Both.

Look it over! Peruse the changes made to your pristine prose by the barbarian interlopers; use the Reviewing pane to witness each change individually. You can click a change in the Reviewing pane to quickly see which part of your document was folded, spindled, or mutilated.

✔ It helps to use unique filenames for both documents. I strongly recommend that you choose filenames carefully. In fact, I name my originals by using the word *org* or *original,* as in `chapter1.org` or, often, `chapter1.dan`. The person reviewing your document should follow suit, appending their name or the word *edited* or *draft,* for example, to the end of the filename. This strategy helps keep straight the different versions of a document.

✔ Scrolling is synchronized between all three documents: original, edited, and compared.

Show/Hide Reviewing pane.

Click an X button to close a pane.

Original document

Compare button menu

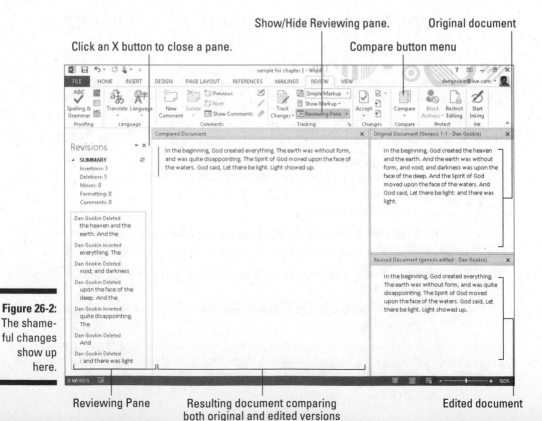

Figure 26-2:
The shameful changes show up here.

Reviewing Pane

Resulting document comparing both original and edited versions

Edited document

Tracking changes as you make them

Comparing documents after they're edited is the defensive way to locate changed text. A more friendly way to do things is simply to direct your editor to activate Word's revision-tracking feature. That way, changes are noted on the screen as they're made.

 Turn on Track Changes by clicking the Review tab and then clicking the Track Changes button. The keyboard shortcut is Ctrl+Shift+E.

After Track Changes is on, the Track Changes button becomes highlighted. As you type and edit, you see a red line appear in the left margin next to your text. This line indicates that you've made edits.

 To see the actual edits, you show all markups in the document: Click the Display for Review button menu and choose the All Markup command.

When All Markup view is active, edited text appears in a unique color. Deleted text appears with a line through it (strikeout). Added text appears underlined. The text color, strikethrough, and underline attributes are applied by Track Changes; they aren't text-formatting attributes.

Word continues to track changes and edits in your document until you turn off Track Changes. To do so, click the Track Changes button again.

 ✔ Seeing text unexpectedly colored, underlined, and so on, commonly frustrates Word users who are unfamiliar with revision tracking. When you're done using Track Changes, turn it off.

✔ The color of the markup text you see depends on who's marking up the text. On my screen, my own revisions appear in the cyan color. Marks from others appear in different colors, depending on who's edited the text.

 ✔ To hide the changes, choose the No Markup command from the Display for Review button menu. The changes are still being tracked, though they aren't visible on the screen.

✔ If you forget to use Track Changes, you can always use the document comparison tools covered in the preceding section.

Reviewing changes

Of course, you want to scrutinize every change made to your document. Word makes the task easy, thanks to the Changes area on the Review tab, as shown in Figure 26-3.

Accept a revision.

Reject a revision.

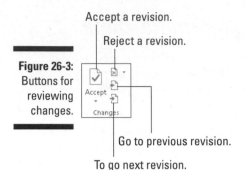

Figure 26-3:
Buttons for
reviewing
changes.

Go to previous revision.

To go next revision.

To review changes throughout your document, use the Next and Previous buttons. Click a button to hop to the next change in the text.

Click the Accept button if you can tolerate the change. To reject a change, click the Reject button. After clicking either button, you instantly see the next change in the document, until all the changes are dealt with.

- ✔ The Accept and Reject buttons are actually menus. They sport menu items that accept or reject all the changes in your document in one fell swoop. The only thing missing is the "Swoop!" sound when you use those commands.

- ✔ You can view a summary of changes by summoning the Revisions pane: Click the Reviewing Pane button, found in the Review tab's Tracking group. The Revisions pane doesn't show the changes in context, but it lists them all. You can hop to a change in your document by clicking its tidbit in the Revisions pane.

- ✔ The Review tab also shows Next and Previous buttons in the Comments group, but those buttons only hop between *comments,* not revision marks.

- ✔ To see the changes in your text, ensure that you chose the All Markup command from the Display for Review menu button.

- ✔ When you goof, you can choose Edit⇨Undo, just as you can undo any other boo-boo.

- ✔ You can also right-click any revision mark to accept or reject it.

Chapter 27

Mail Merge Mania

. . . .

In This Chapter

▶ Understanding mail merge

▶ Building the main document

▶ Conjuring up a recipient list

▶ Making a recipient list

▶ Inserting fields into the main document

▶ Merging (the final act)

. . . .

Here's a little quiz: What do these things have in common? Rocket science. Quantum mechanics. Brain surgery. Levitation. The answer: They're all a lot easier to accomplish on your own than by using mail merge in Word. I'm not saying that mastering mail merge is impossible. True, it's an ancient word processing tradition — something that just about everyone toys with at one time or another. Yet the way Word handles mail merge has been traditionally and consistently frustrating. That's why I wrote this chapter.

About Mail Merge

The term *mail merge* is given to the process of opening a single document, stirring in a list of names and other information, and then combining *(merging)* everything. The result is a sheaf of personalized documents. Sounds useful, right? Peruse this section before making up your mind.

Understanding Word's mail merge jargon

Before taking the mail merge plunge, you should understand these three terms, used throughout the mail merge process:

Main document: This document is just like any other document in Word, complete with formatting and layout and all the fancy stuff you can put into a document. The big difference is that the main document contains the various fill-in-the-blanks items that are used to create form letters.

Recipient list: This list contains the information you use to create customized documents. It's a type of *database file* — basically, names and other information organized in rows and columns. It's this information that's merged with the main document to create customized documents.

Field: Each of these fill-in-the-blanks items inside the main document is a placeholder that will be filled in by information from the recipient list. Fields are what make the mail merge possible.

Getting these three elements to work together is the essence of mail merge. You use the Mailings tab in Word to make it all happen, as explained throughout this chapter.

✔ The main document need not be a form letter. It can be an e-mail message, an envelope, a set of labels, or anything else that can be mass-produced.

✔ The key to mail merging is the recipient list. If you plan to create a mail merge as part of your regular routine, build a recipient list that you can use repeatedly.

✔ A mail merge document can have as many fields as it needs. In fact, any item you want to change can be a field: the greeting, a banal pleasantry, gossip, whatever.

✔ Fields are also known as *merge fields*.

✔ You can use information from the Outlook program, also a part of Microsoft Office, to work as a recipient list for a mail merge in Word. This trick works best, however, when you're in a computer environment that features Microsoft Exchange Server. Otherwise, making Outlook and Word cooperate with each other can be a frustrating endeavor.

Reviewing the mail merge process

The typical mail merge involves five steps:

1. **Build the main document.**

   You can create several types of mail merge documents:

   Letter: The traditional mail merge document is a letter, which is simply a document in Word.

E-Mail Messages: Word can produce customized e-mail messages, which are sent electronically rather than printed.

Envelopes: You can use mail merge to create a batch of customized envelopes, each printed with its own address.

Labels: Word lets you print sheets of labels, each of which is customized with specific information from the mail merge. See Chapter 28 for specifics.

Directory: A directory is a list of information, such as a catalog or an address book.

2. **Decide which fields are needed for the main document.**

You need to know what kind of information is necessary for the recipient list before you create it. This chapter explains how to do that so that you don't end up having to repeatedly modify the recipient list after it's created.

3. **Create the recipient list — the data for the mail merge.**

The recipient list is a database, consisting of rows and columns. Each column is a field, a fill-in-the-blanks part of the document. Each row is a record in the database, representing a person who receives their own, custom copy of the document.

4. **Insert fields specified in the recipient list into the main document.**

The fields are placeholders for information from the recipient list.

5. **Merge the information from the recipient list into the main document.**

The final mail merge process creates the customized documents. They can then be saved, printed, e-mailed, or dealt with however you like.

The rest of this chapter covers the specifics. You can also use the Word Mail Merge Wizard to help you work each mail merge step. See the next section.

Chickening out and using the Mail Merge Wizard

If all this mail merge malarkey is just too intense for you, consider using Word's Mail Merge Wizard: On the Mailings tab, choose Start Mail Merge⇨Step-by-Step Mail Merge Wizard. You see the Mail Merge pane appear on the right side of the document's window. Answer the questions, choose options, and click the Next link to proceed.

The Main Document

Mail merge begins with a document, or what I call the *main document*. It's the prototype for all the individualized documents you eventually create, so it contains only common elements. The specific stuff — the items that change for each document after the mail merge — are added later.

The following sections discuss different types of main documents.

Creating a mail merge letter

The most common thing to mail merge is the standard, annoying form letter. Here's how you start that journey:

1. **Start a new, blank document.**

   Press Ctrl+N.

2. **On the Mailings tab, from the Start Mail Merge group, choose Start Mail Merge⇨Letters.**

3. **Type the letter.**

   You're typing only the common parts of the letter, the text that doesn't change for each copy you print.

4. **Type the fields you need in ALL CAPS.**

   This step is my idea, not Word's. Type in ALL CAPS the text to be replaced or customized in your document. Use short, descriptive terms. Figure 27-1 shows an example.

   I inserted a `PrintDate` field in the document shown in the figure. That way, the documents all have today's date on them when they print. See Chapter 23 for more information on the `PrintDate` field.

5. **Save the main document.**

   If you already saved the document as you were writing it, give yourself a cookie.

After you create your letter, the next step is to create or use a recipient list. Continue with the section "The Recipient List," a little later in this chapter, for more information.

Start here.
Mailings tab
Browse merged documents.

PrintDate field | Work with receipients.
Insert fields | Preview | All done!

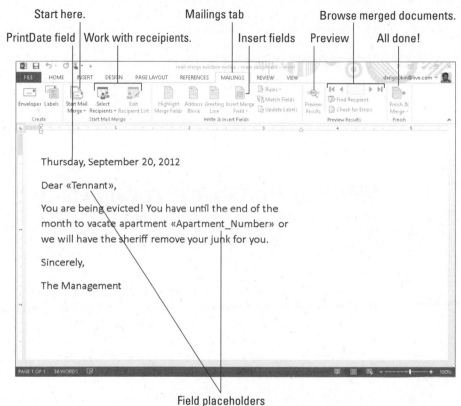

Field placeholders

Figure 27-1:
A mail-
merge main
document.

Creating mail merge e-mail messages

Word lets you spew out custom e-mail messages by using the E-Mail option for mail merge. This option works only when you configure the Microsoft Outlook program on your computer. After that's done, you start the main document for your e-mail merge by obeying these steps:

1. **Press Ctrl+N to create a fresh document.**

2. **On the Mailings tab, choose Start Mail Merge⇨E-Mail Messages.**

   Word changes to Web Layout view, used for creating Internet documents in Word.

3. **Create your mail message.**

4. **If you anticipate inserting fields in the message, type them in ALL CAPS.**

Normally, an e-mail mail merge doesn't have fields in the document, though there's no rule against using them. Still, putting someone's name or other personal information in the message removes the stigma of a mass e-mail form letter.

5. Save your document.

The primary field you use when merging an e-mail document is the recipient's e-mail address. You can't e-mail-merge without it. Continue your mail merge adventure in the later section, "The Recipient List."

Creating mail merge envelopes

To create a stack of mail merge envelopes, which is far more classy than using peel-and-stick mailing labels, abide by these steps:

1. Start a new document.

2. On the Mailings tab, choose Start Mail Merge⇨Envelopes.

The Envelope Options dialog box appears. You can set the envelope size and font options, if necessary.

3. Click OK.

Word's window changes to reflect a typical envelope, a size specified in the Envelope Options dialog box.

4. Type the return address.

Normally, an envelope mail merge doesn't use different return addresses for each envelope. So type the return address where the insertion pointer is blinking in the upper-left corner of the envelope.

Press Shift+Enter at the end of a line in the return address. The soft return you set keeps the lines in the return address tightly together.

5. Click the mouse in the text box found in the center of the envelope.

Word stuck a text box in the middle of the envelope, which is where you place the recipient's address. If you don't see the box, just click the mouse where you think the address should go.

6. If necessary, type any unchanging text in the recipient's address.

Odds are good that each recipient has a different address, so you probably don't have to type anything for this step. Instead, the information from the recipient list — the fields — is inserted here.

7. Save the envelope.

Your next task is to use the recipient list to gather the information for your mailing. Keep reading in the next section.

The Recipient List

To make mail merge work, you need a *database,* which is a list of information to place into the fill-in-the-blanks part of each document. In Word's mail merge ordeal, this database is the recipient list.

> ✔ Using a recipient list is the second step in a mail merge, after creating the main document.

> ✔ Every main document must have its own recipient list. You can create a new recipient list, use an existing one, borrow one from the Microsoft Office Outlook program, or steal one from a database server, which is an option too scary for me to write about in this book.

Creating a recipient list

Unless you already have recipient lists built and saved, you need to make one from scratch. This process involves setting up the list, removing unneeded fields that Word annoyingly preselects for you, adding the fields you truly need, and finally, filling in the list. It's quite involved, so follow along closely.

Follow these steps to create a new recipient list:

1. **Create and save the main document.**

   Refer to the section "The Main Document," earlier in this chapter. Creating the recipient list works the same no matter what type of mail merge document you created.

2. **On the Mailings tab, in the Start Mail Merge group, choose Select Recipients⇨Type a New List.**

   If this option isn't available, you haven't properly created the main document. Start over in the earlier section, "The Main Document." Otherwise, you see the New Address List dialog box, as shown in Figure 27-2.

   Word assumes that you need a dozen or so fields for your mail merge, which is silly because it's more than you need. So the next set of steps removes the surplus fields and replaces them with the fields your document requires.

3. **Click the Customize Columns button.**

   The Customize Address List dialog box appears, displaying fields that Word assumes you need. Such foolishness cannot be tolerated.

4. **Select a field that you *do not* need.**

   Click it with the mouse.

5. **Click the Delete button.**

Fields   Click to sort the list.

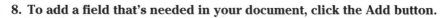

New Address List   ? X

Type recipient information in the table. To add more entries, click New Entry.

Tennant ▼	Apartment Number ▼	
Susie Loudmusic	206B	
Jake Stoner	105V	
Arty Smells	145A	
Hau Manypeoplearelivinghere	406H	
Jane Mysteriousvisitors	271A	
Buddy Neverpaystherent	190Q	
Simon Trashes	380A	
Mildred & Hugh Bickerson	301B	
The Angry Family	145B	
Cindy Loudteevee	250C	
Alfred Grumpy	208V	

New Entry   Find...

Delete Entry   Customize Columns...   OK   Cancel

Figure 27-2:
Making a
recipient
list.

Records   Add/Remove fields.

6. Click Yes in the confirmation dialog box.

The keyboard shortcut for the Yes button is the Y key. Oh, and the keyboard shortcut for the Delete button (refer to Step 5) is D. Typing D and then Y deletes the selected field.

7. Repeat Steps 4 through 6 for each field you don't need.

After removing the excess fields, your next step is to add the fields you need — if any.

Whether it appears in the message body or not, you need the Email_ Address field when you're merging an e-mail message. Word uses this field so that it knows where to send the message. Don't delete the field!

Rather than delete all fields, you can rename some fields to match what you need: Select a field and click the Rename button. For example, I renamed First Name to First; Last Name to Last; and so on.

8. To add a field that's needed in your document, click the Add button.

The teeny Add Field dialog box pops into view.

9. Type the field name and click the OK button.

Follow these rules for naming fields:

- Name the field to reflect the kind of information in it; for example, Shark Bite Location.

- No two fields can have the same name.

- Field names can contain spaces but cannot start with a space.

- Field names can be quite long, though shorter is best.

- The following characters are forbidden in a field name: . ! ` [ ].

10. Repeat Steps 8 and 9 for each new field you need in the main document.

When you're done, review the list. It should match up with the list of ALL CAPS fields in the document (if you chose to create them). Don't worry if it doesn't — you can add fields later, though it takes more time.

11. Click OK.

You now see customized fields appear as column headings in the New Address List dialog box (refer to Figure 27-2).

In the final set of steps, you fill in the recipient list. You need to input *records,* one for each document you plan to create:

12. Type the first record's data.

Type the information that's appropriate to each field shown in the New Address List dialog box: name, title, evil nickname, planet of origin, and so on.

13. Press Tab to enter the next field.

After filling in the last field, you'll probably want to add another record:

14. To add a new record, press the Tab key after typing in the last field.

When you press the Tab key in the last field in a record, a new record is automatically created and added on the next line. Keep filling in data!

15. Review your work when you're done.

You can edit any field in any record by selecting it with the mouse.

If you accidentally add a blank record at the end of the list, click to select it and then click the Delete Entry button. You do this because blank records are still processed in a mail merge, which can result in wasted paper.

16. Click OK.

The Save Address List dialog box pops up, allowing you to save the recipient list.

The recipient lists dwell in the folder named My Data Sources, found in the Documents or My Documents folder. Word automatically chooses (or creates) this folder.

17. Type a name for the address list.

Descriptive names are best. After all, you might use the same recipient list again.

18. Click the Save button.

You return to the document.

Making a recipient list document

Here's a secret: You can create a document in Word and use it as a "data source" for a mail merge. The document contains a single element: a table. The table must have a header row, formatted in bold text, which identifies all the fields. Every row after that becomes a record in the recipient list database.

Using a table as a recipient list provides an easy way to import information into Word and use it for a mail merge. For example, you can copy information from the Internet or a PDF file and then paste that information into Word. Edit the information into a typical Word table, add a table heading row, and save the thing — and then you have a recipient list.

Follow the steps outlined in the nearby section, "Using an already created recipient list," to use the table document as your recipient list. Also see Chapter 19 for more information on tables in Word.

The next step in your mail-merge agony is to stir the fields from the recipient list into the main document. Refer to the section "Fold in the Fields," later in this chapter.

Using an already created recipient list

To use an existing recipient list for your mail merge, follow these steps after creating the main document:

1. **From the Mailings tab, choose Select Recipients⇨Use an Existing List.**

   The Select Data Source dialog box appears. It works like the Open dialog box, though it's designed to display recipient lists that Word can use or that you previously created and saved.

2. **Choose an existing recipient list from the files that are displayed.**

   I hope you used a descriptive name when you first saved the recipient list, which I recommend in the preceding section.

3. **Click the Open button.**

That's it: The recipient list is now associated with the main document.

✔ You can tell that a recipient list is associated with the main document when the Insert Merge Field button (on the Mailings tab, in the Write & Insert Fields group) is available.

✔ Refer to the later section, "Fold in the Fields," for information on inserting fields into your document, which is the next step in the mail merge nightmare.

Grabbing a recipient list from Outlook

Assuming that you use Microsoft Outlook as your e-mail program or contact manager, and assuming that it contains information you want to use in a mail merge, you can follow these steps to create a recipient list:

1. **On the Mailings tab, in the Start Mail Merge group, choose Select Recipients⇨Choose from Outlook Contacts.**

2. **If necessary, select your profile from the Choose Profile dialog box.**

3. **Click OK.**

4. **In the Select Contacts dialog box, choose a contact folder.**

   Contact folders are created in Outlook, not in Word.

5. **Click OK.**

6. **Use the Mail Merge Recipients dialog box to filter the recipient list.**

   The simplest way to do this, if the list isn't too long, is simply to remove the check marks by the names of the individuals you don't want in the list. You can also click the Filter link in the dialog box to do more advanced filtering, which I'm loathe to describe right now.

7. **Click OK when you're done culling the recipient list.**

The next step in the painful experience known as Word mail merge is to insert fields into the master document. Keep reading in the later section, "Fold in the Fields."

Editing a recipient list

If you're like me, you sometimes have One Of Those Days and forget to add a record or field to your recipient list. When that happens, you need to edit the recipient list. Such torture involves these steps:

1. **On the Mailing tab, in the Start Mail Merge group, click the Edit Recipient List button.**

   The button isn't available unless you're working on a main document and it has been associated with a recipient list.

2. **Select the data source.**

   In the lower-left corner of the Mail Merge Recipients dialog box, click the data source filename.

3. **Click the Edit button.**

   You can now use the Edit Data Source dialog box to edit each record in the recipient list or to add or remove columns and perform other chaos. The Edit Data Source dialog box looks and works just like the New Address List dialog box (refer to Figure 27-2).

   Click the Delete Entry button to remove a record.

   Click the New Entry button to create a new record.

   Click the Customize Columns button to delete, add, or rename fields.

4. **Click the OK button when you're done editing.**

5. **Click the Yes button to save any changes.**

6. **Click the OK button to dismiss the Mail Merge Recipients dialog box.**

This technique doesn't work when you create a recipient list from a Word document. (See the earlier sidebar, "Making a recipient list document.") In that case, you must open the document and edit the list by using Word's table tools. See Chapter 19.

Fold in the Fields

A main document and a handy recipient list are two separate things. To make them work together, and make the mail merge happen, you must mix the two. This process involves inserting fields from the recipient list into the main document. Here's how it works:

1. **Select some ALL CAPS text from a field placeholder in the main document.**

   I assume that you followed my advice from the earlier section, "Creating a mail merge letter," and used ALL CAPS placeholders to insert fields in your document. If not (if you're creating an envelope, for example), click the mouse button to place the insertion pointer wherever you want to insert the field.

2. **Use the Insert Merge Field menu to stick the proper field into the document.**

Insert Merge
Field

   Clicking the Insert Merge Field command button displays a menu of fields according to the recipient list associated with the main document. Choose the proper field to insert into your text.

   After the field is inserted, you see its name appear in the document, hugged by angle brackets, such as <<First>> for the First field. This field would replace the capitalized text FIRST in the document.

3. **Continue adding fields until the document is complete.**

   Repeat Steps 1 and 2 as necessary to stick all fields into your document.

   When adding fields to an envelope, you can press Shift+Enter and add a soft return to prevent the recipient's address from looking too spaced out.

4. **Save the main document.**

   Always save! Save! Save! Save!

The next step in your journey through the mail merge underworld is the integration of the recipient list with the main document and its fields. See the next section.

✔ When the Insert Merge Field button isn't available, a recipient list isn't associated with the document. See the earlier section, "The Recipient List."

✔ To delete an unwanted field, select it with the mouse and press the Delete key.

✔ A tad of editing may be required after inserting the field. I typically have to add spaces, commas, or colons after fields as Word inserts them.

Mail Merge Ho!

The final step in the mail merge process is to create personalized documents. The gizmo that handles this task is the Finish & Merge button, the sole item in the Finish group on the Mailings tab. This section describes how to use that button to complete the mail merge.

Previewing the merged documents

I highly recommend using the Preview Results command to ensure that your final, merged document looks good before it's officially merged. Here's how to work things:

1. **On the Mailings tab, in the Preview Results group, click the Preview Results command button.**

   The fields in the main document vanish! They're replaced by information from the first record in the recipient list. What you see on the screen is how the first customized mail-merge document appears. Hopefully, everything looks spiffy.

2. **When things don't look spiffy, click the Preview Results button again and then edit the main document. Start over.**

   Otherwise:

3. **Peruse the records.**

   Review every merged document to ensure that everything looks right. Use the record-browsing buttons in the Preview Results group to move forward or backward through the records. Look for these problems:

   - Formatting mistakes, such as text that obviously looks pasted in or not part of the surrounding text

   - Punctuation errors and missing commas or periods

   - Missing spaces between or around fields

   - Double fields or unwanted fields, which happen when you believe that you've deleted a field but haven't

   - Awkward text layouts, strange line breaks, or margins caused by missing or long fields

   To fix any boo-boos, you must leave Preview mode and then go back and reedit the main document.

4. **Click the Preview Results command button again to exit Preview mode.**

You're now ready to perform the merge, covered in the following sections.

Merging to a new set of documents

When you want to save merged documents and print them, follow these steps:

1. **Choose Finish & Merge⇨Edit Individual Documents.**

   The Merge to New Document dialog box appears.

2. **Ensure that the All option is selected.**

3. **Click OK.**

   Word creates a new document — a huge one that contains all merged documents, one after the other. Each document copy is separated by a Next Page section break. (See Chapter 14 for more information on section breaks.)

4. **Save the document.**

At this point, you can print the document, close it and edit it later, or do anything else you like.

Merging to the printer

The most common destination for merged documents is the printer. Here's how it works:

1. **Choose Finish & Merge⇨Print Documents.**

   A dialog box appears, from which you can choose records to print.

2. **Choose All from the Merge to Printer dialog box to print the entire document.**

   Or specify which records to print.

3. **Click OK.**

   The traditional Print dialog box appears.

4. **Click the OK button to print your documents.**

5. **Save and close your document.**

See Chapter 9 for more information on printing documents in Word.

Most printers require special feeding for envelopes. A printer usually has an envelope slot, in which you can stack a few envelopes. You may have to monitor the printer to insert them.

Merging to e-mail

To send out multiple e-mail messages, abide by these steps:

1. **Choose Finish & Merge⇨Send Email Messages.**

   The Merge to Email dialog box appears.

2. **Choose the e-mail address field from the To drop-down list.**

   Your document's recipient list must include an e-mail address field, whether the field is used in the document or not. If not, go back and edit the recipient list to include the address.

3. **Type a message subject line.**

4. **Click OK.**

   It looks like nothing has happened, but the messages have been placed in the Outlook outbox.

5. **Open Outlook.**

   After you open Outlook, the messages you queued are sent, or they sit ready to be sent when you give the command. (Whether the messages are sent right away depends on how you configured Outlook.)

Yes, this trick works only with Outlook, not with any other e-mail programs.

Unsolicited e-mail that's sent to people is considered spam. Sending spam may violate the terms of your Internet service provider's agreement and can terminate your account. Send mass e-mail only to people who have cheerfully agreed to receive such things from you.

Chapter 28

Labels of Love

. . . .

. . . .

One of the more esoteric Word features is its ability to print sheets of labels. The labels can all be the same or be produced as the result of a mail merge operation. Word's label feature works because the labels are, at their core, merely cells in a table and, unlike most teenagers, Word has no problem setting a table. You won't either, after you peruse the delightful options for creating labels that are presented in this chapter.

The Label Thing

Word isn't a label-making program. Although it can produce labels, as shown in this chapter, it's not your best choice. For those times when you plan to print labels, I highly recommend that you use a label-design program, one specifically geared to print labels — perhaps even some type of database program that lets you manage simple lists as well.

Word prints on labels just as it prints on any sheet of paper. Basically, Word puts a table on the page, making each cell the same size as the sticky labels. Word then fills the cells with information, which fits snugly on each label. When the sheet emerges from the printer, you have a bunch of labels for your peeling-and-sticking pleasure.

✔ Label printer paper can be found wherever office supplies are sold. Label paper comes in packages thin and thick, with various label layouts and designs.

✔ You must buy label paper compatible with your printer. Laser printers need special laser printer labels. Some inkjet printers require special, high-quality paper to soak up the ink.

✔ Of all the label brands available, Avery is the one I recommend. Its stock numbers are standard. So, if you buy Avery stock number 5160 or a similar number, your software and printer know which type of label you have and which format it's in.

Here's a Sheet of Identical Labels

One thing Word does easily and reliably is print a sheet of identical labels. Just follow these steps:

1. **Click the Mailings tab.**

2. **Click the Labels button (in the Create group).**

   The Envelopes and Labels dialog box appears, with the Labels tab ready for action, as shown in Figure 28-1.

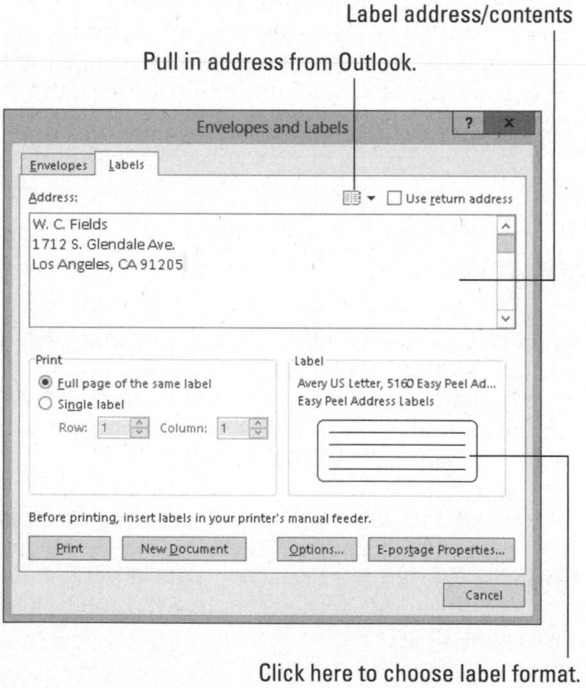

Label address/contents

Pull in address from Outlook.

Figure 28-1:
The Labels
side of the
Envelopes
and Labels
dialog box.

Click here to choose label format.

3. **Use the Address box to type the text you want printed on the label.**

   Keep in mind that you have only so many lines for each label and that each label is only so wide.

   Press the Enter key at the end of each line.

You can apply some simple formatting at this stage: Ctrl+B for bold, Ctrl+I for italic, or Ctrl+U for underlining, for example. If you right-click in the Address box, you can choose Font or Paragraph from the pop-up menu to further format the label.

4. **In the Print section of the Envelopes and Labels dialog box, select the Full Page of the Same Label radio button.**

5. **In the Label section, choose the type of label you're printing on.**

   If the stock number that's displayed doesn't match up, click the sample label to display the Label Options dialog box, from which you can choose the proper stock number or design of your labels.

   For some weird and unexplained reason, Microsoft appears as the label vendor in the Label Options dialog box. Choose Avery from the list when you use Avery (or similar) labels.

6. **Click the New Document button.**

   By placing the labels in a new document, you can further edit them, if you like. You can also save them so that you can use the same document when you need to print a batch of labels again.

7. **Print the labels.**

   Ensure that the sheet of label paper is loaded into your printer, proper side up. Use the Ctrl+P command to print the labels as you do for any document.

On my PC I have a folder full of label documents I print from time to time. For example, one document holds my return address, one is for the IRS, and another has my lawyer's address. They all come in quite handy.

  ✔ When you elect to save the labels to a new document, avoid the temptation to mess with the table, because it's perfectly aligned to the labels. Neither should you adjust the page margins or paragraph formatting.

  ✔ There's no need to make two sheets of labels. When all the labels are identical, simply print that sheet twice.

Print That Address List

Word can take a list of names and addresses and print them all, or a selected few, on a sheet of labels. This trick is more of a mail-merge feature than a true label-making ability; therefore, I highly recommend that you read about the Word mail-merge process (see Chapter 27) before following these steps:

1. **Start a new document in Word.**

2. **Click the Mailings tab.**

   All action in the remaining steps involves command buttons on the Mailings tab.

3. **From the Start Mail Merge button's menu, choose Labels.**

   The Label Options dialog box appears.

4. **Choose the label vendor and product number representing the sheet of labels on which you're printing.**

   For example, to print on a sheet of standard Avery address labels, use Avery catalog number 5160.

5. **Click OK.**

   Word builds a table in your document, one with cells perfectly aligned to match the labels on the sheet you selected. (The gridlines may be hidden, but the table is still there.)

   Do not edit or format the table! It's perfect.

6. **Use the Select Recipients button's menu to create a recipient list for your labels.**

   If you already read the section "The Recipient List," in Chapter 27, it pays off here.

   After you create or choose a recipient list, Word fills in all but the first cell (label) in the table with the `Next Record` field. This field directs Word to duplicate the label layout from the first label onto the remaining labels on the page. Before that can happen, though, you need to build the first label.

7. **Use the Insert Merge Field button to insert fields to help create and format the first label.**

   Clicking the Insert Merge Field command's menu button displays a list of fields associated with the address list you chose in Step 6. Choose a field from the list, such as `First Name`. Then type a space and insert the `Last Name` field from the list. Use the fields, as well as your keyboard, to build the first label. Figure 28-2 shows an example.

   Press the Shift+Enter key combination at the end of each line in a label. Shift+Enter inserts a soft return, which keeps the lines in the label tightly together.

8. **Check the layout.**

   Ensure that spaces appear between the fields that need them, and also commas and other characters.

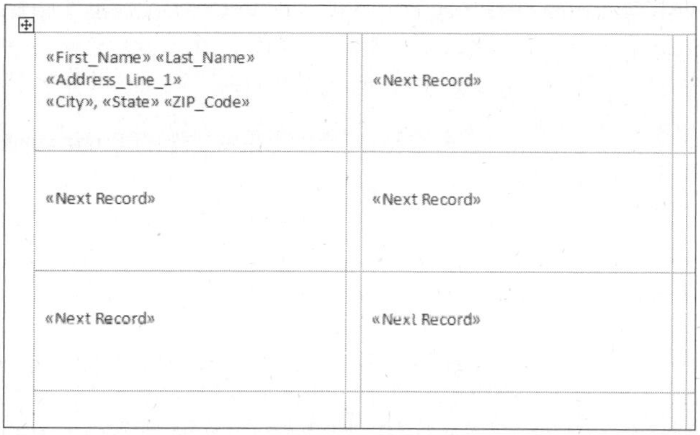

«First_Name» «Last_Name» «Address_Line_1» «City», «State» «ZIP_Code»	«Next Record»	
«Next Record»	«Next Record»	
«Next Record»	«Next Record»	

Figure 28-2:
The first label dictates how other labels are formatted.

9. **From the Write & Insert Fields group, click the Update Labels button.**

   Word populates the remaining cells in the table with the same fields. This is why you check the layout in Step 8: If you find a mistake now, you have to fix every dang-doodle label rather than a single label.

10. **Choose the proper command from the Finish & Merge button's menu:**

    To save the document and print, choose Edit Individual Documents.

    To print only, choose Print Documents.

11. **Click OK in the Merge to Print dialog box or the Merge to New Document dialog box.**

12. **Save. Print. Whatever.**

    If a new document opens, save it. You can then use it over and over and print it any time you like.

When you choose to print the labels, click OK in the Print dialog box to start printing. (Be sure that the printer is loaded with as many sheets of labels as required.)

A Label Trick with Graphics

It's possible to add a graphical image to a mailing label. You can do it to a sheet of labels that are identical or when you're merging names from an address list. I recommend reading Chapter 22, on using graphics in Word, before you proceed.

To stick a graphical image into your list of labels, work Steps 1 through 5 from the preceding section. What you do next depends on whether you're merging an address list or simply making a sheet of identical labels.

✔ When you're merging in an address list, follow Steps 6 through 8 from the preceding section.

✔ When you're creating a sheet of identical labels, simply type and format the label that you want in the table's first cell, such as your own name and address to be used for return address labels.

After making your label, either from an address list's Merge fields or by typing plain text, you're ready to add the graphical image: Click the Insert tab and use the Picture button to insert the image — or use any of the techniques covered in Chapter 22 for sticking graphics into a Word document.

Right-click the image and choose Wrap Text⇨Square. Resize the image and position it so that it's *completely* within the first cell in the table, as shown in Figure 28-3.

Figure 28-3:
Creating a
label with
an image.

When everything looks just right, click the Update Labels button on the Mailings tab. This action populates the entire sheet, duplicating exactly what you placed in the first cell — including graphics.

Unfortunately, this graphical trick involves fooling Word's mail-merge function. And before you can save or print your document, you need to get rid of those <<Next Record>> fields. Here's my suggestion:

1. **Carefully select the text <<Next Record>>, including the angle brackets on either side.**

   You have to select the whole thing; clicking only the field turns it gray. That's not selecting! Drag the mouse over the entire thing to select it.

2. **Press Ctrl+C to copy that text.**

3. **Press Ctrl+H to conjure up the Find and Replace dialog box.**

4. **Click the mouse in the Find What box and then press Ctrl+V to paste.**

   This step pastes the text <<Next Record>> into the box.

   Leave the Replace With box blank.

5. **Click the Replace All button.**

   At this point, Word may replace only the selected text. That's fine: Click the Yes button to continue replacing throughout the entire document.

   Also click the Yes button if you're asked to continue searching at the beginning of the document.

   Click OK when the search-and-replace operation has been completed.

6. **Close the Find and Replace dialog box.**

   All those annoying <<Next Record>> chunks have disappeared from the labels.

Now your labels are ready to save and print.

Chapter 29

A More Custom Word

*I*t's human nature to mess with things. Got a bump on your arm? Odds are good that you'll pick at it. Ever rearrange a room? How about jamming a puzzle piece into a spot where it doesn't fit? Heck, Home Depot wouldn't exist if this innate idea to mess with it yourself didn't exist. The same logic can be applied to Word: You can change the way Word looks, by customizing it to the way you like. This chapter explains what you can do.

My, What Big Text You Have!

When the information in Word's window just isn't big enough, don't enlarge the font! Instead, whip out the equivalent of a digital magnifying glass, the Zoom command. It helps you enlarge or reduce your document, making it easier to see or giving you the Big Picture look.

You have several ways to zoom text in Word, as described in this section.

✔ Zooming doesn't affect how a document prints — only how it looks on the screen.

✔ When zooming moves too far out, your text changes to shaded blocks, or *greeking*. Although zooming out that far isn't keen for editing, it gives you a good idea, before printing, of how your document lays out on the page.

✔ On a touchscreen display, you can pinch two fingers together to zoom in; spread your fingers apart to zoom out.

 ✔ If you have a wheel mouse, you can zoom by pressing the Ctrl key on your keyboard and rolling the wheel up or down. Rolling up zooms in; rolling down zooms out.

Working the status bar Zoom control

For quick-and-dirty zoom madness, use the main Zoom control. It's on the far-right end of the status bar, enlarged (zoomed) for your viewing pleasure in Figure 29-1.

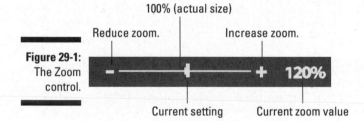

Figure 29-1: The Zoom control.

To make the document appear larger, slide the gizmo to the right (toward the plus sign). To make the document appear smaller, slide the gizmo to the left. The percentage value displayed to the right of the gizmo is the approximate ratio between the size of your document on the computer's monitor versus its size when printed.

Using the Zoom commands

For more specific zoom control, use the commands found in the Zoom group on the View tab, illustrated in Figure 29-2.

Figure 29-2: The Zoom group on the View tab.

Summon the Zoom dialog box.

Good choice for general editing

Zoom document to actual size.

Here are the various things you can do in the Zoom group:

✔ Click the Zoom button to display the Zoom dialog box. It gives you specific control over how large your document appears in the window.

✔ Click the 100% button to display your document at 100 percent magnification, basically the same size on the screen as the document when it prints.

✔ Use the One Page command to zoom out so that you can see the entire page on the screen. The text is too tiny to see or edit, but you can get a good grasp of the page layout.

✔ Use the Multiple Pages command (like the One Page command) to zoom out and show two pages on the screen at one time. You can see more than two pages at a time by using the Many Pages button in the Zoom dialog box.

✔ Using the Page Width command, set the zoom level so that you see your entire document from its left to right margins; it's my favorite setting.

✔ You can also display the Zoom dialog box by clicking the zoom percentage (100%) on the status bar.

A Better Status Bar

Word's status bar is an extremely useful gizmo, lurking at the bottom of the Word window. Chapter 1 introduces the status bar but only hints at its potential. Now it's time to reveal all: Right-clicking the status bar produces the helpful Customize Status Bar menu, as shown in Figure 29-3.

The Customize Status Bar menu does two things: controls what you see on the status bar (informational tidbits as well as certain controls) and lets you turn on or off certain Word features.

From Figure 29-3, as well as on your screen, you can see the current status for lots of optional settings. A check mark indicates that an item is either visible or appears when necessary. To add an item, choose it. To remove a check marked item, choose it.

Here are my thoughts:

✔ Choosing an item from the menu doesn't cause the menu to disappear, which is handy. To make the menu go away, click the mouse elsewhere in the Word window.

✔ The eight topmost items on the menu display information about your document. You can also choose to have that information displayed on the status bar by choosing one or more of those options.

✔ The Selection Mode option directs Word to display the text *Extend Selection* on the status bar when you press the F8 key to select text. See Chapter 6 for more information on selecting text.

✔ The Overtype item places the Insert/Overtype button on the status bar. You can click this button to easily switch between Insert and Overtype modes — if you enjoy that feature. Most Word users prefer to use Insert mode all the time.

✔ The last three items on the menu control whether the View buttons or Zoom shortcuts appear on the status bar.

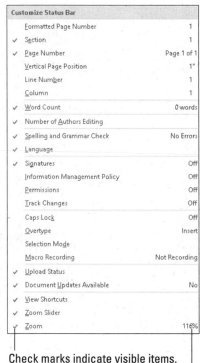

Figure 29-3:
The
Customize
Status Bar
menu.

Check marks indicate visible items.

Current setting information

Fun with the Quick Access Toolbar

Back in the old days, you could really mess with the way the Word window looked. You could add or remove toolbars, modify toolbars, create your own toolbars, and generally use the word *toolbars* over and over again until it lost its meaning. Though Word isn't quite as flexible these days, it still allows you to control a few specific parts of the program window, as described in the following sections.

Discovering the Quick Access toolbar

The *Quick Access toolbar* is a small strip of command buttons dwelling near the document window's title bar, as shown in Figure 29-4. This territory is yours, free to modify at your whim and according to your needs, as covered in this section.

Preset command buttons

Touch Mode button (added)

Control menu   Quick Access Toolbar menu

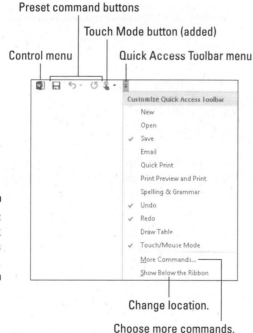

Figure 29-4:
The Quick
Access
toolbar.

Change location.

Choose more commands.

✔ The Quick Access toolbar is preset to dwell above the Ribbon, on the far-left edge of the Word window's title bar (refer to Figure 29-4).

✔ You can change the Quick Access toolbar's location from above the Ribbon to below the Ribbon and back again. To make the move, choose the command Show Below the Ribbon from the toolbar menu (refer to Figure 29-4). To move the Quick Access toolbar back atop the Ribbon, choose the command Show Above the Ribbon.

✔ Put the Quick Access toolbar below the Ribbon when it contains so many custom buttons that it begins to crowd into the document's title.

✔ Three command buttons naturally reside on the toolbar: Save, Undo, and Redo. You're free, however, to remove them.

✔ The item to the left of the Quick Access toolbar is the window control button. It's a part of most windows, not something unique to the Quick Access toolbar.

✔ The last item on the toolbar is the menu button. This menu is illustrated in Figure 29-4.

You can customize icons that appear on the Quick Access toolbar. The key is to find a command you use often, or a command that is otherwise tedious to access, and add it. It's quite easy to do, if you know how to right-click the mouse — and read the next section.

Adding commands to the Quick Access toolbar

To add a command to the Quick Access toolbar, locate its command button anywhere on the Ribbon. Right-click the command and choose Add to Quick Access toolbar from the shortcut menu that pops up.

You can also add a command to the Quick Access toolbar by using its menu (refer to Figure 29-4): Choose a common command from that menu, such as the Quick Print command, to add it to the toolbar.

✔ Word remembers which commands you add to the toolbar. These same commands will be there the next time you start Word, in every document window.

✔ Some commands place buttons on the toolbar, and others place drop-down menus or text boxes.

Removing commands from the Quick Access toolbar

To remove a command from the Quick Access toolbar, right-click its command button and choose Remove from Quick Access toolbar.

Likewise, you can choose a command with a check mark from the Customize Quick Access Toolbar menu. Doing so removes that command from the toolbar.

I don't recommend removing the Undo or Redo commands from the toolbar, unless you've truly committed the Ctrl+Z and Ctrl+Y keyboard shortcuts to memory.

Customizing the Quick Access toolbar

For vast control over the Quick Access toolbar, you summon the Quick Access toolbar portion of the Word Options dialog box, as shown in Figure 29-5. To summon this window, choose More Commands from the Quick Access toolbar's menu.

The Word Options dialog box lets you not only add any of the bazillion commands to the toolbar (including lots not found on the Ribbon) but also change the toolbar's button order, as illustrated in the figure.

When you're done making changes, click the OK button to close the Word Options dialog box. There, you can view and treasure your new Quick Access toolbar.

✔ Choose the All Commands item from the Choose Commands From menu to view every possible command in Word. Sometimes, a missing command that you think could be elsewhere ends up being available in the All Commands list — for example, the popular Save All command or the Tabs command, which quickly displays the Tabs dialog box.

✔ When your command list grows long, consider organizing it. Use the <Separator> item to help group similar commands. The <Separator> appears as a vertical bar on the Quick Access toolbar.

✔ Yes, some commands lack specific graphics on their buttons; they show up as green dots on the toolbar.

✔ My personal Quick Access toolbar contains these commands: Save, Save All, Small Caps, Undo, Redo, Quick Print, and Touch Mode. These commands are shown in Figure 29-5.

✔ To return the Quick Access toolbar to the way Word originally had it, choose Reset⊃Reset Only Quick Access toolbar from the Word Options window (refer to Figure 29-5).

Category list   Add/remove commands.

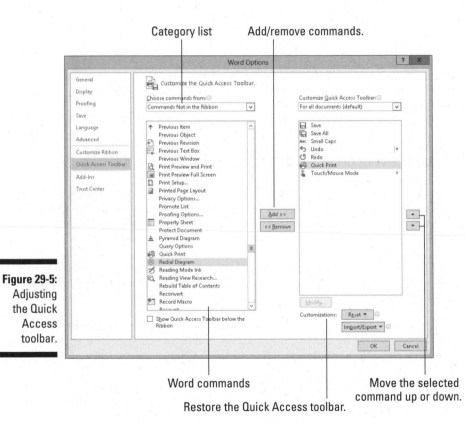

Figure 29-5:
Adjusting
the Quick
Access
toolbar.

Word commands   Move the selected
command up or down.

Restore the Quick Access toolbar.

Part VI
The Part of Tens

Enjoy an additional Word 2013 Part of Tens chapter online at www.dummies.com/extras/word2013

In this part . . .

- ✔ Partake of ten helpful tips on how to work best with Word 2013.

- ✔ Learn ten tricks to improve your mastery of Word 2013.

- ✔ Find out about ten things you might know are possible in Word 2013.

- ✔ Read about ten friendly tips on how to work more efficiently in Word 2013.

- ✔ Enjoy an additional Word 2013 Part of Tens chapter online at www.dummies.com/extras/word2013.

Chapter 30

The Ten Commandments of Word

In This Chapter

▶ Thou shalt remember to save thy work

▶ Thou shalt not use spaces unnecessarily

▶ Thou shalt not press Enter at the end of a line

▶ Thou shalt not neglect thy keyboard

▶ Thou shalt not manually number thy pages

▶ Thou shalt not press the Enter key to start a new page

▶ Thou shalt not forget thy Undo command

▶ Honor thy printer

▶ Thou shalt have multiple document windows before thee

▶ Neglecteth not Windows

I admit that I look nothing like Charlton Heston. Though I'm only guessing, I probably look nothing like Moses, either. Still, I feel compelled to return from Mount Sinai with some basic codes for word processing. I call them my Ten Commandments of Word.

Thou Shalt Remember to Save Thy Work

Save! Save! Save! Always save your stuff. Whenever your mind wanders, have your fingers dart over to the Ctrl+S keyboard shortcut. Savest thy work.

Thou Shalt Not Use More Than One Space

Generally speaking, you should never find more than one space anywhere in a Word document. The appearance of two or more spaces in a row is a desperate cry for a tab. Use single spaces to separate words and sentences. Use tabs to indent or to align text on a tab stop.

✔ Refer to Chapter 12 on setting tabs.

✔ Refer to Chapter 19 for creating tables, which is a great way to organize information into rows and columns.

Thou Shalt Not Press Enter at the End of a Line

Word automatically wraps text. As you type and your text approaches the right margin, the words automatically advance to the next line. Therefore, there's no need to press the Enter key, unless you want to start a new paragraph.

✔ In one-line paragraphs, pressing the Enter key at the end of the line is okay.

✔ When you don't want to start a new paragraph but you need to start a new line, such as when typing a return address, press Shift+Enter, the *soft* return command.

Thou Shalt Not Neglect Thy Keyboard

Word is not Windows. Windows is a graphical operating system. Graphics means using the mouse. So, although you can get lots done with the mouse, some things in Word are done faster by using the keyboard.

For example, stab the Ctrl+S key combo to quickly save a document. Pressing Ctrl+P to print works better than fumbling for the mouse, as does Ctrl+O to open a document. You don't have to know all the keyboard commands, but remembering a few helps.

Refer to this book's online Cheat Sheet for a full-on list of keyboard shortcuts mentioned in this book. You can find the Cheat Sheet here:

www.dummies.com/cheatsheet/word2013

Thou Shalt Not Manually Number Thy Pages

Word has an automatic page-numbering command. Refer to the section in Chapter 13 that talks about where to stick the page number.

Thou Shalt Not Press the Enter Key to Start a New Page

When you need to start text at the top of a new page, you use the *manual page-break* command. Its keyboard shortcut is Ctrl+Enter. That's the best and most proper way to start a new page. Also see Chapter 13.

The worst way to start a new page is to brazenly press the Enter key a couple of dozen times. Although the result may look okay, this strategy doesn't guarantee anything; as you continue to edit your document, the page break moves back and forth and ends up looking butt-ugly.

Thou Shalt Not Forget Thy Undo Command

Just about anything that happens in Word can be undone by choosing the Undo command from the Quick Access toolbar or pressing the popular and common keyboard shortcut Ctrl+Z.

Honor Thy Printer

The biggest printing problem anyone has is telling Word to print something when the printer isn't on. Verify that your printer is on, healthy, and ready to print before you tell Word to print something.

Never (or at least try not to) continue trying the Print command when a document doesn't print. Word tries to print once every time you use the Print command. Somewhere and sometime, those documents will print, unless you do something to prevent it.

Thou Shalt Have Multiple Document Windows Before Thee

In Word, as in most Windows applications, you can work on more than one document at a time. In fact, you can have as many document windows open as you can stand (or until the computer runs out of memory). Word even lets you view a single document in multiple windows. Refer to Chapter 24 to see how things are done.

 ✔ You don't have to close one document to open and view another document.

 ✔ You don't have to quit Word to run another program, either. In Windows, you can run multiple programs at a time. So don't quit Word when you plan to start it again in just a little while.

Neglecteth Not Windows

Word is not Windows. Word is an application, designed for productivity. Windows is a computer operating system, designed to control a computer and to drive human beings crazy. These two different computer programs work together.

Windows is used to help keep *files* (the documents you create in Word) organized. You cannot do that in Word by itself. Therefore, verily I say unto you, don't feel that just because you're using Word, you can utterly skip out on Windows. You need them both in order to control your computer system.

Chapter 31

Ten Cool Tricks

*W*hen it comes down to it, just about everything Word does can be considered a cool trick. I still marvel at how word-wrap works and at how you can change margins after a document is written and all the text instantly jiggles into place. Everything in this book can be considered a cool trick, but when it came down to the wire, I found ten cool tricks barely (or not) mentioned anywhere else and stuck them in this chapter.

Automatic Save with AutoRecover

Word's AutoRecover feature will save your butt someday. What it does is periodically save your document, even when you neglect to. That way, in the event of a computer crash, Word recovers your document from a safety copy that it has secretly made for you. That's a blessing.

Ensure that AutoRecover is activated. Heed these directions:

1. **Click the File tab.**

2. **On the File screen, choose Options.**

   The Word Options dialog box appears.

3. **Choose Save.**

4. **On the right side, ensure that a check mark appears by the item Save AutoRecover Information Every 10 Minutes.**

5. **Click OK to close the window.**

   Whew! You're safe.

Most of the time, you never notice AutoRecover. But when the computer crashes and you restart Word, you see the Document Recovery pane displayed and any files listed that you didn't save before the crash. To recover a document, point the mouse at its name. Use the menu button that's displayed to open and recover the document.

The best way to avoid accidentally losing your stuff is to *save now* and *save often!*

Keyboard Power!

You can use the keyboard in Word to do just about anything the mouse can do. Specifically, you can use the keyboard to work the Ribbon interface.

Each tab on the Ribbon has its own keyboard shortcut, as do commands on the Quick Access toolbar. To see the shortcuts, you press one of two magical keys: Alt or F10. After you press either key, a tiny bubble appears, telling you which key to press next to choose a tab on the Ribbon or a command from the Quick Access toolbar.

After you press a tab's shortcut key, additional shortcut keys appear for each command or group on the tab. Sometimes one character appears as a shortcut, and sometimes two characters appear. Either way, pressing those keys one after the other activates the command or displays further keyboard shortcuts.

For example, to change the page orientation to Landscape mode, you press Alt, P, O to display the Orientation menu and then press the down-arrow key to choose Landscape. Press Enter to choose that menu item.

After you press Alt or F10 to activate keyboard control over the Ribbon, your keyboard is used to manipulate the Ribbon, not to write text. Press the Esc key to cancel this mode.

Build Your Own Fractions

Word's AutoCorrect feature can build common fractions for you. Actually, it doesn't build them as much as it pulls them from a set of existing fraction "characters." Sadly, Word has only a few of these fraction characters. When you need your own, specific fraction, such as ³⁄₆₄, you can create it this way:

1. **Press Ctrl+Shift+= (the equal sign).**

   This keyboard is the shortcut for the superscript command.

2. **Type the *numerator* — the top part of the fraction.**

   For example, type **3** for ³⁄₆₄.

3. **Press Ctrl+Shift+= again to turn off superscripting.**

4. **Type the slash mark (/).**

5. **Press Ctrl+= to turn on subscripting.**

6. **Type the *denominator* — the bottom part of the fraction.**

   For example, type **64** for ³⁄₆₄.

7. **Press Ctrl+= to turn off subscripting.**

There's your fraction.

Electronic Bookmarks

Word allows you to stick electronic bookmarks into your document. They not only help you set your place in a document but also flag specific tidbits of text for other commands, such as Go To. Bookmarks can prove quite handy — better than trying to use the Find command to locate places in your text where the text itself may not reflect what you're searching for. For example, your bookmark might say, "Here's where you stopped reviewing the text."

To set a bookmark, place the insertion pointer where you want to insert the bookmark. From the Insert tab, click the Bookmark button in the Links group. Type a name for the bookmark in the Bookmark dialog box. Try to keep the bookmark name to one word, letters only. Press the Enter key or click the Add button.

Bookmarks don't show up on the screen; they're invisible. But you can use the Go To command to find them: Press the Ctrl+G keyboard shortcut to summon the Go To tab in the Find and Replace dialog box. Choose Bookmark from the Go to What list and then select a bookmark name from the drop-down list on the right side of the dialog box. Click the Go To button to visit that bookmark's location. (Close the Find and Replace dialog box when you're done with it.)

Lock Your Document

When you really, *really* don't want anyone messing with your document, you can apply some protection. The key is to lock your document. Several levels of protection are available, but you start the journey by following these steps:

1. **On the File screen, choose Info.**

   Click the File tab to view the File screen.

2. **Click the Protect Document button.**

   Of the several choices, I recommend these options:

   Mark As Final: The document is flagged as *final,* which means that editing is disabled. Still, you can easily override it by clicking the Edit Anyway button that appears.

   Encrypt with Password: The document is encrypted and a password is applied. To open the document in Word, you must enter the password. You cannot remove a password after it's applied.

   Restrict Editing: You can limit whether a user can edit a document or whether all changes are tracked or restrict that person to make only comments.

3. **Choose an option and answer the appropriate dialog boxes that appear.**

4. **Click OK.**

   The document protection you've chosen is applied.

Locking your document is a serious decision! I cannot help, nor can anyone else, if you forget a password or are otherwise unable to remove the restrictions you've applied to your document.

The Drop Cap

A *drop cap* is the first letter of a report, an article, a chapter, or a story that appears in a larger and more interesting font than the other characters. Figure 31-1 shows an example.

Figure 31-1:
A drop cap.

> S uddenly, the phone rang. Come to think of it, the phone always rings suddenly.

To add a drop cap to your document, select the first character of the first word at the start of your text. For example, select the *O* in *Once upon a time*. From the Insert tab, choose a drop cap style from the Drop Cap button's menu, found in the Text group. And there's your drop cap.

✔ It helps if the drop cap's paragraph is left-justified and not indented with a tab or any of the tricky formatting operations discussed in Part III of this book.

✔ You can undo a drop cap by clicking it and then choosing Drop Cap⇨None.

Map Your Document

The Navigation pane can be used to not only find text but also help you see the big picture on your document. The pane replaces an older feature, beloved by many Word users — the Document Map.

To see the big picture, click the View tab and put a check mark by the Navigation Pane item, found in the Show group. You see a document summary listed by heading style, as shown in Figure 31-2.

Figure 31-2: The Navigation pane document map.

Click a heading inside the map to instantly jump to that part of your document.

To close the Navigation Pane, click its X close button.

Add an Envelope to Your Letter

A quick way to print an envelope with every letter you create is to attach the envelope to the end of the document. Obey these steps:

1. **Type your letter.**

2. **Select the recipient's address in the letter.**

   If the address isn't in the document, you can add it later.

3. **Click the Envelopes button on the Mailings tab.**

4. **If the recipient's address doesn't appear in the Delivery Address box, type the address.**

5. **Click the Add to Document button.**

6. **Type the return address on the envelope.**

   And you're done.

It may not be obvious on the screen, but the first page of your letter is now an envelope. When you're ready to print the letter, the envelope is printed first and then the letter. All you have to do is stuff the letter into the envelope and seal it and then apply the increasingly costly postage.

✔ Most printers prompt you to manually enter envelopes if that's what they want you to do. After doing so, you may have to press the Ready, On-line, or Select button for the printer to continue. (My old LaserJet printer said, "Me Feed!" and, for some reason, it knew when I inserted the envelope because it just started working.)

✔ Check the envelope as you insert it into your printer to ensure that you didn't address its backside or put the address on upside down — as so often happens to me.

✔ When typing an address, use soft returns to break up the lines: Press Shift+Enter at the end of a line. That keeps the address tight.

✔ If you have trouble remembering which way the envelope feeds into your printer, draw a picture of the proper way and tape it to the top of your printer for reference.

Sort Your Text

Sorting is one of Word's better tricks. After you understand this feature, you go looking for places to use it. You can use the Sort command to arrange text alphabetically or numerically. You can sort paragraphs, table rows, and columns in cell tables and in tables created by using tabs.

Save your document before sorting. It's just a good idea.

Sorting isn't difficult. First, arrange whatever needs to be sorted into several rows of text, such as

```
Lemon
Banana cream
Apple
Cherry
Rhubarb
Tortilla
```

 Word sorts by the first item in each paragraph, so just select all the lines as a block. Then click the Sort button in the Home tab's Paragraph group. Mess around in the Sort Text dialog box if you want, but most of the time, clicking OK is all you need to do to sort your text alphabetically.

Map Ctrl+F to the Advanced Find Command

I'm a stubborn old Word user. I'm really disappointed that pressing the Ctrl+F key summons the Navigation pane. No thank you! I want Ctrl+F to bring forth the traditional Find dialog box, the one that's now called the Advanced Find dialog box. To make that happen, follow these steps:

1. **Click the File tab.**

2. **Choose Options from the list of commands on the left side of the screen.**

3. **Choose the Customize Ribbon item in the Word Options dialog box.**

   The Customize Ribbon item is found on the left side of the dialog box.

4. **Click the Customize button, found at the bottom of the dialog box.**

   The Customize Keyboard dialog box appears. You can use this dialog box to reassign all keyboard shortcuts in Word — and even create a few new ones.

5. **From the list of Categories, choose Home Tab.**

6. **From the list of Commands, choose Edit⇨Find.**

7. **Click the mouse in the Press New Shortcut Key text box.**

8. **Press the Ctrl+F key combination on the computer's keyboard.**

   You may notice that Ctr+F is already assigned to the NavPaneSearch command. That setup is about to change.

9. **Click the Assign button.**

10. **Click OK.**

Go ahead: Press Ctrl+F. You see the Find and Replace dialog box with the Find tab upfront. Congratulations!

The Navigation pane can still be accessed: On the View tab, place a check mark by the Navigation Pane item, found in the Show group.

Chapter 32

Ten Bizarre Things

*1*f Word were only about word processing, this book would end at Chapter 17. Fully half the book talks about things I consider to be along the lines of desktop publishing or even graphics, tasks that can be done far better by using other software. But beyond those strange abilities are things I consider even more strange and unusual. Welcome to the *Twilight Zone,* the chapter where I list ten bizarre things I find in Word.

Equations

Here's a feature that everyone demands, as long as everyone graduated from college with a degree in astrophysics or quantum mechanics. It's Word's Equation tools, which you need whenever you're desperate to stick a polynomial equation into your document and don't want to endure the tedium of building the thing yourself.

You can pluck a premade equation from the Insert tab's Equation button menu, as long as the equation you need is shown there. Otherwise, just click the button by itself (not the menu triangle) and two things happen: An equation *content control* is inserted into your document at the insertion pointer's location, and the Equation Tools Design tab appears on the Ribbon. Creating equations was never easier! Well, creating them is easy, but knowing what they mean is a different story altogether.

No, Word won't solve the equation.

Video in Your Document

One showcased feature in Word 2013, but also downright strange, is its ability to embed a video into your document. Obviously, the feature isn't intended for anything you plan to print; inserting a video is something you do for electronically published documents.

To insert a video, click the Insert tab's Online Video button, occupying the Media group. Search for a video by using Microsoft Bing (of course) or YouTube or by pasting in a video link. Eventually, after little toil, the video appears as a large graphical object in your document. You can play it and watch it right there on the screen, which is apparently something people have been demanding in a word processor since the Electric Pencil program debuted back in 1976.

 Videos are best viewed when a Word document is presented in Read mode — which in itself is yet another bizarre thing. To enter Read mode, click the Read Mode button on the status bar (shown in the margin) or click the Read Mode button on the View tab.

Make a Macro

I find lots of people who are curious about macros in Word. While I'd love to write about this topic, it's so big that I'm unable to do it justice in this book. Still, it's kind of a bizarre thing, so it fits well into this chapter.

A *macro* is a teensy program you can write in Word that automates things, such as repetitive keystrokes or tasks. It's actually quite handy — but not simple to create.

You start making a macro by recording it. Here are some steps:

1. **On the View tab, choose Macros⇨Record Macro.**

2. **Give the macro a name in the Record Macro dialog box.**

3. **Click the Keyboard button to assign a keyboard shortcut to the macro.**

   I recommend using this approach over choosing the Button option, which is more work.

4. **Type a keyboard shortcut combination.**

   Most of the good combinations are already used by Word, though many of the Ctrl+Alt+*letter* combinations are not.

5. **Click the Assign button.**

6. **Click the Close button.**

   You're now recording a macro in Word. Everything you do is recorded, from typing text to choosing commands and setting options.

   If you're only testing the waters, type some text. That's good enough.

7. **To stop recording, choose Macros⇨Stop Recording.**

   The macro is saved.

To play back the macro, press the keyboard shortcut you assigned. Word repeats all actions taken while the macro was being recorded, playing them back as though you've just issued the commands or typed the text yourself.

✔ To review macros you made, choose Macros⇨View Macros. You can manually run a macro from the Macros dialog box, or you can rename, edit, or delete the macros. You know the drill.

✔ Macros in Word broach the arena of computer programming. If you want to dig into macros, find a book or resource on the Microsoft Visual Basic for Applications programming language.

✔ Macro is short for macroinstruction. Yeah, whatever.

The Developer Tab

Word's advanced, creepy features lie on a tab that's normally hidden from view: the Developer tab. To display the Developer tab, obey these steps:

1. **Click the File tab to display the File screen.**

2. **Choose the Options command to display the Word Options dialog box.**

3. **On the right side of the window, place a check mark by the Developer Tab item.**

   You find the Developer Tab item in the Customize the Ribbon list.

4. **Click OK.**

The Developer tab is aptly named; it's best suited for people who either use Word to develop applications, special documents, and online forms or are hellbent on customizing Word by using macros. Scary stuff.

Hyphenation

Hyphenation is an automatic feature that splits a long word at the end of a line to make the text fit better on the page. Most people leave this feature turned off because hyphenated words tend to slow down the pace at which people read. However, if you want to hyphenate a document, click the Page Layout tab and then the Page Setup group, and choose Hyphenation⇨Automatic.

Hyphenation works best with paragraph formatting set to full justification.

Document Properties

When your company (or government agency) grows too big, there's a need for too much information. Word happily obliges by providing you with a sheet full of fill-in-the-blanks goodness to tell you all about your document and divulge whatever information you care to know about who worked on what and for how long. These tidbits are the *document properties*.

To eagerly fill in any document's properties, click the File tab and choose the Info item. Document properties are listed on the far-right side of the window. Some information cannot be changed, but when you click the lighter-colored text, you can type your own stuff.

The document's property information can be inserted into your text: From the Insert tab's Text group, choose Quick Parts⇨Document Property to insert various property text information tidbits into a document.

Cross-References

The References tab sports a bunch of features that I don't touch on in this book, not the least of which is the Cross-Reference button in the Captions group. The Cross-Reference command allows you to insert instructions such as *Refer to Chapter 99, Section Z* into your document. This feature works because you absorbed excess energy from the universe during a freak lightning storm and now have an IQ that would make Mr. Spock envious. Anyway, the Cross-Reference dialog box, summoned by the Cross-Reference command, is the place where cross-referencing happens. Page 653 has more information about this feature.

Collect and Paste

Normally, the copy-paste operation is singular: You copy something, you paste it. Using Word's Collect and Paste feature, you can copy multiple chunks of text, paste them in any order, or paste them in all at once. The secret is to click the dialog box launcher in the lower-right corner of the Clipboard group on the Home tab, right next to the word *Clipboard*. The Clipboard pane appears on the screen.

With the Clipboard pane visible, you can use the Copy command multiple times in a row to collect text. To paste the text, simply click the mouse on that chunk of text in the Clipboard pane. Or you can use the Paste All button to paste into your document every item you collected.

Even more bizarre: You can actually select multiple, separate chunks of text in your document. To do so, select the first chunk, and then, holding down the Ctrl key, drag the mouse over additional text. As long as the Ctrl key is held down, you can drag the mouse to select multiple chunks of text in different locations. The various selected chunks work as a block, which can cut, copy, or delete or to which you can apply formatting.

Click-and-Type

A feature introduced in Word 2002, and one that I don't believe anyone ever uses, is *click-and-type*. In a blank document, you can use it to click the mouse anywhere on the page and type information at that spot. *Bam!*

I fail to see any value in click-and-type, especially when it's easier just to learn basic formatting. But click-and-type may bother you when you see any of its specialized mouse pointers displayed; thus:

I≡   I≡   I   ≡I

That's click-and-type in action, with the mouse pointer trying to indicate the paragraph format to be applied when you click the mouse.

The best news about click-and-type is that you can disable it:

1. **Click the File tab menu.**
2. **On the File screen, choose Options.**

   The Word Options dialog box appears.

3. **Choose Advanced from the left side of the Word Options dialog box.**

4. **Remove the check mark by Enable Click and Type.**

   This setting is found in the Editing Options area.

5. **Click the OK button.**

You have now rid yourself of this nuisance.

Word and the Internet

Microsoft went kind of kooky in the 1990s when Bill Gates suddenly realized that his company was behind the curve on the Internet. In response, many Microsoft programs, including Word, suddenly started to bud various Internet features, whether the features were relevant to the software's original intent or not. For example, Word has — even to this day — the ability to create web pages or post to a blog.

Word is an excellent word processor. Word is a lousy web page editor. Though you can write a blog post, the steps involved to configure that process are complex and rarely meet with success. (And, yes, I tried and tried to get it to work.) Therefore, I cover none of that stuff in this book.

This book is about *word processing*. If you want software for e-mail, making web pages, using an Internet fax, creating a blog, or finding pictures of famous celebrities in compromising poses on the Internet, you have to look elsewhere.

Chapter 33

Ten Avuncular Suggestions

*J*ust like Mom wouldn't let you run off to school without ensuring that you were wearing a sweater (especially when *she* was cold) and carrying your books, homework, lunch, and money for milk, I don't want you to march forth with your word processing efforts without reading at least ten more pieces of loving, Word-friendly advice. This chapter is where you can find that advice.

Keep Printer Paper, Toner, and Supplies Handy

The electronic office is a myth. Along with your word processor, you need some real-world office supplies. Keep them stocked. Keep them handy.

✔ When you buy paper, buy a box.

✔ When you buy a toner cartridge or printer ribbon, buy a second.

✔ Keep a good stock of pens, paper, staples, paper clips, and all other office supplies handy.

Get Some References

Word is a writing tool. As such, you need to be familiar with, and obey, the grammatical rules of your language. If that language just happens to be English, you have a big job ahead of you. Even though a dictionary and a thesaurus are electronic parts of Word, I recommend that you keep a few references handy.

As someone born in the previous century, I prefer real books to electronic references. And for electronic references, I prefer eBooks to visiting various web pages. Whatever is your whim, consider the following references:

- Strunk and White's *The Elements of Style* (Longman) is also a useful book for finding out where to place apostrophes and commas.

- Any good college or university dictionary is helpful. Plenty of good electronic copies of those dictionaries are available now. Use one.

- Find a good thesaurus. (I love a good thesaurus. The one I use is from 1923. No electronic thesaurus I've seen has as many words in it.) With luck, a thesaurus is supplied with your dictionary software.

- Books containing common quotations, slang terms and euphemisms, common foreign words and phrases, and similar references are also good choices.

If you lack these books, visit the reference section of your favorite bookstore and plan to invest some good money to stock up on quality references.

Keep Your Computer Files Organized

Use folders on your hard drive for storing your document files. Keep related documents together in the same folders. Properly name your files so that you know what's in them.

One of the biggest problems with computers now is that millions of people use computers who have no concept of basic *computer science*. You can get a good dose from my *PCs For Dummies*, but also consider taking a class on computer basics. You'll enjoy your computer more when you understand how to use it.

Add the Junk Later

Write first, then format, then edit. Keep writing and editing. Save your stuff. Only when you truly finish writing should you go back to insert a picture or a graphical doodad. Doing these tasks last keeps you focused on *writing,* which is the main part of your document. Also, Word behaves better when a document doesn't have a lot of graphics or fancy junk in it. Write first, add the junk later.

Back Up Your Work

You should have two copies of everything you write, especially the stuff you value and treasure. You keep the original copy on the computer's main storage device (the hard drive); this book tells you how to save that copy. A second copy, or *backup,* should also be made, one that doesn't live on the same disk drive as the original.

To back up your work, use an optical disc, a USB thumb drive, a flash drive, an external hard drive, or a network drive. You can back up files by simply copying them in Windows, though using a traditional backup program on a schedule is the best method.

Understand Tabs

The problem most people have with tabs in Word is that the tab has *two* parts to it: There's the tab character itself, which is generated by pressing the Tab key. Then there's the tab stop, which sets how far across the page the tab goes. It's this tab stop that's more important, and properly setting up tab stops in Word is vital to lining up your text, nice and neat.

Review Chapter 12 for more information on tabs and tab stops.

Also remember that any time you feel the slightest urge to press the spacebar more than once, you need to reconsider what you're doing and use a tab and a tab stop instead.

Use Those Keyboard Shortcuts

You should have a repertoire of keyboard shortcuts, representing many of the commands you use often. Though it may not seem so at first, using the keyboard is much faster than getting by with the mouse. Refer to this book's Cheat Sheet at

```
www.dummies.com/cheatsheet/word2013
```

Try New Things

In Word, as in life, people form habits and repeat behaviors. Rather than falling into this trap, consider trying new behaviors from time to time. For example, consider using tables rather than tabs to organize your stuff. If you're an ancient Word user from days gone by, check out some Quick Styles or mess around with themes. Try to explore as much of Word as possible. You may master a new trick or discover a faster way to get something done.

Let Word Do the Work

Word does amazing things. In fact, any time you feel that you're doing too much work in Word, an easier, faster way to get the same job done is probably available. Use this book's index or, if you enjoy agony, the Word Help system to peruse the various tasks you undertake. You may be surprised that a shortcut exists, one that saves you time and makes your stuff look good.

Don't Take It All Too Seriously

Computers are about having fun. Too many people panic too quickly when they use computers. Don't let them get to you! And *please* don't reinstall Word to fix a minor problem. Everything that goes wrong has a solution. If the solution isn't in this book, consult your computer guru. Someone is bound to be able to help you out.

Index

• *G* •

Notes

Notes

ple & Mac

ad 2 For Dummies,
d Edition
8-1-118-17679-5

hone 4S For Dummies,
Edition
8-1-118-03671-6

od touch For Dummies,
d Edition
8-1-118-12960-9

ic OS X Lion
r Dummies
8-1-118-02205-4

ogging & Social Media

yVille For Dummies
8-1-118-08337-6

cebook For Dummies,
Edition
8-1-118-09562-1

m Blogging
r Dummies
8-1-118-03843-7

itter For Dummies,
d Edition
8-0-470-76879-2

rdPress For Dummies,
Edition
8-1-118-07342-1

siness

sh Flow For Dummies
8-1-118-01850 7

esting For Dummies,
Edition
8-0-470-90545-6

Job Searching with Social
Media For Dummies
978-0-470-93072-4

QuickBooks 2012
For Dummies
978-1-118-09120-3

Resumes For Dummies,
6th Edition
978-0-470-87361-8

Starting an Etsy Business
For Dummies
978-0-470-93067-0

Cooking & Entertaining

Cooking Basics
For Dummies, 4th Edition
978-0-470-91388-8

Wine For Dummies,
4th Edition
978-0-470-04579-4

Diet & Nutrition

Kettlebells For Dummies
978-0-470-59929-7

Nutrition For Dummies,
5th Edition
978-0-470-93231-5

Restaurant Calorie Counter
For Dummies,
2nd Edition
978-0-470-64405-8

Digital Photography

Digital SLR Cameras &
Photography For Dummies,
4th Edition
978 1-118-14489-3

Digital SLR Settings
& Shortcuts
For Dummies
978-0 470-91763-3

Photoshop Elements 10
For Dummies
978-1-118-10742-3

Gardening

Gardening Basics
For Dummies
978-0-470-03749-2

Vegetable Gardening
For Dummies,
2nd Edition
978-0-470-49870-5

Green/Sustainable

Raising Chickens
For Dummies
978-0-470-46544-8

Green Cleaning
For Dummies
978-0-470-39106-8

Health

Diabetes For Dummies,
3rd Edition
978-0-470-27086-8

Food Allergies
For Dummies
978-0-470-09584-3

Living Gluten-Free
For Dummies,
2nd Edition
978-0-470-58589-4

Hobbies

Beekeeping
For Dummies,
2nd Edition
978-0-470-43065-1

Chess For Dummies,
3rd Edition
978-1-118-01695-4

Drawing For Dummies,
2nd Edition
978-0-470-61842-4

eBay For Dummies,
7th Edition
978-1-118-09806-6

Knitting For Dummies,
2nd Edition
978-0-470-28747-7

Language &
Foreign Language

English Grammar
For Dummies,
2nd Edition
978-0-470-54664-2

French For Dummies,
2nd Edition
978-1-118-00464-7

German For Dummies,
2nd Edition
978-0-470-90101-4

Spanish Essentials
For Dummies
978-0-470-63751-7

Spanish For Dummies,
2nd Edition
978-0-470-87855-2

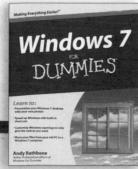

Math & Science

Algebra I For Dummies,
2nd Edition
978-0-470-55964-2

Biology For Dummies,
2nd Edition
978-0-470-59875-7

Chemistry For Dummies,
2nd Edition
978-1-1180-0730-3

Geometry For Dummies,
2nd Edition
978-0-470-08946-0

Pre-Algebra Essentials
For Dummies
978-0-470-61838-7

Microsoft Office

Excel 2010 For Dummies
978-0-470-48953-6

Office 2010 All-in-One
For Dummies
978-0-470-49748-7

Office 2011 for Mac
For Dummies
978-0-470-87869-9

Word 2010
For Dummies
978-0-470-48772-3

Music

Guitar For Dummies,
2nd Edition
978-0-7645-9904-0

Clarinet For Dummies
978-0-470-58477-4

iPod & iTunes
For Dummies,
9th Edition
978-1-118-13060-5

Pets

Cats For Dummies,
2nd Edition
978-0-7645-5275-5

Dogs All-in One
For Dummies
978-0470-52978-2

Saltwater Aquariums
For Dummies
978-0-470-06805-2

Religion & Inspiration

The Bible For Dummies
978-0-7645-5296-0

Catholicism For Dummies,
2nd Edition
978-1-118-07778-8

Spirituality For Dummies,
2nd Edition
978-0-470-19142-2

Self-Help & Relationships

Happiness For Dummies
978-0-470-28171-0

Overcoming Anxiety
For Dummies,
2nd Edition
978-0-470-57441-6

Seniors

Crosswords For Seniors
For Dummies
978-0-470-49157-7

iPad 2 For Seniors
For Dummies, 3rd Edition
978-1-118-17678-8

Laptops & Tablets
For Seniors For Dummies,
2nd Edition
978-1-118-09596-6

Smartphones & Tablets

BlackBerry For Dummies,
5th Edition
978-1-118-10035-6

Droid X2 For Dummies
978-1-118-14864-8

HTC ThunderBolt
For Dummies
978-1-118-07601-9

MOTOROLA XOOM
For Dummies
978-1-118-08835-7

Sports

Basketball For Dummies,
3rd Edition
978-1-118-07374-2

Football For Dummies,
2nd Edition
978-1-118-01261-1

Golf For Dummies,
4th Edition
978-0-470-88279-5

Test Prep

ACT For Dummies,
5th Edition
978-1-118-01259-8

ASVAB For Dummies,
3rd Edition
978-0-470-63760-9

The GRE Test For
Dummies, 7th Edition
978-0-470-00919-2

Police Officer Exam
For Dummies
978-0-470-88724-0

Series 7 Exam
For Dummies
978-0-470-09932-2

Web Development

HTML, CSS, & XHTML
For Dummies, 7th Edition
978-0-470-91659-9

Drupal For Dummies,
2nd Edition
978-1-118-08348-2

Windows 7

Windows 7
For Dummies
978-0-470-49743-2

Windows 7
For Dummies,
Book + DVD Bundle
978-0-470-52398-8

Windows 7 All-in-One
For Dummies
978-0-470-48763-1

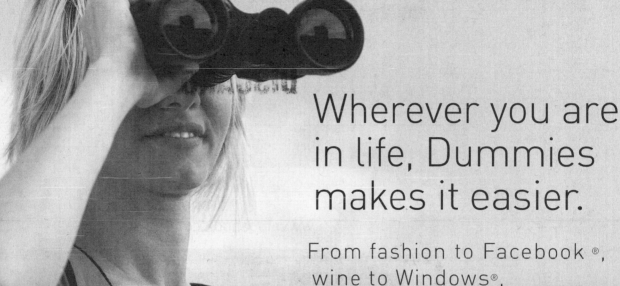

DUMMIES.COM

Wherever you are in life, Dummies makes it easier.

From fashion to Facebook®, wine to Windows®, and everything in between, Dummies makes it easier.